Caroline Fiennes has been a charity Chief Executive, a volunteer, staffer, researcher and trustee. She has advised many donors about effective uses of their resources, including the Big Lottery Fund, BBC Children in Need, some of the Sainsbury Family Charitable Trusts, Nuffield Trust, professional tennis players, the Guardian, Environmental Resources Management (a leading global environmental consultancy), the Private Equity Foundation, Booz & Co., individuals, families and government departments.

Caroline was for five years at New Philanthropy Capital, holds a Shackleton Foundation Leadership Award, and was made a London Leader by the Greater London Authority for her work on sustainability. She grew up in commercial strategy consulting and has a surprisingly useful degree in Physics and Philosophy.

www.giving-evidence.com
www.twitter.com/carolinefiennes

D1375476

It Ain't What You Give, It's the Way that You Give It

Making charitable donations which get results

Caroline Fiennes

ISBN 978-0-9571633-0-0

Published by Giving Evidence 2012
www.giving-evidence.com

Why the quirky price?
It's a nod to the (British) Charitable Uses Act of 1601, which still
influences much of how charities operate, in many countries.

For the twenty four

*'It is more difficult to give money away intelligently
than it is to earn it in the first place.'*
– Andrew Carnegie, Scottish-American philanthropist

*'To give away money is an easy matter and in any man's power. But
to decide to whom to give it, and how large, and when, and for what
purpose and how, is neither in every man's power nor an easy matter.'*
– Aristotle

*'In business, you look for the easy things to do. Philanthropy is...
tackling problems that have resisted great intellects
and often great money. It is a tougher game.'*
– Warren Buffett

*'It's a chilling thought that when we think we are doing good, we may
actually be doing harm, but it is one we must always be alive to.'*
– Dr Ben Goldacre

*'Deeply ingrained "best practices" frequently add cost and reduce
management flexibility in already difficult operating conditions.
We end up hurting organizations we mean to help.'*
– Clara Miller, Founder, the Nonprofit Finance Fund

*'A farmer went out to sow seed. Some fell on rocky places, but the
plants withered because they had no root. Other seed fell among
thorns, which grew up and choked the plants, so that they did not
bear grain. Still other seed fell on good soil. It came up, grew and
produced a crop, multiplying thirty, sixty, or even a hundred times.'*
– Gospel of Mark 4:3-8

Contents

A long time ago, I taught in India, in a village in Tamil Nadu. It had just one road on which were the shop, the temple, the land-owner's big house, and the tree where the erratic buses stopped. All the other tracks were dirt, leading to people's houses and the wells and out into the fields. The school in which I taught, the only one in the village, had about 40 children on the register aged between about three and about eleven (they were often unclear about their ages). Each morning, some 20 or 30 pupils would arrive: it was pretty rare to have a full house. I wondered why they came so sporadically.

There were many children in the village who didn't come to school at all. Some clearly wanted to come: they would stand at the school windows and watch, or even drop in on lessons, more frequently if the lesson was outside under a tree than if we were in the classroom, I noticed. Sometimes I'd see the children out in the fields during school time – maybe working, maybe just playing – or going to the well, or doing errands, or just sitting. I wondered why they didn't come.

Other people have wondered this too. Unlike me, they've done something about it: gone to the trouble of identifying why children skip school in these villages, and researching what happens if those reasons are addressed. Poor transport to and from school is one factor. Another problem is the cost of a school uniform – even in dusty Tamil Nadu it's just too weird for a child to be the only one in the classroom wearing something different. A third is that parents take children out of school, perhaps to deal with the harvest or care for younger siblings. All of these factors were visible from my classroom window. But a fourth factor I hadn't seen. In villages like mine, many children have intestinal worms – amazingly, one in four people globally has some form of worms – which cause anything from malaise and lethargy to severe pain, and which prevent children from doing anything much, including coming to school. Charities run programmes to solve each of these four problems. They all do some good.

But what a variation in how much good they do! One type of programme addresses the issue of parents keeping children out of school, by giving them a payment when the children show up at school. These 'conditional cash transfer' programmes cost about $1,000 to keep a child in school for a whole year (including all the management costs). Another programme distributes school uniforms. There, $1,000 achieves rather more – and not just a little bit more. It achieves ten times as much: for the same amount of money, school uniforms can get ten children into school for an additional year. One child or ten: it's no contest. And even that isn't half the story. Dealing with the worms isn't 'just' ten times as good. Deworming (as it's charmingly called) can keep a child in school for a year for just $40. It's 25 times better. (In fact, even that understates it: some deworming programmes add a year of education for just $4. You read that correctly. They achieve 250 times as much.

For the sake of argument, let's be conservative and call it 'just' 25.)

To put that another way, if you put $1,000 into a conditional cash transfer programme, you'll do some good. But *you could have done 25 times that much good* – there's a whole gaggle of children out in the fields who could have been in school. That is, every time a donor puts $1,000 into the wrong programme, fully 24 children needlessly miss out.

Though deworming is an extreme example, this pattern repeats right across the charity world: some charities are better than others. It sounds almost heretical to say it because we tend to think that all charities are good. But we also think that teaching is a good thing, and so is providing medical care, and yet we're familiar with the notion that some teachers are better than others and some doctors are better than others. The seeds which scattered on stony ground produce nothing, would feed a family if planted in fertile soil.

Our donations to charity could be getting more children into school, eradicating diseases faster, better empowering communities, adding more to our cultural life and so on. 'Don't settle for average' cries the slogan of GiveWell, an organisation of independent charity analysts. Wouldn't you rather that your donations achieved a lot rather than just a little?

This book is about how to do that. Hence it is dedicated to those 24 children who missed out on school because donors made the wrong call, and who are totemic of anyone or anything that has missed out because of poor decisions by donors.

The problem is that, as a donor, you don't automatically know whether a charity is good or not. Perhaps a charity runs a refugee camp badly or doesn't properly protect women escaping from violent partners. As a donor, you're unlikely to realise that because you're not *in* the refugee camp or the domestic violence refuge. We can't rely on what the charity shows us because bad charities use the same pictures of smiling children and cute animals as good charities do. It's not hard to understand why. So to find out which charities are good, we need to go looking.

And to look hard. Even if the charity is totally transparent and tells us everything – indeed, even if we go to the refugee camp or the domestic violence refuge ourselves – what we will learn about is what the charity *does* achieve: the women it does help, children it does get back into school. That still doesn't tell us about what our support *could* achieve: the charity down the road which would have brought 24 more children from the fields into school with the same donation. As a result, donors often choose charities which aren't actually the best. Aristotle was right: deciding to whom to give and for what purpose is not an easy matter.

So we should be alarmed by stories such as this. In 2008, the Big Give ran a programme as part of which it asked secondary pupils school in Oxford to choose charities to which to donate some money. Several students voted for small charities, and some for local ones. The Big Give praised these as 'mature and adult decisions'. Really? Sure, those are the *same* criteria as adults sometimes use but they may not be *good* criteria because those adults may well not realise that other criteria would favour much better charities. After all, it's not obvious that charities of a particular size or location would necessarily be the best – and, as we'll see, there are much better criteria. Perhaps those adults routinely choose charities which miss loads of opportunities and the young people would be ill-advised to follow them. In fact, it's often unwise to just copy other donors.

So how do we choose to whom to give and for what purpose? Happily we've learnt a bit since Aristotle's time and I'm going to share the insights with you. The first step is to get proactive. The single biggest factor in most people's choice of charity is being asked – a charity approaches them in the street, calls them up, or puts a flyer through the door. This is bizarre if you think about it: nobody invests in companies which put flyers through their door. Correspondingly, there's no guarantee that the best charities in the world are the ones which find you, so to be effective you'll need to go looking for them.

Another early step is to get beyond the problem and onto the solution. Overwhelmingly, charities' leaflets and letters describe how awful something is: these Indian children uneducated, this woman abused by her partner, that rainforest being destroyed. But before we reach for our chequebooks, we need to establish whether the charity has a decent solution. And not just any solution, but whether it has the best solution. Perhaps a neighbouring charity would achieve much more. About half of our quest to achieve a lot rather than a little will be about finding great charities which have powerful solutions to important problems.

The other half of our journey addresses the rest of Aristotle's comment – about deciding 'how large, and when, and how' to give. This is just as influential as the choice of charity. We'll see how to grow the value of your donations: a way to increase their value by half, and another way which increases them by more than half – combining those tricks will make your £100 worth as valuable as if you'd given over £250. There are other ways of making it worth seven times as much, or even eleven times as much as you give. We'll also see ways in which donors can help charities hugely: how you can make them more effective, more responsive and better able to improve and share their insights with others. But we'll also see how it's possible to get it wrong. This too sits badly with the received wisdom that giving is invariably good, but just as Ben Goldacre says about medicine, 'when we think we are doing good, we may actually be doing harm'. I'll show you how to waste your entire donation, and how – if you really try – you can waste not only all of yours but parts of somebody else's too.

But you know what? It's very hard to tell whether you're giving well or badly. You get thanked heartily either way. Consequently donors often help less and hinder rather more than they might imagine. In various roles I've had in charities, I myself have been on the receiving end of some of this hindering: common unhelpful 'best practices' include obsessing about charities' administrative costs or foundations asking for applications and bespoke reports. We'll see better practices too – and how they helped one donor move from an 80 per cent failure rate to an 80 per cent success rate. Again, don't just copy.

But what if you haven't got anything to give? Actually, all of us have a lot to give. I'll show you several remarkable tricks for conjuring money for charity out of thin air, which are not only surprisingly easy but perfectly legal and encouraged. And you can give time: we'll see how one person turned just some of their time into billions of dollars for charity, and children who use similar tactics. You can use your teapot, the meeting room at work, your followers on Twitter, your ability to write stories, the cakes you bake, even the very body you inhabit once the sad day comes that you no longer need it... There's a way to give almost anything effectively. (Almost. Not millions of Pop-Tarts®, as we'll see.)

What this book doesn't do

This book won't recommend individual charities, for the simple reason that it wouldn't help. There are nearly 200,000 charities registered in the UK alone, so even if I gave you my view on 2,000 of them – which would be fatally tedious for me to write and you to read – you would still have the choice of, well, nearly 200,000 charities in the UK and countless thousands elsewhere. Furthermore, charities change over time: between my writing this and your reading it, perhaps the entire board and management of any given charity could quit and their replacements adopt a totally new strategy, rendering my analysis obsolete. By analogy, you wouldn't expect a guide to commercial investment to recommend investing in, say, Vodafone or copper, but rather to give the general principles. Similarly, this book will teach you how to analyse charities for yourself – at any time, in any place, and for any cause.

Nor does the book suggest how much you should give. Plenty of others have done so, from God – Jews and Christians are asked to give ten per cent of their income, and Muslims 2.5 per cent of their assets – to the Australian ethicist Peter Singer, who proposes a formula which is basically 5 per cent of income plus a bit extra if you're wealthy. No prizes for guessing what the 50% League suggests. Alternatively, you could decide how much you need to live on and give away the rest. Toby Ord, an academic at Oxford University, has decided that he only needs about £10,000 a year to live on. Since he currently earns around £45,000 and expects to work for another 30 years, he could end up giving over £1m.

Is any of those the right answer? I don't know – it seems to me that the amount you *give* is up to you. But the amount you *achieve* depends on whether you find great charities and give in ways which really help. Let's imagine that Lady Bountiful gives £200 to charity, whereas you give only £100. Let's further imagine that Lady Bountiful is ignorant about the curious world of charities so gives to bad charities and in ways that waste money, whereas you are well-informed and give to great charities and in helpful ways. It's perfectly possible that your £100 will achieve more than her £200 – much more. What can we say then? Her giving might be more generous, but yours is more useful.

So this book won't tell you how much to give because I honestly think that in the absence of insight about how best to help, it genuinely doesn't matter. In terms of making a difference, *it ain't what you give: it's the way that you give it.*

How this book works

This book is organised rather like a driving course.

First, we'll cover the basics which any donor absolutely must know if they're to be safe on the road. Not the pedestrian things (sorry) like what charity boards do and how the tax breaks work, but the crucial issues such as why charities exist at all, why you might support one, and how charities go about making the world better. We'll look at the fundamental characteristic which makes charities' behaviour – and donors' roles – very counterintuitive.

Next, we'll learn how to drive: Section 2 covers what you need to do. First, how to find a great charity – taking the short route if you're in a rush or the long route if you have more time; whether you should give credence to the many popular myths (such as charity beginning at home or small charities being more efficient); and what to do in common situations such as being asked to sponsor your friends. Second, we'll look at the best ways to give – in short, how to help and not hinder. We'll look at giving money, and an array of ways to help beyond money. We'll see how to deploy money you'd not even thought about. This section is for you if you're giving a few tens or hundreds of pounds – up to about £100,000, roughly speaking.

Then we'll learn how to drive big trucks. If you're giving a lot – perhaps you're a foundation, or a wealthy family or a company – the effects of the way that you give are amplified, and some other issues come into play. In Section 3 we dive into those issues, seeing an intriguing range of options beyond giving to charity, and how to devise a process which helps and doesn't hinder. Read carefully: we'll see how 'big' donors waste perhaps £250m of charities' money each year. (Oddly, it's just as easy to waste £10,000 or £10m as it is a humble tenner.) Corporate giving – maligned, vaunted, useless and brilliant – is a little different again, and we'll see how to do that effectively.

Finally, we'll come back to some advanced theory and dynamics: essential if you're giving a lot and interesting even if not. We'll take a close look at charities' results – why are they so hard to understand and compare, and what can you most usefully look for? – see why size and growth are almost totally irrelevant, why most of the folklore around charity mergers is wrong, and unravel why in your dealings with charities you keep bumping into government.

At the end, I'll give you a toolkit which will help in any situation you encounter with your giving. You see, though the advice in the various sections of the book may seem diverse, eclectic and possibly even contradictory, it is in fact all underpinned by a few unifying principles. Once you get the hang of those – and we'll do a few dry runs so that you do – you'll always be able to find the best way to give.

On our way, we'll see the most potent uses of charitable money in history, donors honest enough to admit disastrous mistakes, and hear from myriad charities at home and abroad, analysts, researchers and quirky voices including Private Eye, the Duke of Wellington, the Onion, and an over-representation of Nobel laureates. Most of the guidance will work in any country, though the examples happen to be primarily from the UK. Many are anonymised or disguised: some on request, others because the detail is out of date, some to avoid embarrassment: it's the learning that interests us, rather than finger-pointing. Where calculations are cited but not detailed in the book, the maths can be found at www.giving-evidence.com

But in case you're really in a rush, here is the ten-minute version:

The ten-minute guide to supporting charities

What to know

The three most important things to know about charities:

Charities vary markedly in how good they are
Nobody ever talks about the bad ones, but they do exist. So find a good one!

Admin costs are no indicator of whether a charity is any good
Neither is whether the charity's well-known. You have to look deeper than that – or use analysis by somebody else.

Donors don't know whether they're helping or hindering
It's normally impossible for them to see their own effect. So don't copy other donors, and do ask the charities.

What to do

Find a great charity

Give only to charities which are effective and which share your ambition for improving the world. A good indicator is whether it measures its effectiveness, publishes full details of its research process and talks about the results.

The quickest way to find good charities is to 'borrow' analysis already done by somebody reliable. Some of the big grant-making foundations have great processes for finding effective charities, and publish lists of charities they support. BBC Children in Need, or Comic Relief, or the BBC Radio 4 appeal are examples. There are some great independent analysts like GiveWell who also publish lists. Obviously, those lists aren't exhaustive but they're pretty reliable.

If you want to do the analysis yourself, check first that the charity:

- is a registered charity. For UK-registered charities, that means that it will be on the register of the charity regulator: the Charity Commission for England and Wales, the Office of the Scottish Charity Regulator or the Charity Commission for Northern Ireland; **and**
- reports publicly on how much its work achieves and how it is improving its work. It should have detail about that on its website or available if you ask.

Even if a charity has approached you – say by post or via a fundraiser in the street – check these two things. In Section 2 are six crucial questions which indicate how good a charity is and a process you can do in about an hour to assess a charity's effectiveness in more detail.

Meanwhile, don't look at how much it spends on administration: it's a total red herring – like judging a teacher by how much chalk he uses – and can ruin charities. 'Admin' isn't waste (it often includes time spent learning, which is obviously a good move), it's got nothing to do with effectiveness (we'll see how some charities could waste 95 per cent of their income and still outperform their peers) and anyway, there's no sensible common definition, so it's simply unclear.

Help it
A few pointers here:

- Don't ring-fence your money to particular activities, e.g., don't say that it can only support a day-centre in Hull, or tree-planting near Shanghai or whatever. The charity's management spends all day every day thinking about its work so trust it: your gift will improve the world a lot more this way.
- If the charity does a good job, give again next year. And tell the charity that, because it'll help with planning. There's a myth that donors shouldn't give repeatedly to the same charity, that they should 'spread the love around'. Not true! If it's doing a good job, it needs to continue, so keep supporting it.
- Get together with other donors. It's more fun for you and will make your giving more effective, whether you're giving £10 or £10m.
- Give to just a few charities. Your £50 will achieve much more if you don't chop it up, as will your £50m. In fact, if you chop up your £50 into 50 donations of a pound each, the whole lot may get consumed in bank fees.
- Offer non-financial things too. Be creative here. The charity might need office space, or mentoring, or used postage stamps or somebody to cut the hedge.
- Be nice! Return the charity's calls and answer its messages. It's amazing how few donors do this.
- Don't create work for the charity – in finding you in the first place, or writing bespoke reports for you.
- If you're a major donor, share what you're learning – the good and the bad. Stories of what isn't working may be your biggest asset, because other donors (and charities) need to know the traps to avoid.

Don't hinder it
To be honest, if you just give money, offer other things (such as your time or useful items) and then leave the charity to get on with its work, you won't hinder it. The key rule is: don't act like medieval royalty! Don't make charities waste a load of the resources which you and others have given on dealing with you. This sounds like blindingly obvious advice but large donors often don't follow it. If you are giving a lot, minimise the effort (i.e., cost) for the charity of getting your money/ support. So:

- Best of all is to avoid making a charity apply to you at all: just look at what it does and its published research into its effectiveness. Then make a decision, quickly, and tell it.
- If you must make charities apply, minimise the work for them. Use a standard – and short – application form. There's one in the appendices which almost certainly covers what you need.
- While it's nice for you to meet a charity's staff and beneficiaries, remember that this will take up time. Go easy.

Minimise the effort (i.e., cost) for the charity of telling you what your money/support has achieved. For sure, it should report on its overall effectiveness but don't make it write a report just for you.

The principles of good giving

If in doubt, be guided by the goal of improving the world as much as possible. That means:

- using everything you've got, being creative about resources you can offer besides or instead of money
- making good decisions by choosing charities based on relevant data and advice from suitable people
- helping them and not hindering
- maximising what's available by minimising waste

Sounds obvious doesn't it? But if we all – as donors – stuck to this in all our dealings with charities, we could make world rather better.

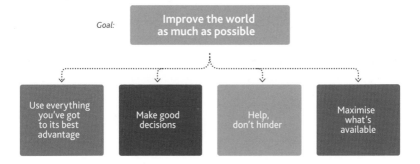

Goal: **Improve the world as much as possible**

| Use everything you've got to its best advantage | Make good decisions | Help, don't hinder | Maximise what's available |

Investors and donors: a word about language

The language around giving isn't great, so I'll be clear.

If you are using money, time or anything else in pursuit of a charitable goal, this book calls you a donor. Strictly speaking, you may actually not be a donor. For instance, if you do a beach cleanup or initiate a conference about homelessness or talk on Twitter about the dangers of skin cancer, to whom are you 'donating'? – technically nobody. But since there's no decent word for 'person using money, time or anything else in pursuit of social or environmental goals', I shall call you a donor.

Sometimes donors prefer to be called 'investors' because they feel that this sounds more active and signals their interest in the results. Personally, I find that confusing because 'investing' normally means using money in the expectation of making money. So it's confusing when the government talks about 'investing in schools': though it expects schools to improve, it doesn't expect the money back. This book uses 'investment' only where you can expect to see your money again.

And while we're here, let's agree to talk about 'giving', rather than 'giving it away'. 'Giving it away' sounds as though the objective is simply to rid ourselves of money, which is obviously not difficult at all. What we're talking about here is finding the best ways possible to improve the world in some meaningful fashion. As CNN founder Ted Turner, who pledged $1 billion to support the United Nations, puts it: 'Don't say philanthropy is giving it away. I consider it an investment in the future of humanity. I'm not giving it away.'

Section One

What you need to know

Chapter 1

Choosing a cause: hearts and minds

'Start with your heart and then engage your mind.'
– Rebecca Eastmond, Head of Philanthropic
Services EMEA at J.P. Morgan Private Bank

Start with your heart

If you ran the world, what would you do first? Provide clean drinking water for everybody? Help single parents in your community? End war? Hand out chocolate in the street?

Charities work on all kinds of issues: global poverty, local sports, eradicating disease, encouraging creativity, making childbirth safer, adapting to climate change (though not, typically, handing out chocolate). And whether you're running the world or not, charities offer you a way to act on the issues you care about.

If you already know which issues those are, then great: this book will show you many ways to be effective in supporting charities which work on those issues.

If not – if you want to 'do something' but are not sure which issues to prioritise – then start with your heart. Your own interests and tastes are important factors. While there's no right or wrong answer to the question of 'who should I help?', there are answers which are markedly better than others. A 'good answer' will speak to your passions: it may be a place you've visited or an issue which has affected somebody you know. It may be something you're particularly well-placed to help solve, perhaps because of your financial resources, skills, contacts or experience. For instance, if you have expertise in health, education, law, heritage or urban planning, it's better to select some of the many areas where that will be disproportionately valuable.

Areas in which charities operate

UK charities must have a purpose which is 'for the public benefit' and which falls within the following areas:

- the prevention or relief of poverty
- the advancement of education
- the advancement of religion
- the advancement of health or the saving of lives
- the advancement of citizenship or community development
- the advancement of the arts, culture, heritage or science
- the advancement of amateur sport
- the advancement of human rights, conflict resolution or reconciliation, or the promotion of religious or racial harmony or equality and diversity
- the advancement of environmental protection or improvement
- the relief of those in need by reason of youth, age, ill-health, disability, financial hardship or other disadvantage
- the advancement of animal welfare
- the promotion of the efficiency of the armed forces of the Crown, or of the efficiency of the police, fire and rescue services or ambulance services
- other purposes that are currently recognised as charitable or are in the spirit of any purposes currently recognised as charitable

The most notable exception from this list is activity related to political or constitutional change, which charities may not undertake.
(The long tradition of charitable activity makes for some quirky history. The list above is defined by the Charities Act of 2006. This replaced an Act passed in 1601 which remained in place virtually unchanged for four centuries.)

Good answers are also around the most pressing problems. Several organisations have opinions about which those are, and you'll have your own views. The Arlington Institute, a non-profit research institute in the US, compiled a list by considering global problems which could escalate into severe crises. It makes scary reading:

'The biggest problems facing humanity' from www.worldsbiggestproblems.org	Charities' work on those problems
Species extinction. Certain species that human beings depend upon for our food supply are going extinct; if their numbers fall too low we may face extinction ourselves.	Charities are involved in conserving species – including those charmingly called 'charismatic' (cute) and others – as well as their habitats.
Global water crisis. Over the last 50 years the human population has nearly tripled, and industrial pollution, unsustainable agriculture, and poor civic planning have decreased the overall water supply.	Charities work on all elements of the water crisis, including raising awareness and developing practical solutions.
Rapid climate change. Despite some debate about its causes, climate change is an empirical fact. The problem is both a curse and blessing, in that people from different cultures will either have to work together or face mutual destruction.	Charities have been involved in funding research into climate change, raising awareness and spurring action.
Peak oil. Petroleum has powered the modern world for almost 100 years; today, many industry insiders say that we may be reaching a permanent peak in oil production.	Charities' responses include the high-risk early-stage development of alternative supply sources, and encouraging resource efficiency.
Economic collapse. Fragilities in the current global economy could tip the developed world into conditions not seen since the 1920s.	Perhaps surprisingly, charities are involved even here, for example by promoting transparency amongst companies and exploring alternative measures of success such as well-being as a complement to measuring economic growth.

Good answers are also around areas which are particularly under-resourced. Work related to crime, mental health, sexual violence or people-trafficking is a good bet because it's hugely needed but struggles to attract donations. The same is true of much of the work on the global problems above. On health specifically, the Global Forum for Health Research reckons that 90 per cent of global health research spending goes to diseases which account for just 10 per cent of the world's health burden – presumably on what Tom Lehrer, the legendary singer-songwriter (and Harvard maths professor) called 'diseases of the rich'. You might want to prioritise diseases of the poor, which are under-researched because they don't hold out the promise of a lucrative market for pharmaceutical companies, such as tuberculosis, cholera, typhoid and malaria.

Another route to a good answer is to focus on people who are doing least well in life. Gallup measures people's well-being in 124 countries on a scale from 'thriving' through to 'struggling'. While it's hardly surprising that people are less cheery in poorer countries, the contrast in the proportions of people who are 'thriving' is shocking. One could easily argue that charitable resource is most chronically needed in the least thriving nations:

Least thriving nations		Most thriving nations	
Chad	1%	Denmark (1)	72%
Central African Republic	2%	Sweden (=2)	69%
Haiti	2%	Canada (=2)	69%
Burkina Faso	3%	Australia (3)	65%
Cambodia	3%	Finland (=4)	64%
Niger	3%	Venezula (=4)	64%
Tajikistan	3%	Israel (=5)	63%
Tanzania	4%	New Zealand (=5)	63%
Mali	4%	United States (13)	59%
Comoros	4%	United Kingdom (17)	54%

Even within the UK, some areas of charitable work are much better funded than others. The graph below shows the annual spend by UK charities for various types of 'beneficiary'[1].

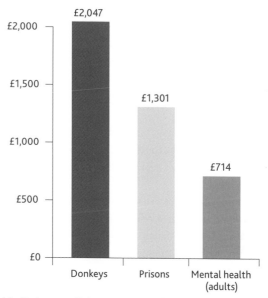

**Charitable spend per beneficiary
for various causes (UK)**

You'll probably find yourself drawn to several issues. Then comes the hard part: choosing a few on which to focus proactively. Why should you limit yourself? Because it'll make you more effective. You'll have time to understand the issues more thoroughly, to make better choices between charities, and to learn the best ways that you can give to them. Though it's quite intuitive that focus is a good move for donors with few resources, in fact there's value in focusing for donors of any scale: even the Bill and Melinda Gates Foundation with its $56 billion – the largest charitable donor the world has ever seen by a long chalk[2] – focuses on just three issues.

Defining and sticking to a limited focus is not without pain. It necessarily means ignoring other causes and charities, despite their importance and effectiveness. Not

---

1 Charities have various terms for the recipients of their services/products, which include customers, clients, service-users, beneficiaries – or indeed terms like people, children, donkeys, buildings. For simplicity, this book refers to them all as beneficiaries.
In the graph, 'donkeys' refers solely to donkeys in the Donkey Sanctuary (in Devon); 'prisons' refers to prisoners and their children; 'mental health' refers to people with 'severe and enduring mental illness'. Calculations are at www.giving-evidence.com
2 Even adjusting for inflation, Gates' giving roundly outflanks that of the two great 19th century US philanthropists Andrew Carnegie and John D. Rockefeller combined

for nothing does our word 'decide' derive from the Latin *decidere* meaning 'to cut off'. Donors sometimes say that focusing feels mean. In fact it's the opposite: it will enable you to achieve much more for the beneficiaries you select.

Many donors report feeling pressure to give based on what we might call 'community obligation' (e.g., to local community, or responding to emergencies) and based on who's asking (e.g., matching employee donations, or requests from friends and family). Yet their focus must not get crowded out. A smart way to deal with these competing pressures is to segment the resources you're giving, designating a proportion for each.

Whichever causes you choose, we will refer to them here generically as 'improving the world'.

Engage your mind

Though your heart may lead you to a cause, you'll need your mind for identifying how to improve the world *as much as possible*. One of the options is to give to charity. Why would you do that? If you'll bear with the rather basic question, we can see several important dynamics.

Suppose you want to help victims of a famine in East Africa. One option is to give money to a charity which works there. Another is to send money directly. When you give to a charity you are, in effect, 'hiring' it to help people in East Africa on your behalf. **You're not giving *to* the charity: you're giving *through* it.** It only makes sense to do this if the charity can do a better job than you could yourself with the same resources: if it can find people in need of aid more quickly than you could, if it has more accumulated expertise on the best ways to help than you do, if it has better political and non-governmental contacts than you do, if it can bring other resources such as volunteers, get bulk discounts on the purchase of equipment and supplies. In short, **good charities add value to the resources they receive**.

I spell this out because people sometimes imagine that charities simply 'carry' money to their beneficiaries, with the main effect of depleting that money along the way. This gives rise to the mistaken question about how much of the charity's money is spent on 'the actual cause'. We can see the absurdity of this view by taking it to its extreme (a technique commonly used in philosophy to test whether a notion makes sense). Suppose you wanted to give £100 to the East African famine and wanted every single penny of it to reach 'the actual beneficiaries'. Well, you couldn't give through a UK charity at all because its staff wouldn't count as 'actual beneficiaries', and you couldn't even send it to an indigenous charity because the foreign exchange process would incur some cost. You'd simply have to post your £100 in cash – and an envelope of UK banknotes in a disaster situation abroad would be totally useless. This way of giving would destroy the entire value of your donation.

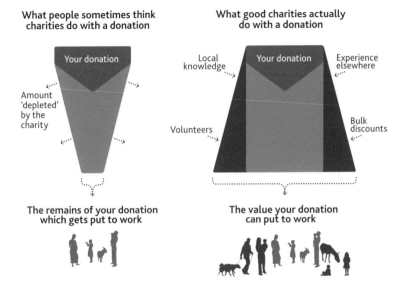

What people sometimes think charities do with a donation

Your donation

Amount 'depleted' by the charity

The remains of your donation which gets put to work

What good charities actually do with a donation

Local knowledge

Your donation

Experience elsewhere

Volunteers

Bulk discounts

The value your donation can put to work

Better than old wives' tales like this is to be guided by what improves the world the most, a criterion to which we'll return time and again. Take for instance the choice of whether to give through a small charity or through a large one. Clearly, your donation will make more difference to the small charity than to the large one. But that's irrelevant: what's important is the difference your donation will make to the *beneficiaries*, and good choices are based on whether that is greater through the small charity or through the larger one.

But we're getting ahead of ourselves. We first need to deal with an even more prevalent misconception.

Chapter 2

Administration costs: the worst way to judge a charity

When people look at how good a charity is, they often ask about its administration costs. Do those indicate whether it's any good?

Professor Dean Karlan of Yale University did the maths to find out. He looked at the set of charities ranked by GiveWell, a US charity which ranks other charities according to their effectiveness. GiveWell's work is hard because charities' effectiveness is far from clear, but its analysis is based on data from many sources and is among the most thorough available on this topic. It's choosy: when Professor Karlan did the analysis in the middle of 2011, GiveWell was recommending only 41 charities of the 294 it had analysed. Professor Karlan looked up each of those 294 charities on Charity Navigator, a US site which reports the proportion of a charity's total budget spent on admin, and he compared the admin spend for recommended charities with that for non-recommended charities. He found that ... drum roll ... the high-performing charities spend *more* of their budget on admin than do the lower-performers. This rather contradicts the conventional notion that good charities avoid 'wasting' money on 'administration'. ('Administration' is also referred to as 'overheads' or 'core costs'.) Because we're looking for high-performing charities, we need to understand how this works.

What do you mean by 'admin'?

Imagine a water charity which operates in several less developed countries to improve irrigation. If it's run well, it will have a system for recording what works and what doesn't in particular circumstances, and for sharing that learning between its various country offices. Now, should the costs of that system count as 'administration'? On one hand, the system isn't *directly* helping people: it probably involves databases and conference calls, rather than pipes and water. As a result, it may well be classified as 'administration' in a charity's accounts (and therefore by sites like Charity Navigator). However, the system will reduce the charity's costs and increase its effectiveness, and therefore certainly isn't waste. Aha – in this example, money spent on administration increases performance.

Let's take a real example. Chance UK provides mentors for primary school children who are at risk of developing anti-social behaviour and possibly being permanently excluded from school (formerly called 'being expelled'). The charity spent some money evaluating its work. It found that male mentors were best suited to children with behavioural difficulties, whereas children with emotional problems responded best to female mentors. Again, the money spent on that evaluation would normally be counted as 'admin', but for the children receiving support from Chance UK which has improved because of that insight, it was money well spent.

Maybe you think I'm cheating by cherry-picking positive examples. So let's be systematic. Charities' overhead costs can be classified as illustrated overleaf. ('Direct costs of front-line activities' might include buying deworming pills or school uniforms. In fact, charity accounting rules allow a surprising degree of discretion about how particular costs are classified):

The costs within a charity

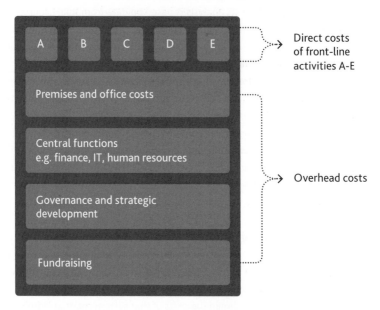

Let's consider 'governance and strategic development' costs. Suppose there is a change in legal obligations, or staff costs rise, or beneficiary needs change or another charity suggests partnering. When the Chief Executive and trustees to meet to discuss those things – that is, to decide how best to respond in the interests of effectively serving beneficiaries – they will incur costs such as travel, refreshments and secretarial support. Those will be classified in the accounts as 'governance and strategic development' costs, but are clearly in the interests of effectiveness.

Let's consider finance costs. Perhaps the Finance Director purchases a better invoice-handling system. Same thing. That system should reduce work for finance staff by reducing processing times and/or mistakes, which frees up their time (and/or frees up money) to improve the quality and quantity of service to beneficiaries.

It even works for premises and office costs. Taking examples from other industries, Google famously has volleyball courts, pianos, and ping pong tables around its offices; retail bank First Direct spends a lot of money on childcare, beanbags and flags at its call centre in Leeds. Are those costs wasted since they don't look like money being spent 'on the cause' of internet search technology or banking? No.

Rather they're integral to those companies' success. People want to work in fun environments, so beanbags and pianos help Google and First Direct to attract fantastic applicants and retain productive staff, and thereby do great work in internet search and banking. The softball pitches and beanbags aren't *separate from* the success: they *contribute to* the success.

So that's all the categories of 'admin' – with the exception of fundraising, which we'll look at in a minute. None of them is necessarily waste, somehow separate from the charity's real work, and so none should necessarily be minimised. We can now understand Professor Karlan's finding that higher 'admin' correlates with better performance: high-performing charities are high-performing *precisely because* they prioritise learning, thinking, planning. Hence GiveWell calls choosing a charity based on the lowness of its admin costs 'the worst way to pick a charity'.

Susan Hitch is a trustee of various organisations including the Sigrid Rausing Trust:
'I'm often a bit worried if a charity claims to have very low admin costs – below, say, five per cent. Either they're fudging it to try to please a potential funder, which doesn't promise much of a relationship; or their admin really is rock bottom, in which case they're unlikely to be very well run. You can't run an effective organisation with barely any core – barely any good people or good thinking. I've learnt that grants are usually more effective if the charity is spending a realistic amount on its core costs.'

This isn't to say that there isn't waste in charities. There is: masses, and much of it totally avoidable. Of course any good charity will try to avoid it, and we'll see many ways in which you, as a donor, can help with that. But if you're looking for the amount of money that a charity wastes on doughnuts or talking about football or even dealing with micro-managing donors, don't expect to find it clearly labelled in the financial statements.

To the question of 'how much of a charity's money goes to the actual cause', the answer is that in a well-run organisation, all of it does. Of course it does: where else would it go? To something totally unrelated? I personally take a rather hard line on this: if a charity says that it spends, say, 83 per cent of its money on 'the actual cause', I take that to mean that either 17 per cent is being stolen or embezzled or otherwise spent on something totally tangential – or that the charity is too stupid to avoid perpetuating the unhelpful myth that admin costs are separate from 'real work' and should be minimised. Either, in my view, is irresponsible and a cause for alarm.

What happens if you choose based on admin costs?

As well as discouraging learning and improvement in the way we've encountered, you might encourage pointlessly expensive work. Suppose you are trying to improve child health in a less developed country by distributing drugs to reduce diarrhoea, which accounts for huge amounts of avoidable mortality. Suppose there are two types of drug: one costs £1 per child, the other costs £10 per child. You want to reach 1,000 children, so your expenditure on drugs will be either £1,000 or £10,000. Either programme will have costs associated with finding and dealing with 1,000 children and their families (for example, hiring and accommodating the team, and managing the finances). Let's put a figure of £1,000 on these 'admin' costs.

Programme A		Programme B	
Direct cost per child	£1	Direct cost per child	£10
Cost of treating 1,000 children	£1,000	Cost of treating 1,000 children	£10,000
Fixed 'admin' cost	£1,000	Fixed 'admin' cost	£1,000
Total programme cost	£2,000	Total programme cost	£11,000
Proportion of spending on 'admin': £1,000 ÷ £2,000 = 50%		Proportion of spending on 'admin': £1,000 ÷ £11,000 = 9%	

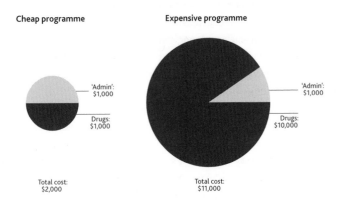

Cheap programme

Expensive programme

'Admin': $1,000

Drugs: $1,000

Total cost: $2,000

'Admin': $1,000

Drugs: $10,000

Total cost: $11,000

Judging by the 'admin' percentages, Programme A looks bad – but that's precisely because it's cost-effective! Looking at it another way, the question of about admin percentage is useless because is doesn't ask 'percentage *of what?*'

Another real-life illustration is provided by the Disability Law Service, a charity which employs solicitors to give advice to disabled people. It found that by employing more secretaries, and thereby increasing its 'admin percentage', it could move administrative tasks away from the solicitors and hence serve more disabled people at lower overall cost.

So as well as being no guide, judging charities by their 'admin costs' penalises cost-effective work. This is one of many examples of where the 'received wisdom' about charities is no wisdom at all.

Even wastage is no guide: how to waste 95% and still be the best

The deworming programme which we met earlier can add a year of education for $40, whereas through a conditional cash transfer programme that costs $1,000. Deworming is so much cheaper that something rather important emerges from the figures.

Let's suppose that the deworming programme is amazingly badly run and wastes 95 per cent of its income (on parties or a swanky office or handbags) whereas the conditional cash transfer programme has no waste at all. Let's give both programmes $10,000 and see what happens. With $10,000, the conditional cash transfer programme can improve school attendance for ten children. Great. But even wasting 95 per cent of its $10,000, leaving just $500, the deworming programme can improve school attendance for 12 children and have some change left over. (See diagram overleaf.) A hugely wasteful programme can *outperform* a less wasteful one.

Surprised? I was. It's because, of course, one programme is much more cost-effective than the other, and the gains in effectiveness easily compensate for the losses through wastage. Here, even where the waste is devoid of any merit at all, as well as on a grand scale, looking at levels of waste would *still* lead us to the wrong charity.

Of course, if you actually found a charity spending 95 per cent of its income on parties and handbags, you'd ask some serious questions. Yet the figures in this example still stand. Suppose that the two programmes to improve school attendance were being run in a war zone and, through no fault of its own, the deworming programme suffered substantial losses from theft, arson or extortion. In a severe case, this might destroy 95 per cent of its resources. Nonetheless, the deworming programme could still help more children than the conditional cash transfer programme. The same effect arises even when the comparison between two programmes is less extreme. Suppose Charity X is twice as cost-effective as Charity B. In that case, even if Charity X loses or wastes nearly half its revenue, it will still outperform Charity B. So much for 'admin costs' as a criterion.

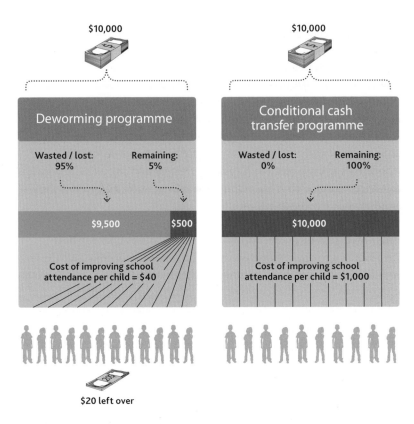

$20 left over

Should you ever look at admin costs?

Yes, but only to compare charities that are very similar. In those cases, you might question charities whose admin costs are particularly high, or indeed suspiciously low. But be cautious even here: programmes which at first glance look similar may in fact differ significantly and requires very different cost bases in order to be effective. (We'll return to this in Section 4.)

What about fundraising costs?

It's just as hopeless to judge charities by their fundraising ratios – the amount they spend on fundraising as a proportion of their total income or their total costs. Professor Karlan looked at those too and found the same thing: high performers spend more on raising funds than do low performers. Why's that?

Well, fundraising ratios say virtually nothing about the charity. What they tell you about is donors. A high fundraising ratio simply tells you that the charity has to spend a lot to raise each pound of income. The ratio might be high because only few donors will support the charity, so it has a low hit-rate: it's easier to find donors for

rehabilitating donkeys than for rehabilitating prisoners. And it's easier to find donors for research into common diseases than for research into rare conditions – because more people have experience of them. That doesn't mean that charities working on rare conditions are necessarily less effective.

Or the fundraising ratio might be high because donors create work and generate
costs for the charity. Large donors sometimes create significant workloads for charities through tortuous application and reporting processes – we'll discuss how to
avoid this in Section 3. It's hardly fair to penalise charities for costs dumped on them
by somebody else. By the way, companies don't have to put up with these processes, and as a result, raising money is much cheaper for them: raising £100 typically
costs businesses around £7 but costs charities about £20-40.

What does this mean for your giving?

What you care about is effectiveness – in improving the world in some way – and
therefore want to find charities which are *effective* in getting things done. As the
deworming-in-a-war-zone example illustrates, this is totally different from *efficiency*,
by which people typically mean lack of wastage. Even if the conditional cash transfer team is marvellously efficient at delivering cash to parents, it remains much less
effective than the deworming team because the approach just isn't as cost-effective.

> Do you invest in companies – either directly or through, say, a company which
> manages your pension? If so, do you look at the 'admin costs' in that compa-
> ny? I thought not. Your concern is with what comes out – what they achieve
> for you with the money that you invest. That's their 'effectiveness'. The same
> applies to assessing charities – look at what they achieve rather than their
> cost base.

Since effectiveness turns out to be pretty independent of efficiency, we can't use
efficiency as a short cut but will need to look at effectiveness itself. To understand
that, we'll need to understand charities' work, for which the tools we'll see in the
next few chapters are invaluable.

Chapter 3

Breadth vs. certainty

'Philanthropy is commendable, but it must not cause the philanthropist to overlook the circumstances of economic injustice that make the philanthropy necessary.'
– Martin Luther King Jr

Once you've chosen the issues you want to work on (say, alleviating poverty in less developed countries or preserving buildings of architectural significance), you have an important choice about how broad you want your impact to be. In the charity world, broader impact normally means less predictable impact. A useful way of looking at this is by placing charitable activity on a triangle developed by New Philanthropy Capital, a consultancy and thinktank. We'll take as an example work which supports disabled adults in employment.

Some charities provide specialist equipment – such as a motorised wheelchair, voice-recognition software or a speech synthesiser for a particular individual. Their support makes a significant difference to that one disabled person, which, though great, has no impact on a neighbour with similar needs. So this type of support, which is very close to the individual, has a very high chance of success (it can be described as 'low risk') but small scope (it helps one person at a time).

No. beneficiaries: one

Supporting an individual e.g.,
via equipment, holidays,
education, housing

Other charities train colleagues of disabled people to understand their needs and to adapt their workplace and practices accordingly. They are a step away from the disabled person themselves, working with the people immediately around them. The training will potentially benefit more disabled people, including employees in that particular workplace, both now and in future, and in other workplaces as the trainees move on, taking their understanding with them. However, there's more risk, since there's some chance that the training doesn't work and changes nothing.

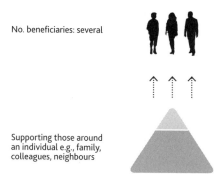

No. beneficiaries: several

Supporting those around
an individual e.g., family,
colleagues, neighbours

A third type of work is another step away from the disabled person, and involves working with professionals and policy-makers to make all employers more supportive of disabled people. This is what happened when charities successfully lobbied for the Disability Discrimination Act 1995, which outlaws discrimination on the basis of physical disability. When this type of work is successful, it has huge scope, influencing many – possibly all – disabled people. However, it also has higher risk because lobbying may not achieve anything at all.

Other work at this level of the triangle includes influencing government spending. Because government is the largest funder in areas such as health, education, criminal justice, influencing it even a little can create a significant change, though again there is higher risk of outright failure.

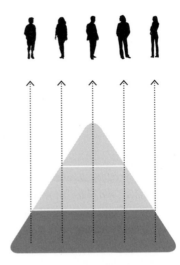

No. beneficiaries:
potentially all in category
(e.g., all disabled people)

Changing universal policy and
practice

A fourth way of working sets out to influence attitudes towards disability across the whole of society, perhaps through education or media campaigns. If they succeed, they will make a significant difference to every disabled person (and their families and carers) – not only by influencing their workplace, but every interaction with anybody anywhere. However, these activities are difficult to pull off and therefore higher risk.

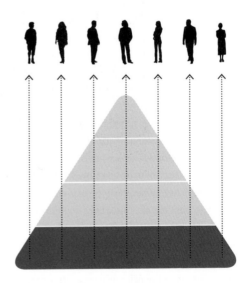

No. beneficiaries:
everybody – whole of society

Changing attitudes and norms

This triangle is useful in virtually any sector where charities operate and we'll use it throughout our journey. At the top, work is close to the beneficiary and therefore has low risk but limited scope; further down, work is more distant from the beneficiary, has a risk of failing completely, but has very broad impact if it succeeds. Notice that as we move towards the base of the triangle, it becomes harder to identify the precise cause of a particular change: policy and societal attitudes are influenced by many factors.

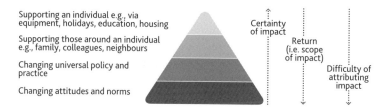

Supporting an individual e.g., via equipment, holidays, education, housing

Supporting those around an individual e.g., family, colleagues, neighbours

Changing universal policy and practice

Changing attitudes and norms

Certainty of impact

Return (i.e. scope of impact)

Difficulty of attributing impact

Let's look at examples in some other areas.

In tackling cancer, some charities focus at the top of the triangle, supporting individual sufferers and their families. At the next level down, charities train health professionals in a particular hospital or region. Further down is work to distribute information about best practice to doctors across the country. And work at the base of the triangle includes raising awareness amongst the whole population about skin cancer.

Or consider the efforts to protect the orangutan, whose habitat – tropical rainforest on the islands of Borneo and Sumatra – is being destroyed by commercial logging. Working at the top of the triangle is the Sepilok Rehabilitation Centre in Borneo which finds new homes for some orangutans. Work at the base of the triangle includes influencing businesses, for example encouraging the food industry away from unsustainable palm oil. (At least a quarter of the destruction of rainforest in South East Asia is to clear land for growing palm trees, whose oil is used in all manner of foods – crisps, chocolate, biscuits are examples – and commonly ambiguously labelled as 'vegetable fat'). It also includes policy campaigners pressuring relevant governments for better rainforest surveillance and prosecution of illegal loggers.

Or let's take education systems which fail to help talented pupils realise their potential. At the top of the triangle, donors and charities sometimes help individual students to 'beat the odds'. At the base is work to 'change the odds' by improving the system for all talented students, perhaps by increasing or re-directing government expenditure on education.

As these examples show, work towards the base of the triangle often involves changing 'a system', which might comprise public perceptions, governments and/ or businesses. The upside is benefit for every person (or orangutan) touched by that system. A downside is complexity. For example, drug companies are supposed to publish results of all clinical trials they run – including where the drugs work, where they don't, and where the experiment wasn't conclusive – in order that doctors and patients can make informed decisions. But they don't: it's thought that around half of all trial results are unpublished. Which half, you may wonder. A clue might be that published studies funded by pharmaceutical companies are four times more likely to give results favourable to the company than are independent studies. As a result, the true effects of loads of prescribed medicines are essentially unknown. There is notionally a system to force full disclosure, but it's manifestly broken. There is now a project to fix that system, which as you can imagine is quite complicated.

Influencing systems, businesses and governments is a powerful way to multiply the impact of limited resources. It's attractive for charities and donors because typically charities – individually and even collectively – are much smaller than the systems which create and perpetuate the problems they seek to solve. Bill Gates has noticed this: he describes his giant foundation as 'a tiny, tiny little organization' (relative to businesses and governments[3]) and therefore endeavours to influence government, other players and public opinion in pursuit of its goals.

But notice: to the question of 'how much of my money goes to the actual beneficiaries?', at the base of the triangle, the answer may be 'zero'. If you were to film the work fixing the health problem outlined above, you wouldn't see any ill people. You'd see doctors and statisticians and computer programmers (and quite possibly a few lawyers). If you observed the work to dissuade business from using palm oil, you wouldn't see any orangutans, you'd see lots of financiers and forestry management people having meetings and writing notes. Does that 'zero' mean that the work isn't worth doing? Hardly. If it enables more evidence-based medical decisions

---

3 The Gates Foundation has roughly $57 billion. At the time of writing, the market capitalisation (i.e., the value) of Microsoft is $227 billion, and of Apple is $376 billion. Total UK government spending in 2011/12 is £703 billion (~$1,134 billion).

or less habitat destruction or more fairness in education, its impact is huge.

What does this mean for your giving?

Again, though there are no right or wrong answers about where on the triangle to operate, there are good and poor answers which these questions will show:

Who is involved in your giving? If you are giving as a family or as a school, perhaps partly to educate children about less developed countries, then activities at the top may be best for you. You might sponsor a child or pay for some specific item, such as a drinking water fountain or a toilet block. Work at the top of the triangle is typically the most emotive, visible and comprehensible, so is a good starting point if you are raising funds from other people – perhaps from neighbours, colleagues or from your industry.

How quickly do you want to see results? If you want to see a change within a school year or a financial year, you probably need to stick near the top of the triangle. Success towards the base normally takes longer because work there is more complicated.

Where is the greatest unmet need? If you don't have those constraints and are solely concerned with making your donation work as hard as possible, a good move is to look for the under-resourced areas. They are almost always lower on the triangle because activities there are complicated and not picturesque. (This underfunding is weird actually, because in a poll, sixty per cent of people in the UK supported charities spending money on lobbying the government, and half cited it as the most cost-effective activity for charities, and yet it remains hard to fund.)

What are your preferences in relation to risk and return? Your own taste for risk is an important factor. As you'll probably have rumbled, my own preference is for work at the base of the triangle: what is the point of paying to dish out more medicines if we have essentially no clue which ones work because half the relevant information is suppressed because the enforcement system doesn't work? Similarly, we could avoid having to rehabilitate any individual orangutans if we prevented their homes being destroyed in the first place. I therefore encourage you to support work at the base of the triangle. And I wouldn't be alone:

> John D. Rockefeller, oil magnate and philanthropist (1839 – 1937):
> *'Instead of giving alms to beggars, if anything can be done to remove the causes which lead to the existence of beggars, then something deeper and broader and more worthwhile will have been accomplished... the gift that matters is not to the individual beggar but to the situation represented by the beggar.'*
> On this logic, both Rockefeller and his contemporary billionaire Andrew Carnegie set up universities so people could help themselves, and Carnegie paid for the building and equipping of some 2,500 libraries globally.

Charitable donors' greatest achievements

UK philanthropy's greatest achievements are dominated by activities at the base of the triangle, according to a list compiled by the Institute of Philanthropy via an open nominations process in 2006. They include:

Provision of social services before the creation of the welfare state. Research in the late nineteenth and early twentieth century, including some in York by Joseph Rowntree and his son, revealed the extent and causes of poverty in Britain. As the Institute of Philanthropy puts it, 'The work of these early social researchers, funded by philanthropy, helped to undermine the myth that the poor were entirely responsible for their own situation and contributed to the reform of the Poor Laws and the introduction of state support for the poor. The Rowntree research helped to create an evidence base for [...] tax-funded, state-organised welfare and is said to have directly influenced the Beveridge Report which set out the blue-print for Britain's welfare state.'

Campaigning which ended the slave trade in Britain. The Society for the Abolition of the Slave Trade comprised thousands of volunteer members who ran local groups, raised funds, distributed pamphlets and worked collectively, inspired and galvanised by William Wilberforce. Their work was crucial to the successful passage of the 1807 Abolition of the Slave Trade Act and the 1833 Slavery Abolition Act.

Famine relief and long-term aid to developing countries. This achievement includes not only relief efforts such as Live Aid, but also the renewed interest in charities and awareness of development issues.

Provision of education for all. 'The advancement of education' was one of four charitable purposes defined by the Charitable Uses Act of 1601. Philanthropic work in education included charity schools for the poor and the nineteenth-century Ragged Schools movement. The government eventually picked up this responsibility on a universal basis.

Health research. The Wellcome Trust, the UK's largest charity, was among donors who ensured that the human genome (the code for human DNA) is publicly available. The impact is just vast and will be felt for generations: one could easily imagine that it will be the most significant use of charitable and public money in the history of the human race. The notion of determining the human genome arose in the 1980s, and the Human Genome Project was launched in 1990, gaining funding from the US government and the Wellcome Trust. When a commercial competitor emerged, with stated intention to patent up to 300 important genes and charge subscriptions for its data, the research turned into a race. The Wellcome Trust piled in money to accelerate the public research programme, which has ensured that the sequence is available in the public domain.

To give a sense of the interest in the human genome, when a 'working draft' was released online in 2000, half a trillion bytes of information were downloaded in the first 24 hours. Activity associated with human genome sequencing projects and research is thought to have generated $67 billion in the US in 2010 alone.

Other social campaigns which have led to major social changes include the banning of handguns after the massacre at Dunblane in 1996, outlawing the production and use of landmines, and granting universal suffrage in 1928.

None of which is to say that work at the top of the triangle isn't necessary. A clever device used by highly effective charities which operate at the top is to wring more value from that work by working further down as well, for example to change the system or laws or attitudes. The charity Changing Faces supports and represents people with facial and other disfigurements. It works at the top of the triangle, providing support to individuals and their families, such as giving advice to parents on how to deal with people's reactions to a child's birthmark. It also amplifies the impact of this front-line experience by lobbying government – its successes include changing the way the NHS delivers care and getting disfigurement included in the Equality Act 2010 – and influencing us all, through campaigns that make us better able to respond to disfigurements.

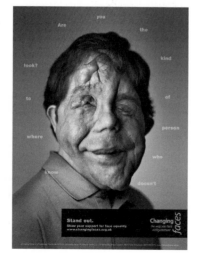

The triangle is one (good) technique for thinking about how charities achieve a particular goal. Next we'll explore another great technique.

Chapter 4

How do you solve a problem like...?
Introducing theories of change

'Lack of clarity is a sin.'
– Karl Popper, philosopher of science

The programmes we saw earlier to improve school attendance in Indian villages rested on the (pretty reasonable) assumption that if school attendance improved, then educational attainment would improve. On that basis, the researchers tested various mechanisms for improving school attendance. You'll recall that they were: providing school uniforms, treating children for worms, making payments to parents if their children attend, and improving transport. Each potential solution is based on what in the charity world is called a 'theory of change' – a causal chain by which some activities (such as buying and distributing uniforms) are supposed to achieve a goal (children with better numeracy).

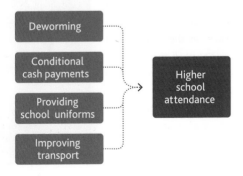

Each theory of change will have begun with some evidence – perhaps some observations like mine about children without uniform being unwilling to come into classrooms, about the erratic nature of the buses, and perhaps interviews with parents revealing a widespread view that children over a certain age should contribute to the family income. From that evidence, researchers come up with a hypothesis (in effect, an informed guess) about a possible solution, for instance that payments could persuade parents to leave children in school.

The four theories of change shown above compete: in a world of scarce resources, donors have to choose between them[4]. How do we know how good they are? Well, with luck we can test them. We run each activity and look at its effect on the goal. You already know the punchline to this particular story, which is that the four theories of change turn out to vary vastly in their effectiveness.

In fact, these four theories of change about improving educational attainment also compete with others which don't rely on increasing school attendance at all. (See diagram overleaf.) They might rely instead on improving school equipment or improving teaching methods. Again, each would also be based on evidence and a hypothesis of how various activities could achieve the goal.

What makes a good theory of change?

Clarity. The work needs a clear goal, and a coherent logic about how each activity contributes to that goal. Every charity should be able to articulate its theory of change even if it doesn't use that term.

Second, it should be based on evidence. Donors and charities must choose between competing theories, and the stronger the supporting evidence, the better, since this reduces the chance that the theory doesn't work.

And third, it should be testable. Testing a theory of change – just like testing a theory in science – will move us from hypotheses (guesses) to reliable data. That may disprove the theory or show other theories to be superior. In many instances, it will enable the charity to refine the work: it's most unlikely that the first hypothesis will be the best conceivable answer. Much more likely is that it can be gradually improved by integrating findings from the charity's own progress and that of others. Theories of change should be dynamic over time.

The ideal tests measure the effect all the way from one end of the chain to the other: if we treat children in a particular district for worms, do their exams results improve? That is perfectly measurable.

---

4 Charities also must choose between theories of change. Indeed, a charity is rather like a donor in that it deploys resources in pursuit of charitable goals. It must decide whether its resources will achieve most if it spends them itself or gives them to another organisation, and must decide between various types of programme it could run.

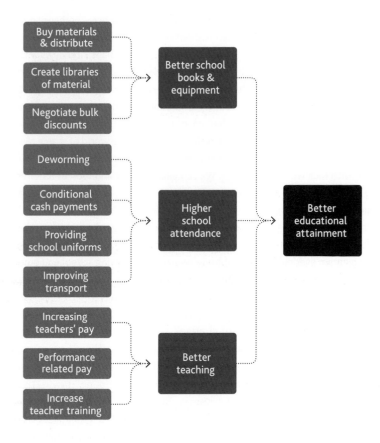

However, returning to our example, we've actually omitted part of the theory of change. Why do we care about educational attainment? Because we believe that better education leads to better life-chances and to people being happier and more fulfilled, which is our ultimate goal (as shown opposite). Great. So to test from one end of the chain to the other, we need to test whether treating children for worms makes them happier and more fulfilled in later life. This is rather harder to measure: we'd have to wait ages for the results, which anyway will be entangled with numerous other factors, and we'll need to keep track of all the children over a long period which will be complicated and expensive – and perhaps impossible.

There are many instances like this, in which measuring from one end of the chain to the other is impractical. Happily, it may be unnecessary. If we have evidence from other situations that educational attainment does eventually improve happiness and fulfilment, then we only need 'our' work to produce evidence for the links in the chain which are still missing, such as the first two links in this chain:

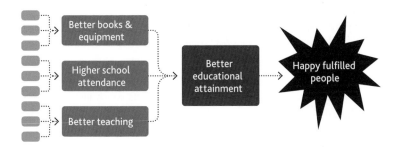

Using theories of change

Theories of change help a great deal with measuring results. Even where it's tough to measure the end goal, it's normally possible to measure progress at intermediate links. Take the example of innovative work, which rightly occupies a lot of charitable time because charities are addressing problems which have so far defied solutions. By definition, innovators will not at the outset have evidence that they will achieve a particular goal. However, they can provide evidence that supports their theory of change, perhaps taking results from analogous work which supports the individual links in the chain. (We'll explore results and intermediate links in detail in Section 4.)

Large charities may have several concurrent goals and therefore several theories of change. For instance, against Oxfam's overall goal of 'working with others to overcome poverty and suffering', it runs broadly three strands of work. First, aid response: work at the top of the triangle and highly time-sensitive. Second, development work, to support communities to become more self-sufficient and resilient. And third, campaigning, both in the less developed countries and in rich countries, to raise political action and public awareness – work at the base of the triangle. Each strand supports Oxfam's overall goal, each with a different theory of change. That's fine, as long as they're all coherent and defensible, and ideally mutually-reinforcing.

Competing theories of change abound in many fields of human activity: economists have multiple theories of how to reduce unemployment; politicians have multiple theories of how to improve the health of the nation or reduce illegal immigration. So how do you solve a problem like poor educational attainment, or climate change, or urban over-crowding? The answer is that there are multiple theories of change for each, and they should compete based on their demonstrable effectiveness.

What does this mean for your giving?

Get a theory of change for *you*! You personally face a choice about the activities through which to achieve your goal. Suppose you are interested in preserving rainforests. The various ways you could help include: lobbying national and international politicians; supporting relevant charities; taking direct action; and using your power as a consumer by avoiding products which include rainforest timber. Each represents an alternative theory of change. Supporting a charity to, in effect, make the change for you, is only one theory of change.

The bulk of this book is concerned with that option, not because it's invariably the best but in the interests of scope. (We touch on another theory – using your financial investments – in Section 2, and in Section 3 will see many further options.)

Theories of your change

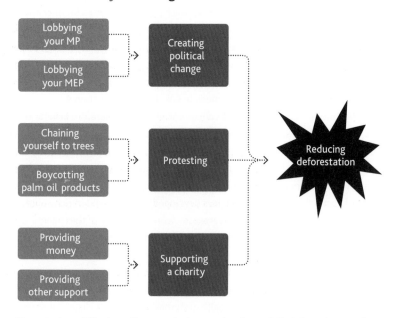

Your choice will be best if you make it consciously, and if it's based on evidence. Suppose you decide to focus on political change. You might decide that an MEP has broader power than an MP, with the potential to effect change across Europe. But if you know that your particular MEP is routinely ignored in Brussels whereas your MP is hard-working and influential, you may choose to pursue change by influencing your MP.

Don't be scared of the unlikely. Doctors aren't grocers. But development economist Professor Esther Duflo discovered that lentils are a good tool for immunisation. Working in Udaipur in India, she found that offering mothers a free kilo of lentils for every child immunised increased immunisation rates more than six-fold, from 6% to 38%.

Professor Duflo had the flexibility to undertake activities (sourcing lentils) which appear quite unrelated to her goal (vaccinating children) – and to great effect. This kind of flexibility is often valuable in reaching a potent theory of change. There are examples of work to improve healthcare in less developed countries where the roads are so poor that drugs and equipment can't be distributed by truck. Charities (and by extension their supporting donors) therefore wind up building roads. Although they didn't set out to build transport infrastructure, they were led there by their goal and the evidence about achieving it.

Don't be scared of the contentious. To reduce sexual abuse of children, many organisations work with children, their parents and schools. They may educate children about 'stranger danger', and educate parents and teachers about signs to watch for in children and adults. These charities use theories of change which involve 'working with the good guys'.

The Lucy Faithfull Foundation also works to reduce sexual abuse of children but, unusually, it works with the offenders and potential offenders – the bad guys – as well as with victims and non-offending family members. The foundation quotes 'Steve', a convicted sex offender: 'When I started offending, I really wanted to ask for help. But it was easier to offend than to ask for help.' Nonetheless it's controversial work, sometimes eliciting negative reactions from local press and public. But if it works, great: you're not half as interested in emotional reactions as you are in improving the world.

Don't be scared of long chains. The UK charity TippingPoint was born from a confluence of observations: that man-made changes to our climate are dangerous and set to worsen; and that the arts have significant sway over popular attitudes and actions. The charity takes its name from the notion of a 'tipping point' in atmospheric carbon levels beyond which the changes are irreversible[5]. TippingPoint brings together performance artists, visual artists and climate scientists in the hope that artists will be inspired to create work in response, raise awareness of the

---

5 For instance, warming is causing the Greenland ice-sheet to melt, putting its (fresh) water into the Atlantic. Up to a point, adding fresh water to the sea doesn't have much effect. But there comes a point when the influx of fresh water is enough to switch off the deep ocean circulation which brings Europe warm water from the Caribbean, which would result in sudden and irreversible changes in climate.

problem and spur action. TippingPoint's events explore climate science itself as well as associated issues such as deforestation, chemical changes to oceans, the effects on sea life, and implications for humans in terms of poverty and migration.

TippingPoint's beneficiaries are people affected by climate change: ultimately, that's all of us, though climate change disproportionately affects people in poor or low-lying countries. Its work starts a long way from 'the action', by convening people who are very distant from those countries.

TippingPoint's theory of change

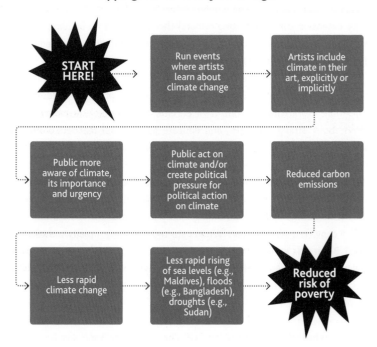

You'll notice that TippingPoint works at the base of the triangle. This is precisely why its theory of change involves a long causal chain, because it influences many organisations and individuals. This gives rise to the sizable risk in its work (it's tough to influence them all) but equally to the sizable potential impact (if it succeeds, it harnesses the power and reach of all those organisations and individuals).

I'd encourage you to be open to these long chains. The length of the chain doesn't matter as long as each link is clear and supported by credible evidence. That evidence may come from the charity's own field (in this example, climate change) or from analogous circumstances. For instance, TippingPoint's theory of change assumes that artistic activity can influence public attitudes and action. This has been powerfully demonstrated for over a century. *How the Other Half Lives: Studies Among the Tenements of New York*, an essay in photojournalism published in 1890, revealed New York's slums to many influential people for the first time, and was credited with inspiring political reforms that improved the lives of millions. Similarly, the 1852 novel *Uncle Tom's Cabin* by Harriet Beecher Stowe is credited with changing American attitudes towards slavery.

The special case of basic research

Basic research is the discipline of finding things out for the sake of it, even when no practical application is envisaged. It is often enabled by charitable money, and I want to address it explicitly because it is a rather special case.

Basic research is, if you will, an extreme case of activity at the base of the triangle: roughly stated, the theory of change says 'let's find out some stuff about XYZ and maybe we'll figure out how to use it'. The evidence for any particular piece of basic research is terrible, precisely because we don't know what it will turn up. However, the evidence for basic research as a whole is stunning. Mathematicians developed a number which doesn't exist (the square root of minus one) which turns out to be invaluable in understanding electricity – and therefore in designing computers and iPods and spaceships and heart-monitors. Physicists who went looking for some unimaginably small particles needed to share their findings with each other and in so doing inadvertently invented the internet. But it doesn't work every time by any means: lots of basic research turns up nothing at all.

Basic research is very high risk but offers potentially vast returns – but returns which are unknowable in advance. I've singled it out because of the danger that in our enthusiasm for achieving and measuring impact, we overlook this important type of work. Charitable money is often uniquely able to take those giant risks and therefore basic research can be a fruitful focus for donors. In the words of Franklin Thomas, the former president of the huge Ford Foundation, charitable money can be 'the research and development arm of society,' providing a service which is invaluable.

Theories of change will be useful throughout our journey in assessing charities before we engage with them, in understanding their impact as we go along, and for understanding our own impact as donors. However, before we spring into action, we need to understand the most fundamental quirk of the charity world.

Chapter 5

The defining feature of charities: separation between donors and beneficiaries

Hairdressers, estate agents, shoe shops, insurers: thousands of companies are involved in the daily lives of all of us. As a result, we have a good background understanding of how companies work, which we bring when we look at charities. But charities differ fundamentally from companies. It's crucial to understand the differences and to realise that our expectations based on our experiences with companies may well be misleading.

Most companies are basically about a swap. I give you cake: you give me money. I use that money to make more cake, which I give to somebody in return for more money. In commerce, the person who wants the product provides the money to create it.

This doesn't happen with charities because charities exist to do work which, by definition, would not happen commercially. They support the poor, save ancient buildings, protect pandas and so on – providing something which the beneficiary needs but cannot pay for. So the money has to come from somewhere else: from donors.

Therefore there is by definition a separation between the donor and the beneficiaries. This has many crucial implications for how charities work, and for the care which you, as a donor, need to take.

a) Charities run two separate operations

Charities have to deal with both donors and beneficiaries. Put crudely, their job is moving resources from one to the other. But donors are normally very different from beneficiaries: roughly speaking, donors have resources whereas beneficiaries don't, and hence the operations to find and deal with them are very different. Serving beneficiaries might involve treating children for worms or fixing church roofs, whereas dealing with donors might involve hosting posh dinners, organising sponsored runs or selling Christmas cards.

You can see this separation by looking in any book about fundraising: it will be full of advice about identifying donors, crafting proposals, actually asking for support and so on – the giveaway is that nowhere will it say 'be good for beneficiaries'.

These different operations often require people with entirely different skill-sets, interests and backgrounds, whose work differs totally. The two teams may not need to be in the same office, and it may even be best if they're not. For example, in many aid agencies, the team raising money from donors needs to be in rich countries whereas the teams serving beneficiaries need to be in less developed countries. Rather comically, the two teams, even if co-located, may have such different work that they even dress quite differently: I've known organisations where fundraisers routinely show up to work in suits because they'll be off to lunch with business people who might give money, whereas their colleagues who run the day-centres in deprived parts of town (which the business people are being invited to support) would rarely be in suits for fear of being mistaken for debt-collectors or undertakers.

One implication of this is that charity Chief Executives are therefore running two almost entirely separate operations. So have some respect for them! Another is the irrelevance of a charity's fundraising costs, which we now see pertain to an operation almost entirely unrelated to the operation you care about, of serving beneficiaries.

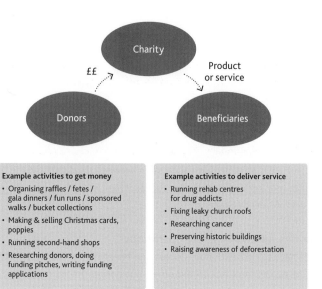

Example activities to get money
- Organising raffles / fetes / gala dinners / fun runs / sponsored walks / bucket collections
- Making & selling Christmas cards, poppies
- Running second-hand shops
- Researching donors, doing funding pitches, writing funding applications

Example activities to deliver service
- Running rehab centres for drug addicts
- Fixing leaky church roofs
- Researching cancer
- Preserving historic buildings
- Raising awareness of deforestation

b) Success in one operation (raising money) implies nothing about success in the other (serving beneficiaries)

Because these two operations are so different, organisations which are good at one aren't always great at the other. Some charities which do fine work with refugee camps, buildings or pandas aren't great at making a big noise to attract funding; and conversely, some charities which are just brilliant at getting people on their sponsored runs don't do a great job for the refugees, buildings or pandas they're meant to be serving. Now that you think about it, it's obvious – there's no reason to believe that skills in two totally unrelated businesses would be correlated.

Charities' success with donors (i.e., at getting money) depends on how good they are at dealing with donors, not on how good they are at dealing with beneficiaries. Consequently, in the charity world, the money doesn't necessarily follow the value: rather it follows the ability to attract money.

From that, we see that a charity's size doesn't necessarily indicate whether it's any good for beneficiaries. If a charity is large, strictly speaking all we can conclude is that it has lots of money, that is, it has a good operation for dealing with donors. (Strictly speaking, we can't even conclude that: it may only have been good at raising money in the past.) That tells you precisely nothing about the quality of the charity's machine for serving beneficiaries[6]. So don't be fooled into thinking that a charity which is large or famous is necessarily good. Growth is no indication

---

[6] It tells you nothing. Not that all large charities are bad at serving beneficiaries, nor that all small ones are good. Simply that size is virtually independent of quality. We'll see this in more detail in Section 2.

of quality either: that just means that a charity is attracting more money than it has previously which indicates nothing about the quality of its work. (By the way, growth in revenue may not actually indicate that the organisation itself is growing: size, revenue and growth work quite differently for charities than for companies, as we'll explore in Section 4.)

c) It won't be obvious whether a charity is any good

As a donor, you will normally only see the operation which deals with donors: the mailings through your door, the requests for sponsorships, the TV adverts. You don't normally see the other operation – the important one – because you're not the homeless person or the forest avoiding destruction or disease being researched. You don't automatically get feedback from beneficiaries about whether the charity is any good. What you get is feedback from the charity, and the feedback that donors get is pretty much the same whether the charity is good or not – pictures of smiling children and cute animals, for example.

As a result, if you want to find the best charities (which you do, since you're trying to improve the world as much as possible), you have to look beyond how good charities are at finding you and asking. There are ways to do this: we'll talk in Sections 2 and 3 about what to look for and what good charities look like, and in Section 4 about the detail of charities' results.

Incidentally, the charity itself doesn't automatically get feedback from beneficiaries either. Whereas companies can tell pretty readily if their customers like their products by looking at the level of demand and the prices they can charge, charities can't. Price signals don't exist in many charities because the beneficiary isn't paying, and the level of demand is a poor indicator because beneficiaries may have no choice about which charity serves them. Therefore charities also have to go looking for other indications of whether beneficiaries are really being helped, which are normally far from obvious.

d) Charity requires subsidy – by definition

Let's return to our insight that a charity provides support which beneficiaries need but cannot pay for. This means that it is in principle impossible to provide this service/product without a subsidy[7]. If it were possible, the provider would be a business. 'The problems philanthropy seeks to address are the very ones that have defied market-based solutions,' observes Phil Buchanan, President of the US Center for Effective Philanthropy. Therefore charities' work needs subsidising forever – the pandas or buildings or refugee camps are unlikely to magically get rich and become able to pay. The exceptions are those rare, halcyon occasions when a problem gets eradicated, such as happened with smallpox.

I'm spelling this out because I've heard people say that donors should only support a particular charity for a fixed period, such as two years or five years, because – and this is a direct quote from a successful business-person – 'any good charity won't need subsidy any more. If it does, then it's not a very good charity'. These donors then migrate their donations from one charity to another in a fanciful quest for a charity which doesn't need external subsidy – which, by definition, is virtually nonexistent.

In fact, when donors migrate like this, they create a problem. The charity simply has to find a replacement: its dependency on subsidy doesn't suddenly disappear. And the process of finding replacement donors can be expensive and therefore wasteful. (This, by the way, drives up the charity's fundraising costs. You see why fundraising costs can be so high, and are no indicator of the charity's quality: this replacement cost wasn't created by the charity at all but rather by the donor.)

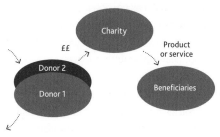

e) The economics are ugly

In fact, the view that 'a good charity won't need subsidy any more' is not only wrong, but normally the opposite of the truth. If a charity is effective, demand for its service will (normally) grow: more schools will want to have its therapy workers supporting their pupils, more families will want to use its toy library etc. Because

---

7 Some charities do earn some of their income from selling products and services. The National Trust sells cake but it can't fund its entire operation that way. 'Social enterprises', which can sometimes fund their own operations, are a different class of organisation altogether, which we'll touch on in Section 2.

none of those schools or pupils or families can pay the full costs, the charity needs a subsidy for each of them. So the more successful a charity is in serving beneficiaries, the more subsidy it needs to raise. More, not less.

Charities are so surprising because they don't live by the laws of supply and demand. They're doing work which, by definition, wouldn't happen commercially because the economics don't work. That's why they need subsidy, and why they get tax-breaks and so on. Success normally creates a hole in the finances, which is painfully counterintuitive given our familiarity with businesses.

Speaking rather brutally, the need to find a subsidy for every beneficiary means that charities (often) have an economic *disincentive* to serve beneficiaries. If you don't believe me, then consider this. You're running a hostel for homeless people which gets a stable income from reliable donors. To keep the example easy, let's suppose that you spend income within the month it's received and you haven't got much in the bank. Suddenly loads of additional homeless people turn up needing support. What do you do? If you serve them all, you'll get through this month's budget in a week and go bankrupt. You can't get more money from your existing donors because they haven't got any more. You can't spend money or divert staff to attracting new donors (it's practically impossible to rustle up new donors *without* spending money or time) because that will leave you even less to spend on beneficiaries – quite possibly preventing you from supporting the ones you've already taken on. You can't apply for a grant from a body like the National Lottery because that will normally take more than a month to come through. And yet you're passionate about helping those people, and your organisation exists expressly for that purpose.

The dilemma is horrible – and entirely realistic. It arises because serving beneficiaries doesn't bring the money with which to serve beneficiaries – one charity CEO described this as there being 'no fuel' in the system. The system in which charities operate does not reward them for serving beneficiaries.

f) The economics of increasing quality or quantity are ugly

Another weird implication of the fact that beneficiaries don't pay is that charities have no *economic* incentive to understand whether they're doing a good job for beneficiaries. Supermarkets, for example, invest a great deal in studying their customers: how they travel to the stores, what they want, how store layout influences purchase patterns and so forth. Supermarkets make those studies because they help sell more products to more people and so earn more money. That economic incentive just isn't there in charities. Serving beneficiaries creates a problem for the charity. As we've seen, charities get money (gather more fuel to do more work) by attracting and serving *donors*. So their economic incentive is to understand whether they're doing a good job for *donors*.

The fact that the fuel isn't attached to beneficiaries makes it hard for charities to invest in improving their services for beneficiaries. Let's take staff training. Our cake company might invest £400 in training staff on the basis that if staff are nicer to customers, the company will get new customers, and the extra profit from those new customers will repay the £400 (and more, with luck). By contrast, if a charity spends £400 on, say, training its panda centre staff to be better at weaning pandas, well, that's nice, but the pandas can't pay for that extra benefit. There's no mechanism by which improved service for beneficiaries brings more 'fuel' (money) to repay the investment which generated that improvement. As a result, there is less training in the charity sector than in the private sector, where improved service does create more fuel: 'The private sector spends more than a billion dollars on executive coaching every year. Yet that wasn't something that the nonprofit sector tapped into,' says Linda Wood at the Evelyn and Walter Haas, Jr. Fund.

Again, let's be precise. I'm saying that charities have no *economic* incentive to increase quality or quantity of serve their beneficiaries: doing a great job for beneficiaries does not bring the money with which to continue doing a great job for beneficiaries. By no means am I saying that charities and the people who work in them aren't interested in beneficiaries, which would be wildly and manifestly untrue.

What does this mean for your giving?

You won't know if you're doing a good job. If you make a good or bad choice of cake company, you will realise pretty rapidly because you're the one consuming the cake. There's a feedback loop, and you're in it. You can use that information in your next cake-buying expedition. But if you make a good or bad choice of charity to support, you won't realise because you're not *in* the refugee camp or the domestic violence refuge. The people who are in the camps or refuges or who are (meant to be) benefitting from the charity's work can't tell you because they've probably no idea that you exist and no means of contacting you. (If you like, or don't like, the art in the Sainsbury Wing of the National Gallery, what are you going to do? Write to Lord Sainsbury? Or you're a child being abused: you can hardly write to some banker or oligarch you've never heard of, berating them for not supporting the Lucy Faithfull Foundation.) There is no feedback loop at all. As a result, donors get no beneficiaries'-eye view on whether they made a good choice, nor on whether their support is helping or hindering.

Everything in this book follows from this insight. It explains why charities are so counterintuitive and hence why you should bother reading a whole book about how to find good ones and how best to help them.

Look under the bonnet. What you will readily see is how the charity deals with donors. But since you will not automatically get information about how the charity serves its beneficiaries, i.e., whether it is making progress at improving the world in the way you care about, you'll need to go looking for that. We'll talk much more about how to do that.

Be choosy about who you copy. Other donors – no matter how much they give or how famous they are – aren't getting feedback from beneficiaries either, so they probably have no more useful information about the charity than you do. Only accept their endorsements if you trust them to have gone looking for that feedback. (We'll see later that some charitable funders do this homework rigorously and taking their endorsements can be a smart move.)

You call the tune. If he who pays the piper calls the tune, then the tune in the charity world is called by donors because they're the ones paying. This may sound odd – even awful, since charities are set up to serve beneficiaries – but the naked truth is that charities have no option but to listen to 'he who pays' otherwise they cease to exist. As such, donors influence charities much more than they probably realise. For example, if donors collectively tell charities to strangle themselves by under-investing in learning systems ('admin'), ultimately charities have no choice. Make sure you call a tune in which the charity has a good operation for serving beneficiaries (as opposed to a good operation for serving you). Support the charity to improve those operations still further, by, for example, understanding its beneficiaries, its impact and refining its work.

Ask whether you're helping or hindering. Sometimes donors unwittingly hinder charities: they move their funding around, making charities incur costs finding new sources, or they create situations in which charity employees have to spend more time dealing with donors than with beneficiaries. The damage is invisible to the donor. As Katherine Fulton of the Monitor Institute astutely observes: 'The problems of philanthropy are not experienced as problems by philanthropists.' But though the damage is real to charities and their beneficiaries, charities rarely give honest feedback to the hand that pays them.

> 'From 1987 to 1999, Paul Brest was the dean of Stanford Law School. A day hardly went by when students, faculty or alumni didn't tell him what he was doing wrong – and at least once in a while they were right. Then in 2000, he became president of the Hewlett Foundation [a large US grant-making foundation] and, within a matter of months, underwent a personal transformation and, by all external signals, achieved perfection.'
> – Paul Brest and Hal Harvey, who worked together at the Hewlett Foundation

There's no external pressure on donors to choose good charities or to help them rather than hindering them. If, as a donor, you enable the expansion of a charity which runs bad refugee camps, you won't feel the pain yourself. But the pain is real nonetheless for somebody else. That means that you have to create that pressure, which clearly will require a bit of determination and brainpower.

Suspend your expectations. It's clear then that the absence of the swap, and the consequent separation of the consumer and the donor, changes everything. It makes charities fundamentally different from businesses, and their behaviour differs in many ways as a result.

If you're a business person, *do not think of charities as just another sector*[8]. Unlike airlines, barristers, oil companies or taxi firms, charities are not in a system in which quality and quantity are rewarded. The economics punish them for doing their job, and the resulting incentives, norms, rewards and frustrations are very different. Prepare to be surprised. I've worked with many donors who've taken a while to adjust to this – and who've learnt that, though their skills are very valuable, they have to be applied in unexpected ways.

This separation makes it hard to find great charities and to know how to support them and how to avoid hindering. But it's not impossible. With the basic theory about charities' goals, theories of change and effectiveness now under our belts, it's time now to look at starting work.

---

8 In the public sector, there is also sometimes a separation between the 'donor' and the 'beneficiary'. For example, UK tax-payers pay for the care of foster children though none of them is currently a foster child themselves. However, in a functioning democracy, the public sector does have a feedback loop: if all tax-payers dislike the service given to foster children, they can express that through elections. The feedback cycle is messy and long – elections give binary choices on disparate baskets of issues, and the full impact of public sector decisions may not be apparent for a long time (perhaps after the government has fallen anyway) – but at least there is *some* mechanism. In the charity world there is often no feedback mechanism at all.

Section Two

What you need to do: how you can improve the world through supporting charities

Who makes the biggest contribution to charities? Perhaps surprisingly, the answer is individual donors. In the UK, individuals give more than all companies and grant-making foundations combined, and 26 times the amount that comes from the National Lottery. Individuals also dominate in the US, where they collectively give 75 times more than even the mighty Gates Foundation. And that's just the money: individuals of course make vast contributions by giving their time. So individual donors are important.

If you're an individual giving small-ish amounts, this section is for you. And you're in great company: over half of personal giving in the UK is by people giving less than £100 a month. That can achieve a lot: a single pound into Marie Curie Cancer Care can provide an information pack for a patient with advice about the Marie Curie Nursing Service, and £20 will cover an hour of nursing care in a patient's home.

If you are a foundation or company or wealthy family giving more than about £100,000, other issues come into play for which you'll need a system. This is covered in Section 3, the additional ideas and insights in which are useful for any donor. Because it's donors who pay the piper, we must make sure to call tunes we really want – tunes which improve the world as much as possible for beneficiaries and which minimise the missed opportunities. In this section, we'll look first at how to find great charities – the practical steps you can take as well as the underlying theory, and then deal with some common situations and some of the folklore around what makes for good charities. Then we'll turn to how you can help: the best ways of using money and anything else, and lastly we'll see how to deploy even money which you're not in a position to give. Throughout, we'll keep in mind the goal, of improving the world – not just a bit, but as much as possible.

Sources of funds for charities, UK and US

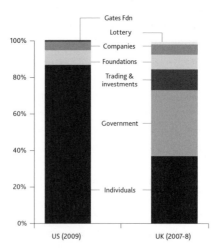

Chapter 6

How to find a great charity

What am I looking for? And what does it look like?

You're looking for charities which do something you feel is important, and which do it effectively. Because charities vary markedly in their effectiveness, you're not just looking for charities that do *some good* but for those which are *the best* – which don't leave children out in the fields when they could be in school. Identifying them is complicated because results aren't readily apparent, so you'll need to go looking. A further complication is that charities' results are genuinely complicated: we'll explore why, and a detailed response, in Section 4.

A charity's impact (its effectiveness) relies on two factors. First, it needs a good idea: an important and clear goal and a robust theory of change for achieving it. As we've seen, some theories of change are more effective than others, and in fact, we'll see shortly how some achieve nothing and others actually create harm. And second, it needs good implementation. That relies on the skill and training of the staff, which varies between charities just as it does between organisations in most walks of life.

For the impact to be high, the level of both the idea and implementation must be high. To put this another way, an organisation could run a deworming programme in India – which is a good 'idea' – but make such a dismal hash of implementation that it creates only low impact. If you're into formulae, think of it like this:

impact = idea x implementation

We can flesh that out into the six questions below, to which any good charity will have strong answers. They are based on a set developed by several UK- and

US-based organisations, and I recommend using them whenever you're reading literature from charities or talking with their staff:

Six questions which any good charity can answer

Idea (goal and theory of change)
- What's the problem you're trying to solve?
- What activities does the organisation do?
- How do those activities help solve the problem?

Implementation (does it seem to be making progress?)
- How do you find out whether you are achieving anything? (i.e., what is the research process?)
- What are you achieving? (i.e., what results does that process produce?)
- How are you learning and improving? What examples do you have of learning and improving?

So what does a good charity look like?

First, it does no harm
This phrase is one of the first precepts of medical ethics and has great relevance to charitable activity. Quite inadvertently, charities sometimes make things worse. Take the idea of providing a 'mentor' to a young person who's having a hard time or who is from a tough background. This work can be very effective at providing stability, boosting self-confidence and improving the attainment of those young people. But it takes time to work – normally at least six months. Providing mentors to young people for periods shorter than this has been found to harm them: it actually reduces self-esteem and increases their propensity to get involved in risky behaviour. There are other examples too, including some programmes to increase agricultural productivity which fail because they sink the water table, or programmes to scare people away from drug use which actually attract people to it.

Second, it achieves more than nothing
Some programmes don't make any difference at all. David Anderson, Assistant Director of the US-based Coalition for Evidence-Based Policy, has written (in a personal capacity) that:

'1) The vast majority of social programs and services have not yet been rigorously evaluated, and 2) of those that have been rigorously evaluated, most (perhaps 75% or more), including those backed by expert opinion and less-rigorous studies, turn out to produce small or no effects, and, in some cases negative effects.'

A couple of example programmes which have proven to achieve nothing are:

Nutrition in a developing country. The Bangladesh Integrated Nutrition Project provided, among other things, supplemental food to malnourished children. Close examination found no difference in malnutrition levels between people included in the programme and people who weren't. (This programme failed because of poor implementation, rather than being a bad idea.)

Educational software products. A rigorous study in the US of 16 leading educational software products for teaching reading and maths – including many award-winning products – found, on average, no difference in reading or maths achievement between students who used them in their classrooms and those who were taught through usual methods.

It is worth checking whether the particular approach (or 'idea') a charity uses hasn't already been proven ineffective. GiveWell publishes a list at www.givewell.org/giving101/Social-Programs-That-Just-Dont-Work.

Third, it maximises what it achieves

I opened this book with the deworming example because it shows an extreme variation in effectiveness. Though it's rare that one idea is 25 times more effective than another, it is common for the variation to be appreciable.

In Kenya, diarrhoea is a major killer of children, and is reduced if water supplies are clean. Several methods have been tried to ensure this. First, reducing contamination from groundwater by encasing village water sources in concrete. Second, delivering chlorine for free to individual households so they can purify their water at home. And third, giving people chlorine when they collect their water from community water sources. (There's a fourth option of delivering uncontaminated water directly to homes, which, for obvious engineering reasons, is substantially more expensive.)

Any guesses which of these three options is the cheapest? It's not obvious to the naked eye at all – they all sound reasonable. As it happens, the answer – at least in Kenya – is providing chlorine at the water source. Why? The researchers think that it's because it makes chlorination part of the routine of gathering water, reinforced by people seeing each other doing it.

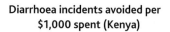

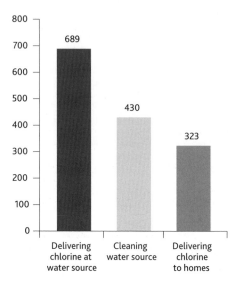

The striking feature of all these programmes is that they all sound like a good idea: none of them is obviously stupid. That's the point: you have to look under the bonnet to find out whether a programme's idea is actually any good.

Common questions about choosing charities

Should I look at its 'admin' costs, or the amount of money that goes to the 'actual charitable work'?
No! Admin costs are meaningless and have almost zero relationship to whether the charity is any good, as we've seen. It's a total nonsense, and will lead you to the wrong place. Do not use this as a criterion. In fact, you could use the fact that you're paying the piper to discourage charities from talking about their admin costs at all, since it so clearly misleads many people.
Can't I rely on the fact that the charity is registered?
Sadly, no. Being registered implies only that the charity is not operating fraudulently and remains within its mission. It does not indicate whether a charity is any good or not.
This charity helped me or somebody I know. Can I give based on that experience?
Great. You're home and dry. Unlike most prospective donors, you're not sepa-

rate from the charity's work – you know exactly how good it is for beneficiaries. If you want to support it to continue and expand, go ahead. It may nevertheless be worth looking at other charities which do similar work. For example, if your friends or family were supported by a hospice, you may want to look at other local hospices, or at hospices elsewhere in the country (perhaps in a region where donations are harder to come by), in case you find one in greater need of your support or which can achieve more with it.

Is it OK to rely on the fact that a charity is large and well-known?
I wouldn't. The fact that you've heard of a charity, or that it's big, is no indicator of quality. 'Large' simply means that the charity is good at raising money (or was in the past), which doesn't prove that it's good for beneficiaries. Similarly, being well-known just means that the charity is good at raising its profile, which is also separate from being good for beneficiaries.

Remember that to have high impact, charities need good ideas and good implementation (hence the formula: impact = idea x implementation). Would you expect large charities to have a monopoly on good ideas? No. Some ideas are impossible without huge resources – managing chunks of coastline as the National Trust does might be an example – but not all: a local lunch club for elderly people or supporting people with a rare medical condition may not take much resource and can perfectly well be done by small organisations. Would you expect large charities to have consistently better implementation? No. Sometimes they will be better, perhaps by deploying a large network of people, or getting economies of scale in purchasing, logistics and learning. But on the other hand, small charities may perform better by being more responsive and personal.

Remember too that a charity may be small simply because it hasn't yet acquired many resources: it might just be young. So size, profile and growth are all poor measures of a charity's ability to improve the world.

What happens if I support a bad charity?
You miss the opportunity to improve the world as much as you could have. But the missed opportunity isn't felt by you: rather, it's felt by the pandas or buildings or children whose lives could have been improved but aren't. Your experience is probably identical whether the charity is marvellous or rubbish, which is precisely why you should do your homework. The Chair of a new charitable foundation once asked me whether it would be sued if it selected bad charities. Sadly, no. There's no drama for you: just an unnecessary problem for somebody else. This entire book is about avoiding that.

How to find a good charity

The quick way is to make use of analysis already done by a judicious person or organisation. Below, I've given a list to start you off. If that doesn't help, there's advice on how to find other reliable analysts or advisors. And if they can't help, you'll need to do your own homework. Fear not – I'll show you a process which only takes about an hour. (If you're giving more than about £100,000, perhaps as a family, company or foundation, you will need some additional steps, outlined in Section 3.)

1) The quick way – making use of somebody else's recommendation

Personal recommendation. Friends and family may be able to recommend great charities, and can be wonderful guides. But remember that donors do not automatically know whether a charity is any good. Therefore, set most store by recommendations from people with a beneficiaries'-eye view: people who've been beneficiaries themselves so have experienced the charity's service or product directly, and donors who have done enough homework to understand what the beneficiary receives and how that compares to what beneficiaries of other charities receive. Experience suggests that donors – even a charity's own trustees – don't always understand that.

> **The Funding Network** is a gaggle of people who get together at weekends or evenings to hear from charities. Their sessions involve chat, wine and food – often in beautiful venues. Charities apply to the network and are selected to make a pitch to about 50-100 donors at a time, who then pledge money to ones they like, typically raising about £6,000 per charity. It's brilliant: the charity applies once, pitches once and reports once, and meanwhile the donors have a lovely sociable time and hear from charities they might not otherwise know exist.
>
> Its founder, Fred Mulder, created it after he noticed that 'giving money is one of the few things people do alone. We work together, eat together, dance together, and I've discovered that giving with others is more interesting, more effective and certainly seems to make money go further.'
>
> Representatives from charities also comment on how rare it is to present in person: applications and selections are often done solely on paper, without discussion or questions. Do go to an event: there are several groups throughout England, one specifically for young people, and, at the time of writing, there's one outside the UK, in Toronto. There's no obligation to give and non-members are welcome. www.thefundingnetwork.org.uk

Third-party endorsement. There is a small industry of professionals who spend their days analysing and evaluating charities. They study the needs which charities serve, their various approaches and relative success. You can make use of these professionals and their analysis to help you select good charities.

Some analysts, such as GiveWell, are independent, publishing the criteria they use and the lists of charities they endorse – you can pick charities from their lists. Others work within organisations which disburse money (known as grant-making trusts or foundations) such as Comic Relief and BBC Children in Need. Again, you can pick a charity from their lists, but you can also give *to* the grant-making trust itself. Why would you want to do that? For the same reason you might give to any charity: if it can add value to your money by doing things which you can't do yourself. Comic Relief and BBC Children in Need, for example, can use prime airtime on radio and television and get major celebrities to publicise causes.

Below are listed strong and established organisations which have a history of finding good organisations, and which publish their sensible criteria. If you support charities recommended by one of these organisations, you're unlikely to go wrong. (The list below is not exhaustive, and it's followed by guidance on how to assess other people or organisations.)

BBC Children in Need

Vision: 'A society where each and every child and young person is supported to realise their potential.'

Focus: Disadvantaged children and young people anywhere in the UK.

Not all teddy bears and Terry Wogan, BBC Children in Need does an amazing job of finding and supporting charitable work throughout the UK. It funds the 'obvious' causes – which tend to be the ones highlighted during its annual appeal – but also some quite radical ones such as countering child trafficking and sexual exploitation, street violence and gangs, and work with young offenders. BBC Children in Need is a very progressive funder. For example, it noticed that some causes were not reached by its existing process, and deliberately fixed that problem; it works with other donors (for example, it ran a £2m fund with Scottish donor Sir Tom Hunter, targeting young people who are not in education, employment or training); and is doing ground-breaking work to reduce the costs that its application and reporting processes create for charities.

BBC Children in Need's process is devolved geographically across the UK, enabling it to scoop up knowledge about the context in which applicant charities work. Applications are first seen by assessors throughout the UK, before going through voluntary committee members in each region who advise the Board based on their expertise and local knowledge. As you might expect, given that it was founded by a

public service broadcaster, BBC Children in Need is open and transparent, even publishing every penny of the CEO's expenses.
A list of charities is at www.bbc.co.uk/pudsey/grants/map.shtml. A video and some examples are at www.bbc.co.uk/pudsey/aboutus/whoyouvehelped.shtml

Comic Relief

Vision: 'A just world free from poverty.'
Focus: Activities in UK and less developed countries, notably Africa but also in Asia and Latin America. Areas include mental health, climate change, street children, HIV/AIDS, older people and sexually exploited/trafficked people.

A very impressive organisation, Comic Relief has, like BBC Children in Need, chosen to work in some tricky areas which are acutely under-resourced, such as young people and alcohol, child labour and mental health. To stay fresh, it reviews its choice of areas every four years. It states clear goals (such as, 'ensure that people with mental health problems are at the heart of decisions that affect their lives') and publishes its strategy for both UK and non-UK giving. It funds work right across the triangle, including work which directly supports individuals and work to influence government policy and raise public awareness.

Not only does Comic Relief report on how much it raises, but it also on what it achieves. And it adds value to donations by using its brand and contacts: persuading Sainsbury's to stock more Fairtrade products, getting Alesha Dixon and Chris Moyles to climb Mount Kilimanjaro to raise money, and working with the BBC to make programmes highlighting abuse of older people.
List: www.comicrelief.com/how-we-help/people-issues-we-support/
search-for-projects

GiveWell

Focus areas: In the US: access to employment, education, children and young people. Internationally: health (tropical diseases, TB, HIV/AIDS, immunisation), economic development (microfinance, employment access) and education.

A US-registered charity set up by some mid-career financiers in New York, GiveWell is not itself a funder but independently evaluates charities to help donors decide where to give. It publishes extensive analysis of each charity it considers, and rates them as 'gold', 'silver' or 'commended'. It's strict: of 83 US charities and over 300 non-US ones analysed by December 2010, only two were rated gold, eight were silver, and about 40 were commended. You can donate through GiveWell's site to charities it recommends.

GiveWell is astonishingly transparent – in my experience, uniquely so. It publishes its rationale for not recommending a charity, a list of its own mistakes and what it's doing about them, full transcripts and audio files of its board meetings, as well as great detail on its objectives, theory of change, plan, metrics for its own success, operations, and responses to objections. Its process is also remarkably open: charities can apply to be analysed, donors can request issues to be covered, and anybody can add to the list of its mistakes.

I particularly love it because of this statement, one of the best I've seen in ten years working on giving: 'We believe that information about how to help people should never be secret. We strive to disclose everything that goes into our decisions, in a way that individual donors can understand and use.' Hurrah.

List: www.givewell.org/charities

Innovations for Poverty Action (IPA) and the Abdul Latif Jameel Poverty Action Laboratory at the Massachusetts Institute of Technology (J-PAL)

Focus: Alleviating extreme poverty in less developed countries. Both organisations look at a wide range of issues, including education, health, sanitation, corruption, governance, agriculture, environment and employment.

These guys are a revolution. Full of economists, these sister organisations both run research to determine the effectiveness of various approaches to international development problems. They use randomised control trials, the gold standard of rigour used in drug trials and evidence-based medicine (which we'll discuss in detail in Section 4. The programmes which IPA and J-PAL evaluate are generally run by other 'operating' charities.) The research is deliberately scientific: studies are led by some of the most recognised names in development economics, many holding faculty positions at universities such as Harvard, Yale, Massachusetts Institute of Technology and London School of Economics, and they publish full details of the research methods and results (normally in peer-reviewed journals). Their results are more robust and reliable than almost anything else in the charity world. We've already seen several examples from their findings: the deworming example where we began, the work giving lentils to mothers who bring their children for vaccination (run by Esther Duflo, a professor at J-PAL), and the water chlorination programmes in Kenya.

They also support other academics running randomised evaluations in development issues, with nearly 300 studies covering agriculture, finance, health, education, governance, environment and energy across the globe. IPA has doubled in each of the last eight years (despite having no marketing budget), and now has about 600 staff and has conducted evaluations in over 40 countries. IPA, J-PAL and their network of academics work with governments, charitable funders and others to ensure that the lessons are learnt and used.

Results: The results of all the studies are all public www.povertyactionlab.org/evaluations and www.poverty-action.org/project-evaluations/search

Innovations for Poverty Action invites donations to its Proven Impact Initiative which supports the roll-out of some of the most effective work it has found, including the three examples mentioned above. IPA passes the funds to the operating charities, taking no cut itself: www.poverty-action.org/provenimpact This is the one entity I would specifically recommend supporting: it funds work which has been proven effective by the most rigorous tools available, and avoids the risk of 'going stale' because the set of charities which benefit can change over time.

BBC Radio 4 Charity Appeal and BBC One Lifeline appeals

Focus: Any cause with either UK-wide scope and/or significance, or international scope and/or significance.

The BBC has broadcast appeals for charities since 1923: currently they are broadcast each week on BBC Radio 4 and periodically on BBC One. Applications are assessed against a published set of criteria by a panel of current and former staff of major funders and charities such as Christian Aid and Scope. You can donate to any of the charities individually or to a fund divided equally between the 52 featured in a year.

List of charities on BBC Radio 4 appeal: www.bbc.co.uk/programmes/b006qnc7/episodes/player and charities featured before April 2009: www.bbc.co.uk/radio4/religion/radio4appeal_archive.shtml

List of charities on BBC One Lifeline appeal: www.bbc.co.uk/charityappeals/money/lifeline.shtml

Global Giving

Focus: Small charities mainly in less developed countries, plus some in the UK and US.

Global Giving enables donors to find vetted projects in over 100 countries worldwide. The 300 projects it lists work in education, health, economic development and the environment. The primary role of Global Giving's vetting process is ensuring that the project is truly charitable and properly constituted. The website works rather like eBay (in fact it has had funding from eBay co-founder Pierre Omidyar): projects are listed with a description and price-tags showing the cost of various activities. The site specialises in projects which can make a difference with tiny amounts of money. For example, one organisation which supports very poor elderly people in Guatemala lists the following:

£7 – Will feed an old person for a month
£91 – Will feed an old person for a year
£101 – Will buy a maize crusher to make tortillas

Founded by two former World Bank executives, Global Giving lists projects run by in-country charities and by international agencies. Organisations can nominate themselves to be listed and can be nominated by others. Global Giving can handle physical cash transfers to the organisation and process tax-relief claims on donations. It has raised over £20m from donors in the US and UK.

Lists: www.globalgiving.org.uk for UK-based donors and www.globalgiving.org for US-based donors.

Community Foundations and LocalGiving.com

Community Foundations gather donors to support effective local organisations in a specific region. They exist in many countries, and the UK has 56, covering all of Scotland, Wales, Northern Ireland and every county in England. Each Community Foundation has strong links in its region, a good understanding of local needs and a record of supporting hundreds, if not thousands, of organisations. Community Foundations explain the local context, help donors to prioritise issues there, and provide a range of services depending on the level of involvement that a donor wants. They can recommend charities working on specific issues (perhaps training young people, supporting young mothers or working in the arts), and arrange visits if appropriate. They can handle the financial transfer and subsequent relationship. Community Foundations root out both large and small charities, and are one of the few conduits to organisations which are too small to be registered with the regulator.

Because they work in local areas, Community Foundations are a good way of meeting other people who are giving to, or working on, issues in your community. In some Community Foundations, donors collaborate on supporting work overseas.

www.Localgiving.com is putting online the organisations recommended by UK Community Foundations, and can take donations from £5 upwards. It is co-owned by the Community Foundation Network, the membership body to which most UK Community Foundations belong.

Kiva

Focus: Micro-loans to entrepreneurs in 59 less developed countries and the US.

Kiva lists entrepreneurs, usually individuals, who need a small loan – for example, a small-scale farmer in Ecuador looking for a loan of $50 for equipment to help grow his business. Kiva works through microfinance institutions in the countries in which it works (local lenders, which may be for-profit or not-for-profit). The entrepreneurs repay the loans, and the microfinance institutions repay you, which of course means that you can use the money again. Kiva claims a repayment rate above 98.5 per cent: for example one of my cousins has now lent the same $100 no fewer than 26 times. Although the entrepreneurs and the microfinance institutions may not be charities, I've included Kiva here because microfinance can be a powerful way of improving the world[9].

List: www.kiva.org

Analysts to avoid

There are some entities which 'analyse' charities on simplistic measures, which I do *not* recommend using. For example, the US-based Charity Navigator analyses charities partly on the basis of their published financial data, which really means looking at their admin and fundraising ratios. As we've discovered, these measures are irrelevant, in fact contraindicating effectiveness as demonstrated by Professor Karlan (who is, by the way, the founding President of Innovations for Poverty Action).

2) Getting a recommendation from elsewhere

If you can't make use of recommendations from any of the organisations listed above – maybe they don't cover the region or issue you're interested in – the next best option is to look at other reliable large funders, fundraising foundations and media organisations. For example, Oprah's Angel Network, founded by Oprah Winfrey, which ran from 1997-2010, gave grants to organisations providing basics such as access to education, books and homes.

You're probably safe to take a recommendation from an analyst or donor if:

- it publishes the list of who it supports or recommends
- it publishes the strategy and/or criteria by which it arrived at that list. This will indicate that it's really serious about what it does, and enable you to decide whether you agree with the criteria. Do those criteria align with the principles of good giving? Are they solely related to merit?
- you like its list. If it includes charities that you think are suspect, the organisation's criteria aren't right for you.

It is worth giving to another donor (as opposed to just picking charities from its list) if it adds value to your donation. Perhaps it brings in lots of volunteers, or leverages its experience by getting changes at the base of the triangle, supports charities in other important ways or avoids duplication. It was this logic which led the world's most successful investor, Warren Buffett, to donate the overwhelming bulk of the

---

9 'Microfinance' is often taken to mean solely micro-loans, but can also include micro-savings and micro-payments (which the poor often need but which often have prohibitively high transaction costs). The precise circumstances in which micro-loans (also called micro-credit) are helpful have been investigated by Innovations for Poverty Action and J-PAL, with some surprising findings. How much interest can the poor really pay? Is it true that it's better to lend to women? Is it better to lend to groups? What is the optimal size of a group? What do people really do with the money? And why are we lending at all: how can we move people from loans to savings? This is all discussed in IPA's book *More Than Good Intentions* (Karlan D., Appel J.)

money he is giving to charity, a cool $31 billion, to the Bill and Melinda Gates Foundation. (We'll pull several valuable lessons from their work in Section 3.)

3) Analysing a charity yourself

If there is nobody whose recommendation you can use, you need to do the analysis yourself. This can be a fascinating process. To find charities with a particular goal or in a particular location, look at:

- The Charity Commission or other regulator's website. Here you can search for charities based on their type of activity (search for a term in their 'charitable objects') and the region where they work – www.charity-commission.gov.uk/ShowCharity/RegisterOfCharities/AdvancedSearch.aspx (The role of regulators is outlined in the appendices.)
- There are various online directories, such as Charity Choice or Guidestar, through which you can search for charities by sector and geography. (Charity Choice's 'geography' doesn't distinguish between where the charity is located and where its work benefits. So it lists the charity Africa Now as an Oxford charity, despite its beneficiaries being, presumably, in Africa.)

Then see whether anybody you respect already funds or supports the charity, for example as a donor or trustee. Most charities list donors and trustees on their websites, and they're usually also listed in a charity's Annual Report and Accounts. Publishing these documents is a legal requirement, and they can be found on the regulator's website (within the UK), and often on charities' own websites. If you trust those donors or trustees to have understood what the beneficiaries need and receive, and how this charity compares to others, you may want to take their recommendation.

And if none of that has helped, use the process below, based on one designed by New Philanthropy Capital. You can do it in about an hour, which isn't bad for improving the world. As a reminder, you're looking for a charity which has good impact because it has both a good idea and good implementation. It should have strong answers to the six questions we met earlier – and sufficient plans, people and financial resources to give you confidence that it will remain strong into the future.

Analysing a charity in one hour

The first 20 minutes: the charity's own website
Ideally, you should find answers to the following questions on any charity's website or public materials. However, small charities may (quite rightly) not have a flashy website.

Basics. What legal form does the organisation have? Is it, for instance, a registered charity or a charity exempt from registration? (Definitions are in the appendices.)

Goals. Is the charity clear about its goals? Do you think that its work is important? Does it show a clear understanding of the problem it's trying to solve? Strong charities provide lots of data about the problems on which they focus and how those problems arise.

Activities and theory of change. At a minimum, you should be able to understand the charity's activities and how they are supposed to contribute to the goals (that is, you should be able to understand its theory of change, even if it's not called that.) Ideally, the charity will cite some evidence for its theory of change. Do you agree with its goals and theory? Is the evidence credible? Are you comfortable with where its work sits on the triangle? If not, stop: find another charity to consider. If yes, continue, looking now for:

Results. Is the charity clear about what it achieves? Charities often talk about the problems they address (dyslexia, forced migration, homelessness) which is important but you're looking for solutions. Does the charity have a sensible-sounding process to discover what it is achieving? (Lack of detail is a bad sign.) I'd usually expect to see some case studies – stories of specific people or pandas helped, as well as an overview of the numbers of beneficiaries served or systematic changes created. Sensible processes do not include saying, 'we did such-and-such and then something-or-other happened'. These sorts of statements are pretty common but broadly useless because they indicate nothing about whether the something-or-other was caused by the such-and-such. (We'll return to this hugely important subject in Section 4, when we explore results in more detail.)

Stronger evidence of a charity's results than its own documentation would be provided by an independent evaluation. The strongest evidence of all would be from a randomised control trial, which would identify the contribution of the charity to that change.

Charities which are very new or innovative may not yet have results, and neither will charities whose work takes a long time to bear fruit. In those cases, I'd want to see some rationale for their work based on evidence from other organisations. Be sensitive to the fact that innovative work may fail; that's quite acceptable, as long as the reasons are understood, documented and shared.

Trustees and management team. Does the charity have the kinds of skills, experience and diversity which you would expect, given its goals? Among the crucial elements noted by the Charity Commission in its guidance *Hallmarks of An Effective Charity* is 'a clearly identifiable board or trustee body that has the right balance of skills and experience, acts in the best interests of the charity and its beneficiaries, understands its responsibilities and has systems in place to exercise them properly.'

Learning and improving. Does the charity publish examples of learning and improving, perhaps changing its activities in response to its own experience and research, or that of other organisations?

Working with others. Most charities' goals are too large and complex for any organisation to achieve alone. Therefore look for evidence of collaboration with other charities, businesses, academics and/or with government agencies.

Transparency. Does the charity make it easy to find basic information, such as annual reviews and accounts, strategic plan, and methods for involving beneficiaries in its work? Is there any honesty about the challenges it faces?

Next 10 minutes: information from elsewhere on the web

Goal, theory and results. Check that the charity is not doing a type of work which has already been proven ineffective. For example, if a dyslexia charity is doing 'bio-neurological repatterning', run some internet searches on that term to see whether there are any relevant case studies or research projects. In interpreting what you find, be aware of the differences between countries and situations: just because treating children for intestinal worms can greatly increase school attendance in India, that doesn't mean that deworming would achieve much in Kensington, because few children there have worms. That is to say, just because an 'idea' has proven effective in one place, it won't necessarily be as effective elsewhere – there may be significant differences in social norms, the economy, infrastructure and available technology. The converse is true too: an 'idea' might fail in one place but work marvellously in a different context. Clearly, the more similar the contexts are, the more likely it is that the results will be replicable.

If a relevant randomised control trial shows the idea to be effective in a similar context, then great: 'all' you have to do is look at its implementation.

Press coverage. Check to see whether anything particularly excellent or alarming is reported – though bear in mind that press coverage is not always terribly precise or reliable.

Backgrounds of Chief Executive and trustees. Do they, collectively, have the experience needed? You may find further information by searching on social networking websites such as www.LinkedIn.com.

Influence. Is the charity publicly discussed by other people such as beneficiaries, volunteers, academics or funders? Is its work cited in books or articles as an example of good practice?

Next 10 minutes: the charity's Annual Report and Accounts for the last two years

Charities must publish accounts which, again, are normally available from the charity itself or the regulator, and for charities with income above £500,000, the accounts will be audited.

The accounts can indicate a charity's financial stability. Ideally, a charity has a spread of funders to mitigate the risk of them migrating away. Ideally too, a charity would have a few months' reserves. Reserves are money the charity has in the bank. The absolute amount (which will be published in the accounts) is less important than the length of time they represent (which you'll need to calculate by looking at its total running costs). Two months' reserves means that the charity has in the bank the costs it incurs in two months – that is, if all funding dried up suddenly, it could keep going for two months. Less than about a month's worth and things can be a bit precarious – though this is sadly not unusual. Short reserves are not a cause for alarm if the charity is well-established and funding is likely to continue. Reserves of more than a year or two and your money will (probably) sit in the bank for quite a while before it's spent, so you may conclude the charity isn't a priority use for your funds[10]. The diagram opposite shows the reserves of a random selection of UK charities.

A charity's Annual Report (typically published with its accounts) gives several useful indications. First, it can show what's most important to the charity. Good charities are passionate about their missions and outcomes, there's a hunger to serve and a strong sense of urgency, so they talk a lot about results and efforts to improve. For example, when raising money or dealing with funding cuts is discussed, it is in the context of improving, growing, or maintaining charitable results, rather than just moaning.

Unrestricted reserves, various UK charities (months)

These are just the 'unrestricted reserves', that is, reserves over which the trustees have complete discretion: we'll look in more detail at unrestricted money later.

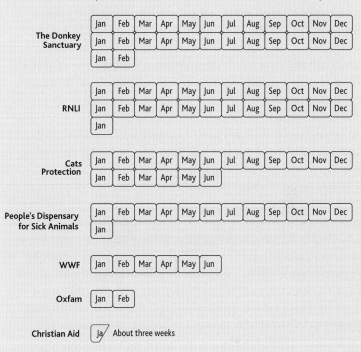

Finally, if you're planning on giving a large amount, you might want a phone call with the Chief Executive or senior management.

> *'The team with the best players wins'*
> – Jack Welch, former CEO, GE

The Chief Executive and senior managers are crucial to a charity's success. (If the charity has no paid staff, the relevant people are the Chair or other trustees.) This phone call has two aims. First to answer any of the questions above which you have been unable to answer from public sources, and second, to help you to assess their leadership qualities.

---

10 The precise analysis is to apply a discount rate. They work like this: if a £100 donation isn't spent for a year during which there is inflation of 5%, the donation will only purchase what could now be purchased for £95. Its value can be discounted by 5%: in other words, it loses 5% of its value whilst waiting.

Clearly, the time of charity CEOs and senior managers is valuable and pressured, and you don't want to distract them. Before you call, do check again for a funder or analyst on whose advice you can rely. To see whether your proposed donation is worth the call, think of a charity CEO's time as being priced at £100+ per hour, depending on a charity's size. So if you're planning to give, say, £500, it's fine to call to a tiny charity, but it would probably not be a great use of time of a manager in a larger charity. Similarly, £5,000 might be a good threshold for a medium charity. Be courteous: book the call in advance.

Below are the questions I suggest. GiveWell also publishes questions specific to various types of charitable work including forest conservation, maternal health in less developed countries, and shelters for homeless people (www. givewell.org/charity-evaluation-questions).

What does success look like for you? I'd want to hear the charity's theory of change (realising that the charity may not call it that), hear some evidence that it works, and sense some ambition. For example, I would be impressed by a statement such as: 'In the long term, success would mean being able to shrink the organisation because we will have helped to reduce the problem of eating disorders in the UK.' Ask about the activities which the charity runs, looking for how each contributes to the goal. Ask what the charity would do if it got a large donation: the answer will indicate what it thinks is a priority.

How do you know if you are succeeding? And are you? A good answer would indicate a sensible process for finding out what the charity is achieving, and concrete examples of past success. For charities with long theories of change, their evidence may be about progress at intermediate stages.

What are the most important lessons you have learnt in the last year, and what will you do differently next year as a result? This indicates whether a charity learns from its results and peers, and whether it is adaptable.

How do you involve your beneficiaries? Because beneficiaries aren't paying the piper and aren't even in the feedback loop, they can end up receiving what somebody else deigns to provide. To ensure that they get what they actually need, good charities involve beneficiaries in planning their work – they might involve young people in planning leisure activities, or consult soldiers' families about priority problems they face. (Clearly this is impractical in some instances, such as when the charity is or serving animals or future generations.)

What is your charity's particular contribution to your sector? Ask how the charity fits with other charities, government agencies and businesses.

A strong charity will be aware of other organisations in its 'industry' (such as mental health, domestic violence or pre-school education), collaborate with others and bring some feature or activity which is meaningfully distinct. A particularly good sign is ability to cite other organisations requesting its services or advice, or using its findings. A bad sign is a senior manager who moans incessantly about everyone else.

Have you ever stopped one of your charity's activities? The answer should show whether the managers know or care which activities work or not, and how resources are allocated. It also shows if he or she is capable of making tough decisions.

Done! You should by now have a sense of the charity's goals, whether they're important and whether the charity is effective in achieving them. Now we need to deal with some common situations and folklore which you may encounter.

Chapter 7

Finding great charities: dealing with particular situations and myths

So you've found an issue which excites you and some charities to support. Fantastic. But life isn't that simple and you may find yourself asked to support other organisations and/or you may also collide with some of the myths about the best types of charity to support. They're mainly useless guides, for the simple reason that they don't look at how good a charity is at serving beneficiaries. This chapter is to help you make good decisions in some common situations and deal with some of the myths.

What if…?
…there's a disaster or emergency

Disaster and emergency situations require rapid and co-ordinated action, and because they are often unexpected, it is rare for any one organisation to already have the necessary infrastructure in place. Therefore the Disasters Emergency Committee (DEC) is your best bet. It comprises 13 humanitarian organisations, including Oxfam, British Red Cross, Christian Aid, Islamic Relief and Save the Children. After an emergency, they collectively fundraise, run adverts in the media, and collect donations at the Post Office and banks (for which they are not charged). The DEC also co-ordinates members' activities on the ground. DEC Appeals raise funds for six months and spend them over two years. The committee has raised over £750m since its launch in 1963, and its process for screening eligible organisations is highly robust: for example, member organisations must meet its published criteria, on which they are re-assessed every two years. DEC publishes its criteria for intervening in a particular situation, and requires organisations to which it gives funds to publish independent evaluations of their work.

...a charity is doing important work but is not very good at it, or is the only charity around

Suppose there's only one hospice in your local area, or one charity supporting parents of children with a rare disease which affects your child. Or perhaps you want to support activity at the base of the triangle in your area of interest, and there are few organisations at that level. It means of course that you're not choosing between several organisations. If you have concerns about the performance of a charity in this kind of situation, I recommend that you do support it but tell it about your concerns and the improvements you would like to see. You might want to share the frameworks about what great charities look like – such as the Charity Commission's *Hallmarks of an Effective Charity* and the set in *The little blue book* by New Philanthropy Capital – and use them to make specific suggestions. You might offer relevant skills or contacts to help the charity to improve, for example, in financial management or risk assessment.

...you're asked by fundraisers in the street or at your door

You might be stopped in the in the street by a tabard-wearing fundraiser (popularly known as a 'chugger', from 'charity mugger'), or a fundraiser might telephone you or knock at your door. These fundraisers normally work for agencies rather than for the charity itself, and in my experience have pretty limited knowledge about the charity's work. Charities use these fundraisers because they recruit donors whom charities don't otherwise reach (notably young people), and so increase the pool of funds available. My advice is not to give via these fundraisers. It is the antithesis of proactive giving, typically ill-informed and ineffective. The charity's ability to put that person on the street or on the phone is utterly separate from any skill in saving pandas or ancient buildings, and is no indication of quality. It's also conspicuous that chuggers almost invariably talk about the *problem* on which the charity works than providing any evidence that the charity is effective at solving it.

My other concern about them is that this kind of fundraising focuses almost exclusively on activities at the top of the triangle. We can understand why, since those are the most emotive, but as we've seen those activities are not universally the best use of resources.

If you're interested in improving the world, then signal to these fundraisers that you will only champion charities with great ideas and great implementation. Instead of signing up, ask the fundraiser the six key questions which any good charity can answer.

...you're asked to support somebody doing a sponsored event

Sponsoring your friend to do the New York City marathon or walk around a field for three weeks is, if you think about it, rather peculiar. Their marathon and your giving money for the church roof are totally separate. In many countries, the concept of charity sponsorship doesn't exist at all. The logic is supposed to be like matched funding: 'I have done my homework on this charity and found that it's effective (at improving the world in some way which I think is important). To demonstrate my conviction, rather than giving money myself – which would naturally give me the right to ask you to match my donation – I'm going to endure sitting in a bath of baked beans for two days. On the basis of my (now demonstrated) conviction, please give to this charity.' Please put your money where my effort is.

Sometimes, this is truly what is happening. For example, at the precise moment I'm in my warm kitchen writing this, several British Army chaps are slogging across the Antarctic recreating the famous Scott-Amundsen's route in order to raise money for the Royal British Legion. And six soldiers who served in Iraq and Afghanistan, three of them amputees, are rowing across the Atlantic to spur donations for Help the Heroes. You can imagine that they feel pretty strongly about supporting ex-service personnel.

However, sponsorship doesn't always follow this logic. For instance, if you want to run one of the big marathons, one of the easiest ways to get a place is through a charity. Runners are sometimes asked to raise a minimum level of sponsorship, so may ask for sponsorship for charities with which they have no connection, conviction or interest.

In deciding whether to sponsor somebody, a good place to start is your relationship with the person asking. You'd be hard-put to turn down the child of a good friend doing a long sponsored swim just because you didn't trust the child to analyse charities. You may well want to support your friend and applaud the child's community spirit. Or you may be willing to pay to enable your friend to do the marathon. The question may be settled simply by the nature of that relationship.

Beyond that, ask the person how they selected that charity. Think about whether you trust them to have done the analysis well and thus found a good charity. If you do, then great, go right ahead. Notice though that the swim or baked beans are totally irrelevant, because your friend has led you to a good charity. For example, I once signed up for a sponsored 10k run in aid of a charity of which I was a trustee. People sponsored me because they trusted my recommendation of the charity: I'd amply vouched for it by becoming a trustee. The weather on the day was atrocious. I remember thinking that nobody would care if I didn't actually run: my sponsors' concern for the charity's work and willingness to support it were quite independent of any concern for my fitness or endurance. (Just for the record, I did complete it.)

Lastly, do your own research in the way described earlier. If you conclude that the charity is effective and its cause important, then great.

If none of those considerations persuades you to sponsor the person, I'd encourage you to ask them the key six questions, and/or to pass the questions to the charity. Again, this will signal to charities that donors value clarity of mission and effectiveness, which should improve performance. You could of course applaud your friend's effort by giving money to a different charity. Alternatively, if you haven't got any money or want to support your friend but aren't convinced about the charity they've chosen, go to The DoNation, a new sponsorship platform that replaces cash with action, and pledge to do some pro-environmental actions instead. www.thedonation.org.uk

...you're asked for a donation by your school or university

You might be asked for money by your old school or university. Several factors might incline you to give to it, and we'll consider them in turn. (Note that, whereas under the charity law of 1601, any activity related to education could be considered charitable, this is no longer the case: since 2006, independent schools have had to demonstrate defensible 'public benefit'. Many responded by offering bursaries, which a judicial review in October 2011 ruled not necessarily adequate.)

It's for extras. Schools often seek funds for musical instruments, sports equipment and so on. In the state school system, the school is largely funded by the state but private donations enable these 'extras'. (The relative roles of government and private money are discussed in the chapter about government in Section 4.)

Peer pressure. Some clever universities divide students into groups, and only if each member contributes does the whole group get invited to a snazzy dinner. If you experience this kind of pressure to give to an institution which you genuinely suspect would use a donation badly, you could do a service to the beneficiaries by pointing this out to your peers, dissuading them from giving, and telling the school or university about your misgivings.

Gratitude. It's great that you want to express your gratitude. But if the institution charges fees, then arguably you (or somebody) has already paid your dues, so perhaps that's a curious reason to pay again. (And even if the school or university was state-funded, your dues have already been funded by the tax-payer, so again that's rather curious.) Either way, if what you're really saying is that you'd like others to benefit from this fine institution in the way that you have, then we need to look at whether it's meritocratic.

To improve the world. Ah, this is more like it: you truly believe that the institution improves the life-chances of its students. Well, in that case, we need to ensure that it distributes those important opportunities fairly, on merit rather than reinforcing existing privilege or rewarding insider knowledge. This will show up in the data about its admissions process.

Most selective institutions do claim to select students solely on merit. For instance, the Admissions Policy of Durham University states: 'Our admissions policy is fair and transparent and we seek to recruit the most able and most motivated students who can best benefit from a Durham University education.'

One education analyst takes the view that a university which admits solely on merit and goes out of its way to find and attract those candidates, there would be similar proportions of less privileged people amongst people who (a) could apply, e.g., who get adequate A Levels (or equivalent) in relevant subjects, (b) do apply, and (c) get admitted. (See diagram below. This analysis will work for any count-able definition of 'less privileged people', such as entitlement to free school meals, household income decile, and so on.) Big discrepancies between proportions in these stages implies that selection is influenced by factors other than merit – in which case the school/university needs to work harder to get less privileged people to apply, and/or to counteract the biases in its selection process.

Most selective institutions which solicit donations claim that those donations are very important. In which case they'll listen to the person calling the tune, so donors collectively can have considerable influence. If we all ask for this analysis, the insti-tution will probably start to manage it rather actively. The questions earlier in this section are also useful, as are further questions available from GiveWell.

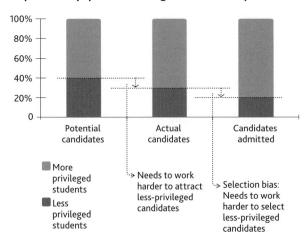

Composition of populations throughout admissions process

...you want to leave a bequest of money in your Will

More than a third of us leave money to charity in our Will, and many more donate our bodies or valuable objects. This is wonderfully generous, but again the ways you give can influence the bequest's effectiveness.

Some issues are specific to Wills. First, you need a charity to outlive you, which with any luck means that it'll be around for quite a while yet. And second, you want to ensure that the charity is large enough to absorb your donation. If your gift is more than about a third of its annual income, you might want to let the charity know that it may be coming and discuss with them how they might use it. (I don't mean prescribing a specific use, but rather that the charity may need additional management in order to use the funds well.) For both of these reasons, larger charities may be safer bets. If you want to support smaller organisations – community groups, for example – a good option is giving to a grant-making foundation or Community Foundation which does a good job of passing funds to smaller organisations.

Ideally, tell the charity about the bequest. This makes it a great deal easier for them to plan. (As we'll see in Section 3, charities can be bizarrely penalised for receiving bequests.)

Let the charity use your gift however it sees fit. This is always good advice – as we'll see later – but it's particularly important with Wills because charities can't call you up to discuss any problems, and dealing with executors can be complicated.

Restoration non-comedy

An art gallery in a medium-sized town received a sizable legacy out of the blue, with an instruction to use it to purchase 'a group of paintings, but not a collection'. Paintings rarely become available in groups so this was problematic. Furthermore, the gallery already owned many more paintings than it could display: what it really needed was help restoring its existing works and with the costs of the heating, lighting, insurance and staffing to keep the gallery open. 'A group of paintings' would simply have added to the restoration backlog.

The gallery couldn't accept the bequest as written, so ended up in a protracted discussion with grieving executors to get the restriction lifted.

Ensure that your Will includes the charity's precise name and charity number. For example, if you want to give to Cancer Research UK, make sure to write 'Cancer Research UK': writing just 'cancer research' can cause confusion and delay.

Advice on drafting Wills is available from any law firm and there is masses of advice online. Will Aid is a scheme through which lawyers waive their fee for creating a basic Will, in return for which customers are invited to make a donation to the nine charities involved in Will Aid. Over 150 charities have collectively formed Remember A Charity which encourages people to leave a gift to charity in their Will and provides advice. (Though its advice pertains to gifts to any charity, searches on its site only include its member charities. The list is rather curious: for example, it has no charities working on the environment or human rights.) www.rememberacharity.org.uk

Cancer Research UK offers a free Will-writing service, without obligation to give to it. http://legacies.cancerresearchuk.org/adding-us-to-your-will/

Advice for people writing Wills in Australia, Belgium, Canada, Ireland, Spain, Switzerland and Norway is available here: www.rememberacharity.org.uk/pages/our-international-partners.html

...you want to donate your body in your Will

If you wish your body to be used for medical purposes, you also need to use the correct form of words because, for very good reasons, the use of human tissue is regulated in the UK by the Human Tissue Authority. Sadly, many people who kind-heartedly make provision in their Will for their body to be used after their death use a form of words which prevents it being used in the way they had hoped. The form of words recommended by the Human Tissue Authority is this:

> *'I wish to donate my body after my death. I understand that it may be used for: anatomical examination; education or training relating to human health; and/or research in connection with disorders, or the functioning, of the human body.'*

This should increase the likelihood of your donation being accepted. However, if you wish your body to be available to train healthcare professionals, the Human Tissue Authority prefer you to complete and return a consent form from the medical school of your choice or include your consent in the Will. The consent forms allow you to make other choices about, for instance, how long your body can be kept, and registering with a specific medical school means that you and your family are fully informed and supported. The Human Tissue Authority provides contact details and general information on its website: www.hta.gov.uk.

...you want to bequeath objects to a gallery or museum

The way that you give is important even for bequeathing Grandma's Stradivarius violin or her set of antique teapots or the stately home that your family no longer needs. (You can, by the way, leave paintings, furniture or even the entire contents of your home to the National Trust.) If possible, make contact with the organisation to which you're considering leaving an object: knowing that Grandma's fiddle is on its way, it may hold off on buying another Strad. Alternatively, it might not need your objects: perhaps it's closing its teapot wing or has an abundance of violins already. This is more complex than it seems: if a gallery or museum receives something it can't use, it may be obliged to sell it – and so your object might end up in private ownership, which might not have been your intention. If your wish was that the gallery or museum use the object itself or failing that gives it to another institution, you would do well to state that explicitly in your Will.

...you are wondering whether to give anonymously

This topic generates quite strong passions, and attitudes vary markedly between countries and cultures. My advice is to do whatever will most improve the world in the long-term, that is, assessing what's in the best interests of the charity – or, better, its beneficiaries.

There are two types of anonymity. 'Total anonymity', wherein you don't tell the recipient charity who you are; and 'public anonymity', wherein the charity knows but doesn't disclose it. Public anonymity can be attractive if donors fear ending up on a list which gets passed or sold between charities. Any well-organised charity will respect a donor's expressed wish for non-disclosure.

Total anonymity is required or applauded by some religions and cultures, and some donors like the fact that nobody else knows. There's an attractive purity to knowing that the gift is given solely to achieve results, rather than from desire for personal gain or recognition. Other advantages include the fact that you won't be bothered by calls or follow-up letters – an appealing route if you are sure that your donation is a one-off because the charity won't spend any of your donation on contacting you. The demerit of total anonymity is that if the charity can't contact you, it can't tell you about its achievements which many donors enjoy hearing. Totally anonymity also precludes donating time and skills, thus limiting the value of your donation to 'just' its financial value, whereas many financial donations are considerably enhanced by accompanying non-financial support.

Either type of anonymity is useful if you yourself are controversial, such that association with you won't help. Be aware though that it may attract suspicion. For example, a lawsuit was brought (unsuccessfully) against the University of Wisconsin in 2010 to force disclosure of the source of a $15m donation so 'they could be questioned about their finances'.

The major drawback is of giving anonymously is that you can't inspire or shame other people into giving to the great organisation which you've found. Research and experience both show that people do what they perceive as 'normal' in their communities, and people often act out of competition and one-upmanship. Here's Bill Gates on this matter (in a private email to a friend of his):

'Scott Oki (ex-Microsoft) and Jeff Brotman (Costco) decided they were personally going to STRONGLY encourage people who [have] been successful to give to United Way at a high level. I hear they have signed up almost 40 people at the Emerald Level which I think is $1M over 5 years. This is unprecedented and fantastic. When people see that Bezos, Allen, Glaser, etc. are all giving **it draws more people in**. *Scott and Jeff make sure to get help from all the givers to get more givers.'*

Tapping that motivation can be a fruitful way to improve the world. In the book *Philanthrocapitalism*, Matthew Bishop and Michael Green quote Bernard de Mandeville's *Fable of the Bees*: 'Pride and vanity have built more hospitals than all the virtues together', concluding, 'So raise your glass, at your $10,000-a-head black-tie gala charity dinner, to those great fundraisers, Pride and Vanity.'

Myths and misconceptions

Having dealt with some common situations, we'll now turn to some common misconceptions. In any which you meet, remember that you're not giving *to* the charity, you're giving *through* it, so your sole concern is its ability to improve the world on your behalf.

'Since my contribution is small, it will make no difference to a large organisation'

It is probably true that your contribution will make a bigger difference *to* a small charity than to a large one, but you don't care about that: you care about whether it makes a bigger difference to the world if given *through* a small charity than *through* a large one. So, which are better at that?

It varies. We've already seen that size is no indicator of quality: sometimes, larger charities can add more value to donations because they can make economies of scale, have better networks, access, experience and so forth. Some types of work are simply impossible for small charities. On the flip-side, small charities may be more innovative: it's well known that in commerce, innovation tends to come from small companies, and there's no reason of which I'm aware to doubt that for charities too. Yet large charities are often portrayed badly in the data-free folklore around charities. We should have no preference other than for effectiveness.

Even if you're giving a little, a large charity may be able to use it well. For example, Oxfam, whose income in 2010 was £318m, claims it can train a teacher for £27, or train a health worker for £31. For only £11 it can deliver a bednet in Kenya which may saves somebody's life by protecting them from malaria[11].

---

11 Distributing anti-malarial bednets is one of the activities proven effective (in some circumstances) by IPA's evaluations and included in its Proven Impact fund.

12 This too is a manifestation of the separation between the source of funds (the donor) and beneficiary. Any organisation pays VAT on (some) of its purchases, such as heating, stationery and insurance, and adds VAT to the fee it charges its customer. This covers the VAT paid on its own purchases. The effect on the organisation itself is therefore nil: the VAT bill is eventually footed by whoever's at the end of the chain, which is normally an individual customer. However, charities often don't charge their 'customers' because by definition they can't pay, so at the end of the chain is the charity.

'Small charities are more efficient: they don't have all the overheads that large charities do'

Now we know that size is no indication of effectiveness, and that overhead costs are normally a red herring, this myth is already losing credibility. We can kill it once and for all with some proper maths which will demonstrate that it's not even true that small charities have lower overheads.

We'll compare two charities, one with annual costs (including admin, fundraising and everything else) of £500,000 and one with annual costs of £5m. For this discussion, we'll consider just two items of 'admin' costs, the costs of the directors and of accountancy, and we'll make some reasonable assumptions about each. The smaller charity has a director paid perhaps £50,000, and it buys in accounting help for £600 per month. In the larger one, the director is paid perhaps £80,000, and an accountant is paid £30,000 per year. Here's what happens:

	Small charity	Large charity
Total annual running costs	£500,000	£5m
Cost of Director + cost of accounting	£50,000 + 12 x £600 = £57,200	£80,000 + £30,000 = £110,000
% of revenue spent on Director and accounting	= 57,200 ÷ 500,000 = 11%	= 110,000 ÷ 5,000,000 = 2%

Oh look: the larger charity spends a smaller proportion of its revenue on these two items of cost. Why? Because it can spread them across more activities. Large charities often benefit from economies of scale like this: the audit fee of the larger charity won't be ten times that of the smaller charity, and the larger charity may well get cheaper stationery or computers by virtue of its scale. Other 'overheads' don't depend much on the charity's size either: the telephone bill, for example, will probably be about the same per employee irrespective of the organisation's size.

So that's clear then. Let's never discuss admin costs ever again!

(If you're watching closely, you'll notice that this example omits some details such as National Insurance on the staff and VAT (UK sales tax) on the accounting support. It actually doesn't matter because they're virtually linear with the organisation's size. And if you're a tax nerd, yes, I did intend to include VAT there because charities normally can't recover VAT[12]. It costs them about a billion quid every year. At the time of writing, you don't pay VAT if you get a boob job but you do if you're a charity serving the homeless. Marvellous.)

'Charity begins at home'

Sometimes people prioritise organisations or needs which are geographically proximate to them. They may feel a responsibility for their neighbours; they may want to 'give back' to the community, country or region which enabled them to be successful; and/or they may be moved by the pockets of deprivation which surprisingly enough, exist in even affluent parts of the affluent West. These are all very understandable motivations.

My advice is that when you start giving, start near you. It will be easier to understand the issues you're addressing, easier to visit charities and therefore learn more and easier to meet other donors and see progress. But don't stop there.

'I was not lucky in the sense that I found the [operating code] system on a desk, but in terms of circumstances. That I could write the best code and hire the best people was in part due to the country I was born in,' says Microsoft founder Bill Gates. Perhaps this suggests that donors should focus *away* from where they live. The logic is that if the meritocratic system where you live was favourable to *your* talent, it will probably be favourable to other people's talent. Is it not better, then, to put your resources to finding and nurturing talent in places which don't have a meritocratic system – in autocratic regimes, or underdeveloped education systems in other countries?

Going a step further, an unintended consequence of donors supporting causes and organisations near them is that disproportionate amounts go to poor people who happen to live near the workplaces or homes of the wealthy. For example, people on grim housing estates in the east end of London benefit from a good deal more charitable activity than do people in similar circumstances in the east end of Glasgow: they just happen to live nearer money, from the City or Canary Wharf.

And going further still, one can argue that if donors fund only locally, their money stays near where the money is – and often a major factor keeping poor people poor is their distance from money. Some of the most under-resourced and horrible issues remain out of reach to local donors. Consider conscripted child soldiers in the Democratic Republic of Congo, or girls facing (or who have 'had') female genital mutilation in north-east Africa: if all the charitable money was spent physically near the donors, none would ever reach these people.

You may need to stick to charities near you if, for example, you're providing physical resources, or need to visit – perhaps because you're volunteering for them, or want to show your colleagues or family. In fact, if you want to provide professional skills or your time, you can do that remotely – through www.i-volunteer.org.uk/ for example. If you are solely providing money, aim to gradually ditch geography as a criterion.

'Local charities are the best'

Let's first be clear about what we mean, because 'local' has two quite different definitions. One is that the charity is based near where you live. It's your neighbour. The other is that its work improves the world in a smallish geographical area (not necessarily the area where you live). Perhaps it's a hospice serving people in Wakefield, or a charity that preserves forest by Loch Lomond. In neither case does being 'local' remotely prove that it's effective.

In the first definition, where it's your neighbour, it's pretty unlikely that all charities based within, say, 20 miles of your home are magically better than those further away. Some near you are probably great, and some probably less great – and the same for those further away.

In fact even if all charities near you were great, this wouldn't help you choose between them because they're so numerous and so eclectic. For example, within only two miles of where I happen to live are: the head office of VSO (Voluntary Service Overseas, an international development agency); Action on Prisoners' Families (which lobbies for better treatment for prisoners and their families across the UK, since among other things, this reduces the re-offending rate); the Royal Hospital for Neuro-Disability (a national centre for people with brain damage) as well as Girl Guide groups, choirs, a Tudor palace and several churches. Even to choose between charities right on my doorstep, I'd need some further criteria.

The second definition, where the charity operates solely at a local level, wouldn't help much either. It encompasses virtually every hospice, centre for homeless people, Girl Guide group and faith-based group. Clearly some are better than others.

Either definition raises another complication. Choosing charities with tight geographic focus often restricts you to the top of the triangle, and some problems don't yield to work at the top of the triangle, because they require work at national or international levels. Suppose you routinely see disabled people unable to enter public buildings in your town. Solving that may require campaigning for a change in the national law (as happened with the Disability Discrimination Act 1995) rather focusing on the problem locally.

All these myths illustrate that when selecting a charity, the sole valuable criterion is its effectiveness at improving the world: if you want to encourage effectiveness, then only use criteria which pertain to effectiveness. That, as we've seen, relies on having a good idea and good implementation. Everything else is irrelevant.

In fact you can help a charity's effectiveness more than you can imagine, as we'll see now.

Chapter 8

How to help and not hinder

Now you've found a cracking charity, your job is to help it as much as possible and hinder as little as possible. This chapter will show you how to increase the value of what you give – just by paying attention to the *way* you give. We'll see some (completely legal) wizardry for increasing the value of money you give, before turning to giving almost anything else.

Money
Step one: make sure to start!
However much you intend to give, you'll be much more effective if you do actually give something! Various studies of human nature, particularly from the new-ish field of behavioural economics, tell of how peculiar we all are, and give some insights about how we can best manage ourselves to ensure that our giving does really happen.

We're terrible at getting round to things. The book *Nudge* cites many examples of inertia getting the better of our good intentions, even when it's against our own self-interest. One example is from Yale University, where final-year students were given information about the dangers of tetanus. This persuaded most of them to plan to get inoculated. Despite knowing full-well where the campus medical centre was, only 3 per cent of them actually got around to it: a dismal 97 per cent never got their act together.

Sadly inertia isn't unique to Yale's students. To state the obvious, if you're going to give, you need to get active and make a decision at least once: all the analysis and good intentions in the world don't help unless you force yourself to get around to making a decision and acting on it.

We stick with what's easy. We overwhelmingly take the course of action which involves the least work. Organ donation programmes have become a famous example. Germany has an opt-in system, (in other words, the 'default' is to be out). There, 88 per cent of people stick with the easy option, meaning that only 12 per cent of the population are enrolled. By contrast, their neighbours in Austria have an opt-out system, that is, the easy option is to be in. Fully 99 per cent of people take the default option by remaining enrolled as organ donors.

Clever donors use this inertia to benefit their giving. Make giving your default setting, by setting up a standing order or direct debit while you're in energetic mode.

We're averse to loss. Research shows that people will work harder to retain £100 which they already own than to gain £100 that they don't own – they value £100 which they already own as much as about £200 which they could gain. This makes no sense if you think about it, because the money has the same value either way. Again, you can use this to benefit. In payroll giving, your charitable gifts are deducted directly from your salary before you see it, so you feel no loss. Your donation can still benefit from tax relief (which we'll cover later). If you want the flexibility to swap the charities you support through payroll giving, give into an account with the Charities Aid Foundation or the Charities Trust from which you can give to any charity. (But beware of your in-built laziness! Make sure that you define some recipient charities, lest the money just accumulate in there, not improving the world at all.) Payroll giving needs to be arranged by your employer: see www.hmrc.gov.uk/businesses/giving/payroll-giving.htm

Organising your giving to maximise its impact

While you're in busy-mode and setting up your giving, pay attention to the *way* that you give it, which will make tremendous difference. Your giving will achieve the most if you: give a lot; give without strings; give without fuss; and give again. We'll examine each in turn.

1. Give a lot

'What if I don't have a lot?' Irrespective of the amount you have to give, I suggest that you share it between just a few charities rather than dividing it into many small sums. This will be more fun for you as well as increasing your impact. Why is that?

First, reducing the number of charities you're trying to select reduces the number you need to analyse. You'll have more time for each analysis which will tend to lead to better decisions. (The converse strategy of making loads of small donations is known by professional grant-makers as 'spray and pray', and is about as reliable as it sounds, as we shall see.)

Second, consolidating your gifts reduces the amount which gets lost in charges for bank transactions, fees for presenting cheques (charities often have to pay for this, as do most businesses) and credit card fees. Some of those costs are independent

89

of the donation size, so four donations of £10 would generate four sets of charges, whereas one donation of £40 would attract only one charge. I promised to show you some ways to make your giving achieve nothing at all, and now we can see one: take your £50 and write 50 cheques (or make 50 credit card transactions) each for £1, and the whole lot may get consumed in transit.

And third, since you'll have fewer charities in your 'brood', you can have a deeper relationship with each one, learning more about them and finding effective ways to help. It can also be more fun for you. For example, many charities host events exclusively for donors who give above a certain threshold. If you give £1,000 to one charity, you might well get invited, but if you 'spread the love' between 10 charities, you'll perennially be below the cut-off and won't get to attend any such events.

People sometimes believe that supporting lots of charities is lower risk than supporting just a few – it avoids 'putting all your eggs in one basket'. Actually, the opposite is true: the way to manage risk is to spend time on choosing few eggs and then look after them properly. To take an analogy from biology, it's like raising offspring: people don't maximise the number of children who survive them by having loads of children none of whom they can feed properly, but rather by having a few and looking after them adequately.

> *'Put all your eggs in one basket and then watch that basket'*
> – Andrew Carnegie

2. Give without strings

This simply means recognising that the charity you chose so carefully has a better sense of what it needs than you do. Because you know that it's a great charity – your analysis said so – you can just give it money or other support and allow it to get on with improving the world.

Donors sometimes 'restrict' what a charity can do with a gift – in other words, they ring-fence it, stipulating that it must be used, say, in the next six months, or in Tanzania, or to hire a school teacher. Almost invariably, this reduces its effectiveness – it destroys value. Charities say that 'unrestricted' donations are worth just over half as much again to them as 'restricted' donations: in a study, charities said that £660,000 of unrestricted income is as valuable as £1m restricted. This is one of the tricks I promised you about how to increase the value of your donation by half.

Why is restricting donations so destructive? There are four main reasons.

First, it **prevents charities from responding** to changes in needs or situations, removing the flexibility which can be literally vital. Imagine an aid agency operating in Malaysia, Indonesia and Thailand, and imagine – for simplicity – that each country's operation is funded by a separate restricted gifts. Imagine now that costs in the

Malaysia programme turn out to be lower than budget, but that there is a natural disaster in Indonesia. A sensible response would be to spend some of the savings from Malaysia in Indonesia. The restrictions prevent this. Instead, they force the charity to go back to the donors and negotiate and haggle – which takes time and effort which frankly would be better spent helping. No kidding – this goes on all the time. It happens too with unexpected opportunities. Sometimes the opportunities – 'Madonna's free on Tuesday to shoot a video for your campaign if you can get a camera crew here' – pass by while charities are trying to de-restrict enough money to take them up.

No-strings money... four Nobel Prizes

In 1874, the University of Manchester was given £10,000 with the delightfully vague instruction for a professorship 'to encourage discovery in physics'. Its flexibility has enabled it to be remarkably fruitful: holders of the professorship have won four Nobel prizes between them. They include Ernest Rutherford, who first split the atom but actually got the chemistry prize; a chap called William Bragg, the youngest Nobel Laureate in any subject ever, who shared not only his prize but also his name with his father (but sadly wasn't a singer-songwriter); and Andrei Geim who shared the physics prize in 2010. It's hard to imagine that if the donor had added strings to the gift, the results would have been so spectacular.

The trick has worked with the Nobel Peace Prize too. It was unrestricted money from the Global Fund for Women which enabled organisations founded by Liberian activist Leymah Gbowee and Yemeni journalist Tawakkul Karman to push for a deal ending the civil war in Liberia. They had the flexibility to do whatever the rapidly-changing situation required: at one point, linking arms and blocking the doors of a hotel room in Accra in neighbouring Ghana until the Liberian politicians inside had made a deal. Similarly, unrestricted support for Tawakkul's organisation of female journalists in Yemen held weekly sit-ins to demand the release of political prisoners, and is credited with a central role in Yemen's democratic uprisings, which spread throughout the Arab world. Tawakkul and Leymah shared the Nobel Peace Prize in 2011 with the Liberian president Ellen Johnson-Sirleaf. 'The flexibility and significance of the general-support grant cannot be overemphasized,' wrote Leymah.

Second, it *disempowers the management*. It's as though the donor says, 'I know better than you do how this money can best be spent'. Really? That seems a little odd since most donors have never worked for a charity and don't know much about saving pandas, whereas the charity's managers think about it every day. We saw in Section 1 that good charities add value to your gift precisely because they know things that donors don't. If you trust the management, then back them; and if you don't, don't. Panahpur, a UK family trust established in 1907, has concluded that 'restricted giving unintentionally becomes a vote of no-confidence in the judgment of the charity. It says that the donor does not trust the management and trustees.' Not only does this disempowerment have practical effects such as the inflexibility we just saw, but it also has a rather pernicious repercussions. Who wants a job in which they're not trusted? Moreover, who wants a career in a sector in which managers are routinely untrusted? I suspect that this kind of continual vote of no confidence, together with some of the other problems we'll encounter, deters some good people from working in the charity sector.

> '*In* Good to Great *(2001), Jim Collins rigorously analyzed thousands of corporations to uncover the ingredients that permitted a few 'good' companies to become 'great' companies. He concluded that no single element of success is more important than the quality and fit of the individuals in the organisation. Average performers, it turns out, deliver average results; great results demand more.*
>
> *Collins articulates an insight that is often repeated in business schools, boardrooms, and private equity firms. Achieving excellence requires an excellent organisation. In most businesses, most of the time, people matter most. The people you pay are more important than the people who pay you. This may be the one business principle that transfers directly from the for-profit to the non-profit world.*
>
> *Yet it is a principle that philanthropists (most of whom earned their money in business) generally ignore. Only 20% of foundation grants are unrestricted. Grantmakers send an unambiguous signal (backed up by money): do not invest to recruit, retain, and develop the best people. Do not invest in the infrastructure necessary to support those people. Do not focus executive time and energy on management and organisation-building.'*
>
> – Thomas Tierney, Co-founder and Chairman of The Bridgespan Group, the US non-profit consultancy specialising in charities and non-profits, a spin-out from management consultancy Bain & Co.

Third, **donors generally all want to fund the same bits of an organisation**: the most visible, glamorous, front-line activities and 'projects' such as teachers, minibuses, and vaccines. Nobody wants to fund the overheads, such as the rent, phone bills, audit fees, bookkeepers. But guess what? If there's no money for the audit, then the audit doesn't happen, and since that is a legal obligation, the charity will be shut down. No teachers, no vaccines, no minibuses, no 'projects'. Even if there is money for some of the overheads, there normally isn't enough, which is daft given that overheads are necessary for performance.

The effect of restricting funds to the front-line is to routinely starve charities of the ability to properly support their work with beneficiaries.

Jim Collins, the author whom Thomas Tierney quotes, went further in a sequel to *Good to Great* specifically about the social sector: 'Restricted giving misses a fundamental point: To make the greatest impact on society requires first and foremost a great organization, not a single great program.'

And fourth, *it's a nonsense which just sets up an expensive circus*. Your gift is like a tributary flowing into a river: it contributes to the river but asking which pieces of the river came from that particular tributary is simply meaningless. At the end of the day, money is all the same. You actually cannot ensure that 'your' £50 goes towards the teacher's salary. As a man working for an international aid agency in Kolkata in India told me years ago, 'it's not like you actually label your five-pound notes'.

The circus arises because charities must fund their overheads somehow. So they resort to ridiculous measures: I have known charities claim that their Chief Executive is a 'project'. It's just a lie and everybody knows it. Or take rent or audit: a charity working with homeless people needs to pay rent on the buildings it uses as centres – or it will become homeless itself. It may use portions of 'restricted' donations to pay the rent. I'm not blaming charities at all: they're not trying to pocket the money, but rather just keep their important services on the road. They're forced into this nonsense by donors. As Fiona Ellis, then Director of the Northern Rock Foundation (a highly-respected charitable foundation established when the Northern Rock Building Society demutualised in 1997) said of restricted donations, 'The charities pretend to use the money as we've said, and we pretend to believe them'. This pretence has a cost – charities' time spent squeezing necessary overheads into project-shaped-moulds. Spot the irony: restrictions, often born of donors' allergy to funding overheads, often increase those very costs.

So restricting is rarely a good option. And it's never a good option for donations below £20,000 – the circus just consumes too much, as well as demotivating the management. If for some reason you do need to restrict a donation, please have a good discussion about it with the recipient charity first, and be open to de-restricting it, very rapidly if necessary.

If you think about it, the notion of restricting money is peculiar to charities and only arises because of the separation between donor and beneficiary: nobody who buys cake demands that their money is spent solely on ingredients. You just judge the quality of the cake and don't care how the cake company uses the five pound note you give it.

Restrictions are a great example of a common practice which is actually very destructive – a problem of philanthropy which isn't experienced as a problem by philanthropists. Don't just copy.

3. Give without fuss

This simply means don't create work for the charity – work such as making it apply to you, making it report to you on its work, or inflicting 'help' which it doesn't need. These problems mostly arise when people are giving a lot, so we'll look at this in Section 3. If you're just choosing good charities and giving them things which they need, you'll be fine.

4. Give again

Since you have gone to all the trouble of finding a good charity, support it again and again if it's doing a good job. Members of the Sainsbury family have sometimes supported the same organisations for ten years or more through their charitable foundations, because they appreciate the need for solutions and know that the problems are complicated. They don't want the charities to waste time and money shopping around for other funders, risking failure in the process. Similarly, veteran venture capitalist Sir Ronald Cohen, who is heavily involved in charities, has noticed how short-term funding hinders them:

> 'The majority of the organisations in the [charity] sector ... can't look beyond one year because that's their fundraising timeframe, which means they are completely unable to build sustainable organisations.'

An easy way to give repeatedly is to use your inertia by setting up a direct debit or standing order. Make sure you tell the charity because this will help it to plan.

And now, some more useful tricks. First, how to increase the value of the money you're already giving, then some ways to generate money out of thin air, and finally some ways to give without giving money at all.

How to increase the size of donations you're already giving

Get Her Majesty to chip in. Unless you particularly love HM Treasury, make sure that you're not giving money to it which could be going to charity. If you pay UK tax at all, there are various ways to get HM Treasury to augment your donations:[13]

Gift Aid. This is one of the easiest tricks. If you pay income tax in the UK, ask to 'Gift Aid' your charitable donation because the government will add to it the

---

13 These rules generally only apply to UK registered charities. For avoidance of doubt, this book is not a lawyer and is not intended as a substitute for legal advice.

income tax you've paid on that sum. If you pay basic rate tax (20 per cent), this increases your donation by a quarter, and if you pay higher rate tax (40 per cent) it increases it by two-thirds[14] at no cost to you. Look out for a tick box on donation forms, or ask the charity for a 'Gift Aid Declaration' form. Donations to charity shops can also benefit from Gift Aid: the charity can reclaim your income tax on the money raised from the sale of your donated items if you sign a declaration. Full details of Gift Aid are at www.hmrc.gov.uk/individuals/giving/gift-aid.htm.

Shares. Income tax and capital gains tax can be reclaimed if you give shares to a charity. Guidance is at www.hmrc.gov.uk/individuals/giving/assets.htm

Owners of private companies who intend to issue shares can donate a stake of the company to charity. It's a lovely way to give because it has no cash cost to the donor, and is a favourite of dot.com companies. For example, when Salesforce.com was founded, it put 1% of its equity into its foundation which will receive that money when Salesforce.com eventually issues shares. And eBay's founders gave $1m of equity very early on which produced $40m for charity when eBay issued shares.

Land and property. Any building or land given in its entirety attracts tax relief, i.e., reduces your tax bill by the market value.

The rules on tax-efficient giving change relatively frequently: the most recent guidance is here: www.hmrc.gov.uk/individuals/tmacharitable-donations.shtml and the Institute of Fundraising has a good guide: www.tax-effective-giving.org.uk

Money out of thin air

Now comes the bit when we generate money out of thin air! There is lots of money around which isn't earmarked for charitable giving but which you can make available for charity if you're creative. I hope the following stories will spark some ideas you can use yourself.

Friends. Starfish helps HIV/AIDS orphans in South Africa. It is supported by a lot of young-ish South African professionals living in Britain. They raised a good deal of money by hosting dinner parties at home and asking each guest to donate the money they would have spent if the party had been in a restaurant. Genius: Starfish tapped into 'personal entertainment' budgets which hadn't been earmarked for charity.

Neighbours. Fred Mulder, who founded The Funding Network, was in a dispute with his neighbours in London over access to some land that he owned. There was every chance that he and they would all hire expensive lawyers to resolve it. Instead, Fred offered to give his neighbours perpetual access if they each (Fred included)

---

14 Yes, the numbers are weird. For lower-rate tax-payers, the £100 in your pocket has had 20% taken off, i.e., it was £125 pre-tax, so when the tax (£25) gets added back, that increases your £100 to £125, i.e., by 25%. For higher-rate tax-payers, the £100 in your pocket has had 40% taken off, i.e., it was £166 pre-tax, so adding back the tax (£66) increases your £100 by 66%.

donated £25,000 towards an educational project in Zambia. This move generated over £100,000 for charitable work – none of which had previously been designated for charity. And furthermore, it's *improved* his relationship with the neighbours – which a legal fight would never have done – because they have a shared endeavour. Clever, isn't it?

Clients. Fred Mulder is full of these ideas. He's an art dealer, and sometimes when negotiations with clients have become stuck, he suggests that the difference between his price and the offering price be donated to charity.

Timpson, the UK's largest shoe repairer, key cutter, engraver and watch repairer, has a good mechanism. 'A customer comes into the shop, wants a quick job, say a hole in a belt, and in the old days you'd charge them a couple of quid. But now, instead of charging, we ask them to put a pound in a box for ChildLine', says Managing Director James Timpson. It's not trivial: the company has raised £887,300 this way.

In memoriam gifts. These are a lovely way to remember and honour a deceased person. You might make a donation instead of giving funeral flowers, and sometimes friends and family come together to raise funds for a specific charitable purchase or goal. A Community Foundation might be a good option for remembering someone with strong links to a particular area, as might art galleries they enjoyed or organisations from which they benefitted.

Weddings. Sometimes couples request donations rather than gifts for themselves. A couple can invite guests to make donations to contribute towards particular items (for instance through Oxfam Unwrapped – see below), or a use a website such as www.giveit.co.uk to organise the process.

Loose change. Pennies for Peace provides education in Pakistan and Afghanistan, and materials for children in the US to learn about its work. Children donating pennies has always been core to its funding. With its slogan 'Collect only pennies – no nickels, no dimes, no quarters, no dollars', it engages all students, including those of very limited means, and teaches them about the difference they can make to the world.

More than money

> *'You give but little when you give of your possessions. It is when you give of yourself that you truly give.'*
> – Khalil Gibran

You can give virtually anything. Again, below are some ideas which I hope will inspire, and some clangers to avoid.

Blood. Find your nearest blood donation session at www.blood.co.uk/Session Searcher/search.aspx

Bone marrow. Some tissue types are more common in certain ethnic groups of the population, meaning that a patient normally needs a donor from a similar ethnic background to her own. There's a particular need for stem cell donors from African, African-Caribbean, Asian, Chinese, Jewish, Eastern European and Mediterranean communities. You can register as a bone marrow or stem cell donor when you give blood or at www.nhsbt.nhs.uk/bonemarrow/

Business clothes. Disadvantaged women trying to get back into work need business clothes – as well as training and confidence – for interviews and when they start work. Dress for Success works in nine countries, and has now helped over 550,000 women. www.dressforsuccess.org

Cars. Several organisations will collect an unwanted car and turn it into money for charity through www.giveacar.co.uk.

Computer equipment. *Which?* has a useful guide to recycling computers: www.which.co.uk/environment-and-saving-energy/environment-and-greener-living/guides/recycling-computers/pc-recycling-tips/

Coupons and free stuff. You can donate the buy-one-get-one free items you don't want. I know some business people who are constantly travelling and give the complimentary toiletries from hotels to a domestic violence refuge: if you're on the run from a violent partner, it's nice if somebody's been thoughtful enough to provide some decent shampoo.

Cycles. A number of non-profit organisations refit unwanted bicycles to send to countries such as Haiti and South Africa, in the process training people in the UK to repair bikes. www.re-cycle.org and www.recyke-y-bike.org

Furniture. The Salvation Army will take furniture to sell in its shops or pass on to homeless people settling in a new home. www.salvationarmy.org.uk

Gardens. Landshare brings together people who want to grow their own food but have no place to do it and those who have land to share but lack time, experience or muscle-power. www.landshare.net

Glasses. Visionaid Overseas organises a nationwide recycling scheme for unwanted spectacles. www.vao.org.uk

Musical instruments. Can go to school music programmes, senior citizens, talented young students, community groups, and charities can use them at events and as prizes to help raise money.

Paint. Community RePaint schemes collect unwanted, surplus paint and re-distribute it to individuals, families and communities in need, improving the wellbeing of people and the appearance of places across the UK. www.communityrepaint.org.uk

You can even give your hair! If you have more than ten inches of hair cut off, take it home and donate it to make wigs for people who've lost hair due to medical treatments. www.charityintersection.com/donatehair.html

The curious incident of the goat in the catalogue

Oxfam Unwrapped is a kind of gift catalogue from which you can 'buy a goat' or various other items as a gift. A goat costs £25: you give Oxfam £25, which it uses to provide a goat to somebody in a less developed country, and in return Oxfam gives you a card picturing a cheery-looking goat to give your friend. Jolly good.

What do you notice about this donation? It appears to be restricted – to buying a goat. In fact it isn't, for this good reason. Theoretically, each of the 50m adults in the UK could 'buy a goat' tomorrow, and it would be just crazy if Oxfam suddenly rained 50m goats onto the unsuspecting communities it serves. So, sensibly, Oxfam's small-print says that your £25 will go to 'either your chosen gift or something else in the same category.' (Goats are in the 'livestock' category whereas 'training a teacher', for example, is in the 'education' category, predictably enough.) 'This kind of flexibility means that poor communities worldwide can get exactly what they need if and when their circumstances change.'

Oxfam has weakened the restriction. But not enough, in my view. The gift-purchaser is extremely unlikely to have done a load of research into international development from which they conclude that agriculture is invariably the best theory of change. (Gift-purchasers don't even specify the country to which their 'goat' is delivered, and as we've seen, the effectiveness of particular theories of change often varies between countries.) Of course not: the purchaser is a teacher or an accountant or a student saying that they want to help but probably wants the big decisions made by somebody who knows what they're talking about – such as Oxfam.

So why does Oxfam have a restriction at all? Because it works: we like to buy some notionally-identifiable 'thing' so that's what we get. However, Oxfam is clever, so it enables customers to tick a box to de-restrict the donation: 'I am happy for Oxfam to use my money to fund any part of its work.' Tick it: Oxfam knows what it's doing. (And given that charities value unrestricted money half as highly again as restricted money, ticking the box means that your £25 in effect buys a goat and a half. Bargain.)

Some charity 'gift catalogues' don't even offer this option. The Good Gifts Catalogue, for example, says that 'your money buys the gift described we guarantee it'. Even if it's no longer needed or the recipient community has enough of those items already or something else has become more urgent since the catalogue was printed? Isn't it important to give communities – *anybody* – the right to some control over their life in real-time? They get that much more if they can influence decisions to respond to changing circumstances.

The rest?

- Charity shops take clothes, books, records, CDs, DVDs and jewellery, and some take furniture and electrical goods. Remember to fill in a Gift Aid form.
- Primary schools and nurseries can use all sorts of things for craft projects: fabric, knitting wool, rolls of wallpaper, old Christmas cards, jars and bottles. Just ask first.
- Find a new home for almost anything on Freecycle and save it from landfill. www.freecycle.org
- Lend to people in your neighbourhood through www.streetbank.com
- Sell it and donate the proceeds. Through the online marketplace eBay you can donate the proceeds from selling virtually anything to a charity of your choice. Secondhand books can also be sold through Abebooks www.abebooks.co.uk and Amazon.

Give while doing something else...

Searching online. Some internet search engines, such as EveryClick in the UK or GoodSearch in the US, make a charitable donation for every search made. You can either choose specific charities to support, or support the whole basket of charities they list. www.everyclick.com

Buying online. Various portals make donations for every purchase made. For instance, www.easyfundraising.org.uk and www.TheGivingMachine.co.uk can generate donations for every purchase from retailers including John Lewis, Mothercare, Debenhams, Apple, Wallis, Fat Face, Expedia, Aviva, Dell and LateRooms. In Australia, www.auscause.com.au is similar.

Turn your time into money

A friend of mine whose day-job is in IT is also a semi-professional photographer. He does photos at weddings and donates his fee to charity. Even children can turn time into money. For example, the kid brother of a friend used to wash his neighbours' cars to raise money for charity.

One of the partners at an investment firm in Manchester is passionate about child refugees in Asia. He gives money to that cause but since he also has a talent for writing for children, he is writing a children's book to be sold in Europe, with the proceeds going to support those refugees.

He's following in celebrated footsteps. The author JM Barrie loved children but he and his wife had none of their own. For many years, he supported Great Ormond Street Hospital, which in 1929 approached him to sit on a committee to help buy land for a much-needed new wing. Barrie declined but said that he 'hoped to find another way to help'. Two months later, the hospital board was stunned to learn that he had handed over his rights to *Peter Pan*. The hospital receives royalties every time the play is staged, as well as from the sale of *Peter Pan* books and other products. At Barrie's request, the hospital has never revealed the amount raised from *Peter Pan*.

Working for the cause

Bill Clinton wrote his book *Giving* 'because everyone can give something. And there's so much to do. It's never too late or too early to start'. He includes this inspiring story:

> 'At the ripe old age of six, McKenzie Steiner organised her friends in California to participate in her second beach cleanup. She did the first cleanup with her school but was concerned because there was still trash on the beach. So she decided to enlist her friends to do another one. She brought gloves and plastic bags for other kids to pick up bottle lids, containers, bags and other trash. She plans on doing a cleanup on her next birthday and several after that. "Sometimes animals die from littering in the ocean. I felt better for helping animals and people coming to the beach to swim."'

At the other end of the scale is a chap we'll call Bob, who is a finance director. He happened to meet the Chief Executive of a charity which works with children. Though Bob was interested in its work, he was unsure about how he could really help. The Chief Executive told him that the charity was trying to appoint a new Finance Director – a crucial appointment, about which she was nervous because her own understanding of finance was weak. Bob, who has recruited dozens of finance professionals in his career, helped design the recruitment process and did some of the interviewing. It was a great use of Bob's time, because he could prevent a disruptive mistake with relatively little effort on his part.

If you're supporting several charities, you can follow the example of Shameet, a business person in his 40s, with expertise in growing organisations. He is interested in grass-roots charities, and realised that a young community-based organisation in Bristol was facing issues which another organisation he supports in Glasgow had been through a few years earlier. Simply by putting them in touch, Shameet helped significantly: the older organisation was able to mentor the younger one, which learnt from the older one's mistakes.

You can donate any amount of time through www.do-it.org which lists volunteering opportunities according to the type of cause (human rights, museums, music and so on) and the location. Timebank also finds opportunities for volunteers: www.timebank.org.uk.

How your organisation can help

If you work in a business or a public institution, there are additional ways you can help. For one thing, many charities have to convert some of their financial donations into purchases such as office space, stationery or lorries. You may be able to short-circuit that process by providing equipment and resources directly. (This is particularly brilliant if it saves the charity paying irrecoverable VAT when buying such items.) Unwanted filing cabinets, envelopes in a size that's no longer needed after a corporate rebranding, fleet vehicles and computers have all found happy new homes with charities.

Access to meeting rooms. Practically everybody who works in an office can get access to meeting rooms out of hours. This can be surprisingly useful. For example, the church of St Bartholomew the Great in the City of London always had its council (board) meetings in the church hall. The Rector, the Rev'd Dr Martin Dudley, felt that meetings could be better: there was usually lots of paper everywhere and much confusion about the financial figures being presented. The church is next door to a large company, whose boardroom is usually empty in evenings when the council meets. So the Rector asked whether the council could use it. The Rector reports that the council has much higher quality discussions in the boardroom than in the church hall, simply because the room feels so professional.

Spare office space. Unused office space, including ends-of-leases, can be very valuable to charities because it saves them the expense of rent. Many charities have few staff so can be accommodated in relatively small spaces. In fact, donating empty floors or empty buildings can sometimes save companies money: rates are payable on empty commercial space whereas they may not be if the space is occupied by a charity.

Bulk purchasing arrangements. A global financial services company based in a medium-sized British town has strong IT infrastructure for processing the huge quantities of data it holds and analyses. One of the ways in which it supports local charities is by including them in its IT purchasing processes, so that they benefit from the company's volume discounts.

Making expertise available. Investment bank Morgan Stanley has a long-term relationship with Community Links, a charity in East London. As part of the arrangement, Community Links can get advice from Morgan Stanley's in-house specialists such as its IT helpdesk or HR department. It uses this advice only a few times a year, but it is helpful to go straight to an expert without having to worry about professional fees when there might not really be a problem. Morgan Stanley can provide this assistance at practically zero cost.

The danger

The danger is that you give items which the charity doesn't need. Aid agencies run an annual competition for Stuff We Don't Want (SWEDOW). Past winners have included second-hand knickers(!), and the 2.4 million Pop-Tarts® airdropped onto Afghanistan by the US government in 2002. Far from being amusing tales, these items create costs for charities because they need storing and sorting, and simply become a hindrance. It's not difficult to check that a charity needs an item before sending it.

If you're volunteering your time, then you are a superstar, but again, please ensure you're doing what's needed. I could tell you dozens of stories of volunteers who will only work in the museum shop or feed the donkeys or arrange the flowers when what is actually needed is somebody to do a couple of hours of the boring stuff: sort through receipts, stuff envelopes or get quotes from insurance companies. These volunteers are effectively restricting the donation of their time to the glamorous front-line activities, in precisely the way that financial gifts get restricted to those items and every bit as unhelpful. Equally donors sometimes foist their 'help' onto charities when it's not needed at all. (Like most problems, this effect is amplified when donors are giving a lot.) Charity staff are often too polite to say anything, and/or are not in a position to say anything because of their dependence on donors.

So offer, don't foist, and check that you're helping and not hindering.

What can you expect from the charity in return for all this? At a minimum you should receive the type of treatment and care outlined in the Fundraising Promise, a code to which charities can sign up, created by the Fundraising Standards Board, the independent self-regulatory body for fundraising in the UK, reproduced in the appendices.

The final way to help doesn't involve *giving* anything to a charity at all.

A cautionary tale

A grant-making foundation was managing a grant to a charity delivering educational work in rural parts of Brazil. The foundation had allocated a manager – let's call him Bill – to oversee the grant, which was pretty sizeable. But neither Bill nor any of his colleagues in the foundation were experts in education or Brazil, or even poverty: this grant was an anomaly for the foundation.

Bill insisted on going to Brazil twice a year to see the charity's work in rural villages – on trips which resembled state visits – and insisted on signing off the budgets for the programme in each region. Not only did this cost a lot of time (and carbon, in all the flights to and from Brazil) but it was laborious for the charity, which had a strong and competent team and didn't need the 'help'.

'We did try to tell Bill, but we think he liked to be involved in development. He made [that foundation] the most difficult of our funders to deal with.'

Only if Bill and the foundation had something useful to add to the charity's team or work should they have been so involved. Notice too the charity's difficulty in telling Bill and the foundation that they weren't helping. This is common: the fear is that honest feedback will damage the chance of further funding. But the problem would have been revealed if Bill – or somebody else at the foundation – had simply asked.

Chapter 9

Before it goes out of the door: using money without giving it

'How the honours system works...

Knighthood for David Newbigging, chairman of Cancer Research UK, for 'voluntary services to cancer research' over a decade

Knighthood for Martin Broughton, chief executive and chairman of British American Tobacco, for a decade selling the causes of cancer'

– From Private Eye, January 2011

Most of us divide money which we're not spending immediately into two complete-ly separate pots. One we invest, through our bank, pension and other savings and investments, to give us a financial return. The other we spend or give to charity to improve the world through what's called a social or environmental return.

Improving the world is the domain solely of the second pot. And since that pot is usually the smaller, most of our money isn't improving the world at all, but just sitting in financial investments. This is hardly consistent with our objective of im-proving the world *as much as possible*. Surely it would be better to ensure that your bank or pension company is investing your money in ways that support your values rather than working against them?

Don't create your own mess
If your charitable passion is eradicating cancer, it's perhaps rather counterproduc-tive to invest in tobacco companies. Similarly, if you're giving money to charities

which address climate change, all your efforts might be neutralised if you invest in oil companies at the same time.

These kinds of mismatches are rather like investing in a process that makes a mess, only to donate the investment proceeds to clean it up again. Therefore some investors avoid companies or governments which fall below certain social or environmental criteria. These 'socially responsible investors' sometimes 'screen out' entire industries. The Methodist Church, for example, has long screened out any company involved in alcohol and gambling, and the Jessie Smith Noyes Foundation, which supports environmental and reproductive rights work, excludes any company involved in tobacco, nuclear power and pesticides.

Other socially responsible investment strategies involve screening out individual companies in any industry if they have poor performance or policies in, for example, labour rights, bribery, safety or environmental damage. For example, several churches divested stock in Caterpillar, the tank manufacturer, over concerns that it was supplying machinery to Israel which was deployed in hostilities with the Palestinians.

Beyond screening, socially responsible investors frequently engage with companies to influence their behaviour, typically around environmental, social and governance issues (collectively called ESG). They may meet with the company, request disclosure of records on, for example, labour standards or use of harmful chemicals, and create pressure around important issues such as animal testing. They may use their vote at the company's Annual General Meeting to advance this agenda. Clearly the theory here is that investors have significant influence with companies – which are of course (among) the most powerful machines humanity has created.

For the record, Bill Gates thinks this is nonsense. Despite his foundation's enormity, his view is that its stakes in companies are too small to provide any influence. He argues that 'the tobacco companies didn't say, "Oh no, the Gates Foundation won't buy our shares. Let's make candy,"' and that therefore the foundation should focus on maximising the financial returns which it can deploy charitably. That view has not been without controversy – such as when an allegation arose that pollution from an oil company in Nigeria in which Gates Foundation had invested was damaging health in some regions where the Gates Foundation itself was trying to improve health.

How to invest socially and environmentally

Practically speaking, it's easiest to ensure that your investments fit with your social and environmental values by using a relevant firm. Charity Bank or the Co-Operative Bank are good places to start for savings products (savings accounts, current accounts) which only invest in screened companies and governments, social enterprises (see below) or charities. For investment products such as ISAs, the mainstream finance houses such as Henderson and Jupiter offer many products with a range of social and environmental criteria.

Pension funds can also be invested using social and environmental criteria. From July 2012, all occupational pension schemes will be required to disclose 'the extent (if any) to which social, environmental or ethical considerations are taken into account in the selection, retention and realisation of investments.' For the first time, pension trustees will have to consider ethics even if they do nothing about it.

Rather, put the capital to work

> 'You're investing in Mayfair to make money which you give to
> the poor of Hackney. Why not invest in Hackney?'
> – David Carrington, consultant in charities and philanthropy

If you think about it, a donation is like an investment which will never come back – it has a guaranteed financial return of minus 100%. By contrast, every other investment you've ever seen in your life has aimed to have a positive return. Why the huge no-man's-land, when there are so many numbers between minus 100 and the positive numbers? Actually, there is a spectrum of types of investment which can improve the world:

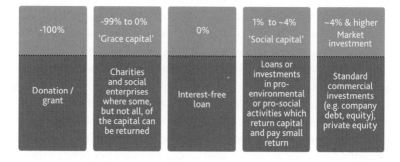

-100%	-99% to 0% 'Grace capital'	0%	1% to ~4% 'Social capital'	~4% & higher Market investment
Donation / grant	Charities and social enterprises where some, but not all, of the capital can be returned	Interest-free loan	Loans or investments in pro-environmental or pro-social activities which return capital and pay small return	Standard commercial investments (e.g. company debt, equity), private equity

Starting on the left of this diagram are donations (grants), which we've discussed. Next come 'investments', which repay *some* but not all of your capital. Then in the middle are opportunities which repay all the capital but no more (that is, which have a zero return. If that sounds unappealing, remember that zero is a lot more than minus 100). Kiva (discussed earlier) is an example, because your investment is returned to you. On the right-hand side of the diagram are investments in companies or organisations which both improve the world in the ways that you want (creating a social and/or environmental return) and make a positive financial return, and finally are standard commercial investments which may or may not be screened using ESG criteria.

Investing in the middle three portions of this spectrum – i.e., in investments which create positive social and/or environmental impact and return at least some of the capital – is known as 'impact investing' or 'social investing'. Entities in which you might invest there include:

Projects within charities which pay a financial return. For instance, loans to a housing association to build new accommodation (repaid through residents' housing benefits); setting up charity shops, or Christmas catalogue businesses.

Social enterprises. These are businesses which create social or environmental benefit through their choice of employees, the materials they use or the products/ services they create. They have a financial transaction at their core which puts their beneficiaries in the feedback loop, reducing the separation issue. They can generate high social and environmental returns as well as financial returns, and include:

- *The Big Issue* magazine: sold and part-written by homeless people, creating work, income and opportunities for them.
- Enterprises which offer training and opportunity for disadvantaged people, and also counter prejudice against them by making them visible to everybody else. They include Jamie Oliver's Fifteen restaurants which employ and train disadvantaged young people; the Working Together Café in Ludlow, which is partly staffed by people with learning disabilities; and the Learning Café in Leicester, partly staffed by ex-offenders.
- Fairtrade businesses: creating economic benefits for the workers through 'fairer' pricing for their goods and spending in their communities.
- Micro-credit: typically involves tiny loans in less developed countries ($40 to buy a weaving loom, or an ox yoke to improve productivity of ploughing) which increase economic activity and so create jobs and independence.
- Charity Technology Trust which earns revenue through services which help charities use technology better; and organisations which sell services to schools to improve education.
- Environmentally-conscious businesses (sometimes called 'eco-mmerce'!). The fashion label From Somewhere is an example because it uses offcuts of luxury materials, 'up-cycling' them into something more valuable.
- Businesses in disadvantaged areas. Bridges Community Ventures is a full-on venture capital fund specialising in businesses which create employment, opportunity and wealth in disadvantaged areas of the UK.

Like any business, social enterprises normally need capital to grow, but they often struggle to find it because they fall between two stools. On one hand, they can't attract commercial venture capital because they're too small, too risky, and insufficiently profitable; but on the other, they can't attract charitable donations because most donors won't give to a business.

For-profit companies. These include companies producing renewable energy, advising on energy efficiency, producing and selling organic food.

How to put your capital to work

To find social enterprises and projects within charities, it's again often easiest to go through a fund or specialist bank. In the UK, the field is led by Charity Bank, the Co-operative Bank and CAF Venturesome, which is one of the world's first funds to invest in charities and open to any client of the Charities Aid Foundation (http://bit.ly/tkOpEA). Other good places to look are:

- UnLtd: a charity set up with £100m from the Millennium Commission which finds and supports social entrepreneurs in the UK
- Ashoka: which finds and supports social entrepreneurs across the globe
- ClearlySo: an online platform for investors to find social enterprises, and for social enterprises to find each other and other useful resources
- Some social enterprises are technically Community Interest Companies, a legal form created especially for them (others are incorporated as charities or normal companies). Community Interest Companies in the UK are listed here: www.bis.gov.uk/cicregulator/cic-register

To invest in for-profit businesses, find a fund which specialises in them. Triodos Bank, for example, runs funds dedicated to renewable energy and microfinance.

For donors in England and Wales, the Charity Commission issues guidance about these types of investments: www.charitycommission.gov.uk/Publications/cc14.aspx

What about the money? Won't I make less money this way and have less to give?

Probably not. Lots of studies have compared the performance of socially responsible investment products and conventional investment products, i.e., screened and unscreened investments on the right of the diagram. To make sense of them all, a meta-study (a study of studies) in 2007 looked at 20 such studies, covering various geographies, time periods and screening criteria. It found that half of the studies found that socially responsible investment outperformed conventional investment, seven found no significant variation and three found socially responsible investment to underperform.

But in any case, is this not the wrong question? Surely the right question is which mechanism is best at improving the world in the way that you want. Even if investing in socially- or environmentally-useful businesses creates less money *to give away* than conventional investment would, it is surely better than making investments which exacerbate the very problems which you're trying to solve. We'd like our net effect to be more than nil, so we can't generate money for social and environmental causes at any price.

The advice we've covered in this section should make you safe on the road driving small vehicles. We'll turn now to the particular issues if you're giving a lot, in which some of the advice will be relevant to any donor. Then in Section 4, we'll look in more detail at charities' results, further background on the charity sector, and the principles which will guide you through any situation.

Section Three

What to do if you're giving a lot

What if you've just won the lottery, are an endowed foundation, a corporate foundation, a community foundation or are otherwise in a position to give a lot? (We'll roughly define 'giving a lot' as giving over £100,000.)

I advise that you don't think about 'giving money to charities'. Rather, figure out a goal – something that you would like to improve in the world – and think of money (and anything else) as your resources for achieving that. Some goals are achievable by giving money to charities, whereas for others there are better tools – such as partnering with a government department, commissioning a playwright, or going on TV yourself, to name just a few. Experience indicates that framing your work as 'achieving a goal', rather than as 'giving to charities', will make you more effective and resourceful as well as making the whole exercise much more fun and rewarding for you.

Everything we've covered so far in the book applies to giving a lot, but there are some additional opportunities and traps which we'll outline in this section. Corporate giving is a little different again and we'll come to that at the end of this section.

The five tips for using a lot of resources to improve the world:

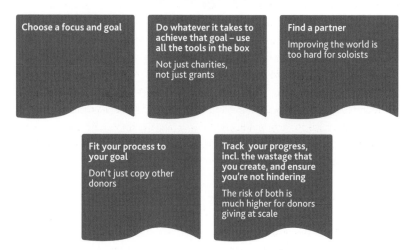

This section will cover each in turn. We'll look first at getting started: how to find a focus, take a whistle-stop tour of the various tools in the box, and see why and how you might partner with somebody else. Then we'll look in detail at the process you'll need if the tool that you choose is supporting other organisations (whether charities or not). This isn't because that tool is invariably optimal but rather to avoid the book being a thousand pages long[15]. Towards the end of this section, we'll look at tracking and improving your own impact irrespective of the tool(s) you use. If you are new to giving, work through all this to decide how to operate; if you are already giving (even if you're in a foundation which has been giving for centuries), review all this periodically to check that your giving is effective – not just a bit but as much as possible. Don't settle for average.

Legal issues if you're starting out

If you're a new donor, you need two important pieces of advice which donors often say they wish they'd known earlier.

First, choose your goal and then talk to a good lawyer before putting money into a charitable foundation. Only a few of the tools we'll discuss can be used by charitable foundations – others require different structures – and therefore a charitable foundation may not be right for you at all. The Charity Law Association, a membership body of people who use or advise on charity law, is a good place to find one. www.charitylawassociation.org.uk

Second, if you do set up a foundation, give it very broad 'charitable objects'. These define the remit within which it must remain by law. Suppose you want to support mental health work in the lovely Scottish highlands. You make that your foundation's charitable object. In later years, you decide you also want your foundation to support work on, say, environmental protection in Costa Rica or to help victims of an earthquake in Haiti. Oh dear: this is outside the foundation's remit. You'd have to change its objects, which requires permission from the regulator and can be a drama. That is avoided if the foundation has broad objects: you'll have the option (but not the obligation) to work in any area encompassed. A good phrase to include in the foundation's governing documents is '...and other charitable purposes'. Though this is good advice for any foundation, it's particularly important if you're planning your foundation to last a long time, because constrained objects can prevent a foundation from responding to new needs which emerge over time.

What is different about giving at this scale?

First and most obviously, you have much greater potential for improving the world. You'll best realise that potential by **focusing on just a few goals**. Though focusing increases effectiveness for any donor, the gains are much more pronounced for donors who are giving a lot. And, although there are no right or wrong answers for your focus, there are again better and worse answers: **good answers are those which speak to your passions and which make good use of all the resources you bring**, particularly any which are unique or unusual. As Andrew Carnegie wrote, the do-

---

15 There are considerable, and very good, resources about some of the other tools available from FSG Social Impact Advisors. www.fsg.org

nor's heart 'should be in the work. It is as important in administering wealth as it is in any other brand of a man's work that he should be enthusiastically devoted to it and feel that in the field selected his work lies.'

Second, giving a lot creates much **greater potential for damaging charities and wasting resources**. As you increase the amount you give to an organisation, you increase the difference that you make, both positive and negative. Take promptness of payment as an example. Suppose you're supporting a £2m charity. If you tell it that you're making a £100 donation and then you delay for a month or two, the effect isn't that huge. But if you promise £500,000 (which it might earmark for the salary bill for a few months), a delay of a month or two could be catastrophic. The potential for damaging charities is no flight of fancy: the cost to charities of just one process – reporting to funders – is calculated at getting on for £1 billion per year, of which around a quarter is probably avoidable (the calculation is at www.giving-evidence.com). That sum could fund some major UK charities, such as the British Red Cross or Barnado's, and that's even before we've included the costs of application processes. Putting all these costs together, we'll see how a bad process can waste your entire donation. Not that damage will be readily visible to you, so you'll need to go looking.

Third, giving a lot is more involved and complex than giving smaller amounts (just as managing a large company is more complex than managing a smaller one). Consequently, **you need a more organised process** for dealing with numerous organisations and managing your knowledge. If you choose to support charities and/ or other organisations, you'll need a process with the stages shown below. We'll use this diagram for navigation throughout this section:

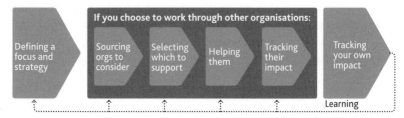

This process needs to work both for you and for your charitable goals. It needs to work for you because it will take more of your time and brain-space: it will probably involve numerous organisations[16], may involve having a network and a team, and you may want to involve others in your life – family members, neighbours, colleagues and employees, for example. So a consideration for the process is that it

---

16 To keep track of all this, you may want to use Salesforce.com's 'customer relationship management' software. Used by thousands of organisations globally, it can hold all your contacts and track your entire relationship with any organisation or person. The software is donated to non-profit organisations. www.salesforcefoundation.org/products/donation

should be engaging for you: don't design a process which involves loads of travel if you hate travel, for example. For the process to work for your charitable goals, **each stage needs to be designed to fit the goal(s)**. If you want to support community-based organisations in India, the way that you would source organisations to consider would be quite different than if you were looking for university research programmes. I know this sounds obvious, but despite the huge range of donors' goals, their processes are dominated by the 'application-and-reports-on-paper' approach. There are many alternatives, lots of which improve upon the 'deeply ingrained 'best practices' which Clara Miller, founder of the Nonprofit Finance Fund, thinks 'frequently add cost and reduce management flexibility in already difficult operating conditions [and] end up hurting organizations we mean to help'. We'll see how one donor has used these alternatives to convert an 80% failure rate into an 80% success rate.

But first, in a horror story compiled from real experiences, let's see...

How to waste your entire donation

Start: You have £10,000 to give charities.

1. Be hard to find, and unresponsive to enquiries.

If you don't have a website, or your site can't be found using obvious search terms, and you're not in the normal lists of funders, it might take a charity quite a while to discover your existence. Let's say a day or two. Then it needs to talk to you. If you don't respond to enquiries and only deal with charities whose representatives you've met in person, they'll need to hang around lots of conferences and networking events trying to bump into you. All in, this might take two days. A charity staffer's time – including National Insurance and the relevant part of the charity's rent, phone bill and so on (people typically cost about twice their actual salary) – could be £350/day, so that's at least £700 wasted before we've even started.

2. Make charities apply to you, and have a complicated and bespoke application process.

This could easily generate a couple of days' work for the charity: drafting answers to your unusual questions, downloading your form whose weird template doesn't quite work properly, drawing the organisational chart in the particular format you want, writing out the charity's registered address (which is requested on every donor's form, so why charities can't just send a standard form with this basic information to all donors is a mystery). That might take another two days. You can waste even more if you make the charities present to you in person and your office is somewhere really inconvenient – especially you don't reimburse the travel expenses. (Sometimes donors behave as if charities ought to be honoured to be granted an audience, rather like medieval royalty.) The meeting, including travel, might take half a day. So this stage is two and a half days, so another £875; the tally's now £1,575.

3. Attract far more applications than you need, so you reject the majority of them.

A good ploy is to be vague about what you fund. If you only fund one in every six applications (which is actually pretty high by industry standards), the total cost borne by applicant charities for every successful application is £9,450 (=£1,575 x 6).

4. Make small grants, and make lots of fuss.

Require complicated reports on progress. These are most wasteful if you insist that they are bespoke to you, because this prevents a charity simply writing one comprehensive report for all its donors. Get the charities to come in person to see you once or twice a year. That's easily another couple of days per charity over the course of the grants: another £700 each.

Restrict your donation and be inflexible. That way, every time the charity sees any significant change in demand for its service (or supply of labour or parts, or changes in legislation, or a new potential partner appears – or in fact pretty much anything), it'll need to negotiate with you. And if you're unresponsive, it'll take several attempts to get hold of you, so that could easily be another couple of days over the life of the grant. Another £700 each.

Make only small grants – say £5,000 each. You'll get two grants from your £10,000, so two charities incur the costs we've calculated. At £1,400 per charity, that's £2,800 all in.

Bingo! You've now wasted the entire £10,000 you had to start with, plus some other donors' money: the charities you've dealt with have now incurred costs of £12,250.

You can make this worse still if you won't fund the charities again for a couple of years after your grant expires – so they have to repeat the whole process to find a replacement, just to stand still.

In this example, the whole lot got wasted because the cost of dealing with the fuss (application and reporting processes and a low hit-rate) outweighed the donations themselves. It's abundantly clear now why 'giving a lot' and 'giving without fuss' were two of the central guides discussed in Section 2.

None of the errors in this scenario is unusual. For instance, as I'm writing this, the bank NatWest has a giving programme which will reject 14 of every 15 applicants – a cracking 93 per cent – and only gives grants of £6,000 after all that. Donor-instigated fuss commonly consumes a good chunk of donations, leaving what is rather soberingly called the 'net grant'. I would guess that net grants are on average about 80-90% of the total grant; bad cases would be below 50 per cent; I personally have seen grants where the net value has been around 25 per cent of the total. As we saw above, it's quite possible for the net grant to be nil or even negative. (An experimental physicist at Columbia University found some of his grants to be net negative.) Crucially, the donors themselves probably don't know about this wastage, and don't themselves feel the missed opportunities which inevitably ensue. Don't just copy.

Chapter 10

Get a focus

'A single, unambiguous aim is the keystone of successful military operations.'
– First of the British Army's principles of war, as taught to all
officers in the Royal Navy, Royal Air Force and British Army

Almost invariably, donors find that being focused helps them to achieve more and to enjoy it more. In this chapter, we'll see the case for focusing, some lovely examples of how successful donors operate, and how to select a focus for your own giving.

To reiterate, the value of focusing isn't confined to donors with relatively small resources. Social and environmental problems are fantastically complex – they have already 'resisted great intellects and often great money,' as Warren Buffett observes. Solving them is hard, and will require understanding them well and knowing what works: as we've discovered, many proposed solutions which look perfectly plausible to the untrained eye turn out to be ineffective or even counterproductive. All of this is easier with a limited focus. Consequently, the UK's largest charity, the Wellcome Trust, focuses solely on 'extraordinary improvements in human and animal health'. The Gates Foundation, the world's largest charity ever, focuses on just three issues: global health, international development, and secondary and post-secondary education in the US. The Rockefeller Brothers Fund focuses on 'advancing social change that contributes to a more just, sustainable, and peaceful world' within which it works in three areas. To take a corporate example, UBS's grant-making Optimus fund has a single focus on children in need, within which it works on education and upbringing, protection from violence and sexual abuse, child health, and neglected tropical diseases. Roger Federer only plays tennis – he doesn't also try to be a swimmer and a runner – selectiveness which seems to have served him rather well.

How to manage a billion dollars

In 2006, Warren Buffett gave a headline-grabbing donation to Bill Gates' foundation. Though it garnered rather less attention, he also gave $1 billion into the charitable foundations of each of his children. (Rather quirkily, he reportedly informed them by fax.) Part of Mr Buffett's advice to his children was to 'focus the new funds and your energy on a relatively few activities in which [you] can make an important difference'.

His son Peter and his wife Jennifer spent two years deciding where to focus and what success would mean. Jennifer reflects: 'The need seems endless. I consistently say: We'd really love to be doing these five other things, but we don't have the resources for them... So we're constantly talking about priorities. What are the greatest levers? How can we get the best results?'

They decided to tackle prison rape and sexual abuse, not exactly the easiest or cutest issues ever. And they're using their influence to amplify the effect of the money: 'We feel strongly that we might actually focus attention and resources on combating some of these entrenched problems, and then others may not be as afraid to go there.'

Jennifer and Peter laudably put great emphasis on planning carefully, being selective, and looking to change the system.

The MELMAC Education Foundation funds statewide educational initiatives in Maine, US. The foundation was struck that although Maine has strong graduation rates from high school, it has low graduation rates from college. It learnt about various underlying reasons and potential solutions. For instance, many school students express a traditional view – 'I want to go to college' – but don't connect this to specific, real aspirations for their lives. They therefore don't take sufficient time to choose the right college or course for them, nor really learn what college actually offers and entails. As a result, they are unprepared for the financial commitments, often enrol in a course with only limited interest for them, and drop out before the course even starts. Research showed that greater parental involvement in the process of planning and deciding about college can ameliorate this. MELMAC created a suite of programmes, one of which involved working with parents to better inform them about college, the commitments and options. The programmes had remarkably quick success: within two years, the rate of students matriculating into post-secondary education rose over 10 per cent, whereas the rates at other schools in Maine were unchanged.

Evidence that not focusing reduces a donor's impact includes the experience of the

Diana, Princess of Wales Memorial Fund. It noted in 2005 that one result of its 'open programme' (i.e., responsive, application-based) was that 'voluntary organisations themselves have selected their own priority proposals, with their own individual intended outcomes' and that 'the impacts are diverse and dispersed and do not necessarily add up to more than the sum of the excellent, individual parts.'

Focusing creates a practical benefit for donors too. Once you become known as a donor, you will get approached by many charities and need to avoid being besieged by requests. Clarity about what you do and don't support helps considerably: many donors report that excluding some areas is actually rather empowering.

We encountered in Section 1 the pain of choosing a focus, and that is just as true for donors giving a lot as for anybody else. That pain is offset by the rise in effectiveness which it enables. Rodger McFarlane, who ran the Gill Foundation, which focuses on civil rights in the US, put it this way: 'There is an unlimited amount of injustice and suffering out there that I cannot mitigate.... Part of the demand of this job is relentlessly focusing on exactly what we said we're trying to do, and staying there.' It's rather similar to running a business in one sector and seeing an opportunity in some totally different area – it might look somewhat attractive, but if it isn't your remit, it will distract you perhaps to the point of precipitating failure.

A field to play in, or a specific goal?

Some donors support work in particular areas. To take one example, the Esmée Fairbairn Foundation, one of the UK's largest grant-making foundations, will fund charities in the arts, environment and education.

Others go a step further and look to solve a particular problem. Google.org, the search giant's non-profit entity, has a programme called RE<C which aims to make the unit cost of renewable energy less than that of carbon-based energy, and the Gates Foundation is aiming to eradicate polio once and for all. This allows the donor to deeply understand what to prioritise: when Bill Gates talks about polio, he's strikingly full of recent statistics about incidence and research about progress. 'My favourite book is *Disease Control Priorities in Developing Countries*,' he says.

Where to focus

Here, ladies and gentlemen, is the first heart-warming tale about an investment bank I bet you've heard for a while:

Last night a banker saved my life

Globally, we lose 2.3m children each year to preventable diseases such as pneumonia, diarrhoea and yellow fever. Various governments have pledged money for developing and delivering immunisation over the next 15-20 years, though the timing of their funding is somewhat unpredictable.

Goldman Sachs, an investment bank, provided a small group of bankers on a pro bono basis to create the innovative International Finance Facility for Immunisation (IFFIm). This takes the governments' commitments and, by issuing bonds secured against them, makes the money available up-front. This enables better planning which accelerates research and development, reduces vaccine prices and speeds delivery. Vaccinations enabled by the bond are expected to protect *more than 500m children* in about 70 of the world's poorest countries, and the bonds themselves are credited with saving at least 3m lives.

This is a beautiful example of an organisation using its virtually unique resources in such a way that they make significant progress on a very substantial problem. 'IFFIm is an intriguing fit for our skills and interests ... a perfect example of how the capital markets can be tapped for the public good. Every bond sold will help save more kids' lives ... The opportunity to marshal the resources of Goldman Sachs to help improve the lives of millions of children is profoundly meaningful,' says Michael Sherwood, co-CEO of Goldman Sachs International.

(Goldman Sachs is one of several banks which sell the bonds commercially. It's been criticised for this, though not, I notice, by any of the half a billion children.)

Now, Goldman Sachs could have donated those financiers' time by having them paint walls in a local community centre. They wouldn't have had nearly as much impact: it would be like using the Crown Jewels as a doorstop. This is precisely analogous to the choice with which we began between increasing the school attendance in India of one child or of 25 children: how you give and where you give are more influential than how much you give. The best ways of using resources enable donors not just to make *some* improvement, but rather to make *the greatest improvement possible*.

So when you define your focus, look not for where to make *some* impact but *for where and how your resources will make the greatest possible impact*. Two questions arise immediately:

- **What are your resources?** They include your skills, passions, interests, experiences and values, as well as funds, contacts, software, equipment and premises. Your resources are almost certainly more varied and extensive than they first appear.
- **What needs doing in the world?** For this, we need to understand priority needs in the world (which we could think of as demand), and what's already being done by other charitable donors, businesses and government (which we could think of as supply).

This useful diagram shows how a good focus lies at the intersection of the answers to those two questions. We'll call it the 'Kramer Diagram', after Mark Kramer, co-founder of FSG Social Impact Advisors, the organisation which developed it:

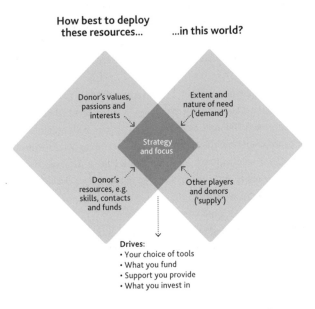

The four factors weigh differently for different donors. For example:

An analysis of the **donor's skills and resources** drove two quite similar businesses – both management consultancies - to different ways of deploying their professional skills to support charities.

In 2006, the UK office of global management consultancy Booz & Co. wanted to focus its pro bono efforts on a single deep and long-term relationship, rather than the multiple but somewhat diffuse engagements it had had to date. The (good) idea was to find a charity which had the breadth to benefit from the full gamut of skills which Booz & Co. delivers to commercial clients.

Because employee engagement was important, Booz & Co. asked its London-based staff to recommend charities which it might support. Suggestions included the British Red Cross, a large and complex international organisation, and several smallish charities looking to grow dramatically.

Booz & Co.'s commercial work is dominated by large companies with complex operational and systems issues (for example, it has many large clients in energy, industrials, consumer goods and transport). It has relatively limited expertise with smaller organisations. Therefore Booz & Co. chose to support the British Red Cross which could make better use of Booz & Co.'s experience. The relationship is proving fruitful to both sides.

By contrast, the Monitor Group, a global strategy consultancy, frequently works with rapidly-growing companies and clients entering new markets. Its skillset is therefore very relevant to the kinds of charities supported by 'venture philanthropy' funds, which provide money and strategic support to smallish high-impact charities to enable them to grow. As a result, Monitor has for some years had a successful relationship with New Profit Inc., one of the early US venture philanthropy funds, in which Monitor advises both the fund itself and the charities which it supports.

We saw the donor's resources at play with Jennifer and Peter Buffett's selection of issues. Their choice of prison rape was clearly influenced by their ability to raise awareness by virtue of their own profile.

Personal passions and interests can determine the area of charitable focus. After spending time in the southern African kingdom of Lesotho in 2004, Prince Harry founded a charity, Sentebale, with Prince Seeiso of the Lesotho Royal Family, to support the country's orphans:

> 'We came up with the name Sentebale because we wanted one in Sesotho, the language of Lesotho, and the idea of 'forget me not' [which sentebale means] seemed perfect. The charity is a way that both Prince Seeiso and I can remember our mothers who both worked with AIDS and orphaned children. I really feel that by doing this I can follow in my mother's footsteps and keep her legacy alive.'

Steve Kirsch, an internet entrepreneur, was diagnosed with Waldenstrom's Macroglobulinemia, a rare blood cancer in 2007:

> 'It's possible that whatever I do to find a cure may likely be too late to save my own life. But that doesn't mean I shouldn't try. I remember as a kid learning the old saying that "nobody ever won a chess game by resigning." Who knows. Maybe I will get lucky. I believe that people make their own luck. I think my best chance of survival is to advance the science by intelligently directing funds into research that is likely to do the most good including bringing in fresh eyes from outside the field.'

Subsequently, the board of the $75m Kirsch Foundation decided to change its focus to funding research into rare cancers. Kirsch himself did not vote, but the decision was clearly informed by the personal connection.

Since the passions, interests and values of the people involved in your giving (your family, company, board) are so important to your charitable work, it's worth being clear about them. Below are various reasons which donors sometimes cite which may be helpful prompts:

If you're giving as an individual or family	Expectations from your community	If you're giving as a company	Needs in the external world
To teach my children the value of wealth.	Having been successful, I'm expected to give.	To demonstrate our commitment to our local area.	To eradicate polio.
To bring my family together and give us a shared project.	I want to encourage others to give, so am leading by example.	To enable our staff to use their skills for the benefit of others.	To keep the opera open in my local town.
To build my network / reputation / visibility.		To demonstrate our corporate responsibility – good for staff morale, retention, recruitment, and reputation.	To improve lives of AIDS orphans in Malawi.
To fulfil a religious obligation.			To increase women's participation in democracy in West Africa.
To honour my mother's memory.		To build our network.	To speed research into treatment of stroke victims.

Other, 'supply-driven' reasons:

The money I have exceeds my requirements.

This company has a great product which we want charities to be able to use for free.

We are a foundation: giving is our role.

Extent and nature of needs we have discussed already, particularly the rationale for prioritising significant, under-resourced needs. When Bill and Melinda Gates decided to concentrate on eradicable diseases, including polio, TB and malaria, they were responding to a situation in which need ('demand') is huge, with the activity (or 'supply') in response currently quite inadequate. The enormous needs related to climate change are clearly behind Google.org's RE<C programme.

An analysis of what other donors make available, or the **'supply'**, can highlight under-resourced areas. One donor who lives in an affluent part of Britain chooses to support hospices in poorer areas which have a particularly tough time raising funds. Supply is also germane when funding for a necessary activity comes to an end, as happens sometimes with government funding. On the extraordinary occasion when the Diana, Princess of Wales Memorial Fund was unable to meet its financial commitments due to legal action against it by the Franklin Mint over use of the late Princess's image, supply was suddenly constrained, so other charitable donors stepped in.

If you do not have to raise your money from anybody else – for example, if you are endowed, or giving as an individual or family – I urge you to consider supporting work at the base of the triangle, on changing whole systems for everybody. As you'll recall, 'supply' is normally more abundant at the top of the triangle than at the base, because it's more tangible, easier to understand, more immediate and more photogenic. It is therefore disproportionately attractive to individuals: Oxfam can sell notional goats as gifts but it can't sell notional researchers. Donors who don't have to raise money from individuals are almost uniquely able to support that work.

Process for choosing a focus
There are three main methods of choosing a focus: democratically, analytically or experimentally. Whichever you choose, you're not locked-in forever: you can work in your area(s) for a while, and periodically review your effectiveness.

Democratically
Deciding democratically has the obvious appeal of giving beneficiaries a voice, which the lack of feedback loop normally denies them. However, it is rarely done. Consequently, donors often prioritise problems which beneficiaries don't think matter that much: for example, in the field of health, a huge study of 2,800 grants from private foundations across 27 countries found a marked mismatch between what the foundations were doing and what people in those countries want done. Eva Harris, professor of infectious diseases at the University of California believes that 'the real problem is other people deciding for other countries what is in their best interests. One needs to develop partnerships and listen, as well as to tell.'

An honourable exception is the Wikimedia Foundation, the organisation behind Wikipedia. In 2010, its tenth year, it ran a project to develop its strategy using a characteristically open process on the basis that it 'would result in a smarter, more effective strategy. Just as Wikipedia is the encyclopaedia anyone can edit, we wanted to invite participation from anyone who wanted to help. More than 1,000 people from around the world contributed in more than 50 languages. The project lasted a full year and resulted in 1,470 content pages on the wiki'.

Deciding analytically

If you already have a good understanding of the area in which you're interested, you might use a process of elimination for defining a focus within it.

Draw a map of the issues which might be candidates. For example, if you're interested in health in a particular country, draw up or get hold of a list of the constituent issues: various medical conditions, public information about prevention, clinical research, accessibility of drug trial data, care for patients, care for families, recuperation, palliative care, doctor training, nurse training, hospital equipment and so forth. (New Philanthropy Capital publishes good guides to some UK sectors in which charities operate, such as domestic violence, mental health, homelessness.)

Exclude any which are a poor fit for your priorities and passions. Perhaps they don't enable you to involve all the people you'd like to involve, for example staff members who'd like to volunteer, or if you'd like family members to see the work. Exclude too any about which nobody in your team feels passionate – good giving relies on tenacity and passion.

Amongst the remaining issues, work out where your resources will be particularly valuable, thinking back to the Kramer Diagram. You may do well to involve beneficiaries in this process, for the reasons we've just seen. Catalogue your resources, prioritising any which are unique to you, and include the less obvious ones such as knowledge, relationships with charities, reputation, relationships with other donors, knowledge of technology. Then research where those resources might be valuable – and be open to some unexpected answers. For example, if you're an architect, health charities might not seem an obvious fit, but Maggie's Cancer Caring Centres, a charity which builds and runs drop-in centres for people affected by cancer, deliberately works with great architects to create buildings which are welcoming and supportive, unlike many health-related buildings.

Looking at the shorter list you now have, check against other criteria important to you, such as whether there are other donors with whom you could partner (which we'll cover later). If the list which that yields is still too long, I suggest choosing based on the interests and passion in your team: don't chicken out of making a choice altogether.

Deciding experimentally

If you don't already have an understanding of the issue(s) on which you might focus, you could experiment for a while.

John Stone, a self-made entrepreneur in the insurance industry, established the Stone Family Foundation in 2005 after selling his business. It holds over £45m. 'When we began, we didn't have a passion for any particular cause, we really started with a blank piece of paper. We were more inclined to support developing countries where there's no welfare state and our money can achieve more.'

They decided to choose experimentally. They aimed to 'experience being involved in all types of charities', and so started with a deliberately diverse 'pilot portfolio' of ten organisations of differing sizes, issues and countries across Africa and Asia. They visited each one. They have now defined their focus areas based on that experience: they elected to support microfinance, water, vulnerable children (primarily for education) and mental health in the UK.

The knack with experimenting is to be disciplined and systematic. Define a duration for the 'experiment' to ensure that you do eventually make a decision. Keep a log of your experiences, impressions and results, so that when the clock eventually strikes midnight, you have a decent set of data to inform your decision.

Once you have a focus, we can rummage in the box of tools to find the best one for achieving your goal – there are many more than meet the eye.

Chapter 11

Use all the tools

'We didn't want to be limited to one tool, traditional grant making: we wanted an expanded toolkit.'
– eBay co-founder Pierre Omidyar

'You really need to play all the keys on the keyboard.'
– Larry Brilliant, the first Director of Google.org

The classic way that major donors give is by supporting existing charities. Whilst this is just perfect for some goals, it doesn't suit them all. There are a hundred and one alternative tools, and the best choice depends on who you are, the resources you have and the issue you're trying to solve. We'll now canter through some of them. The purpose is not to showcase donors whom you can blindly copy but rather to illustrate the diversity of tools available and thereby encourage and embolden you to be inventive about the tools you use yourself.

Setting up organisations

If no organisation does what you want to see done, you may need to set one up.

ARK (Absolute Return for Kids, a foundation which raises funds from the UK hedge fund industry) was one of four partners who set up Teaching Leaders. It was in response to the insight that teacher performance – and therefore, pupils' educational attainment – is hampered by lack of a strong tier of 'middle leaders': heads of department or of year who have the potential to become head teachers. Teaching Leaders trains these emerging leaders to take more senior positions in particularly challenging schools.

HRH The Prince of Wales has set up many organisations to respond to unmet needs. They include the Prince's Trust, which started working with disaffected young people in 1976, ahead of many other charities; Business in the Community, which encourages and supports pro-social and pro-environmental behaviour amongst businesses; and Duchy Originals, an organic food and drink business which provides a route to market for organic producers.

Marcelle Speller OBE is the co-founder of HolidayRentals.com, an online catalogue of holiday cottages. The charity sector might not seem an obvious fit for her skills in setting up and marketing online catalogues but she's found a way to use them to great effect. Partnering with the Community Foundation Network, the membership group of Community Foundations, she created LocalGiving.com, the online platform we met in Section 2 which promotes charities discovered by Community Foundations which cannot afford to market themselves to potential donors.

A word of caution. There is no shortage of charities and – as we'll see in Section 4 – the charity world is already fabulously fragmented. It's only worth starting a completely new charity if you're certain that no organisation already does what you want to do (or can be persuaded to do it).

Supporting social enterprises (non-profit businesses with social and/or environmental missions)

Jeff Skoll, the other co-founder of eBay, is a believer in the ability of film to communicate and engage people. As well as starting a foundation, he founded Participant Media to create 'entertainment that inspires and accelerates social change', i.e., films about social and environmental issues. It's a company: its 2006 film *An Inconvenient Truth* netted a neat profit as well as engaging hundreds of thousands of people in the challenges of climate change. Participant Media has also created films about state school education, Darfur, homelessness and mental illness.

The Shell Foundation, which focuses on 'global development and environmental challenges linked to impact of energy and globalisation', works only with entities which generate all their own revenue, i.e., (non-profit) businesses:

> *'We believe it is important to treat the poor as customers and not beneficiaries. This helps focus on delivering products and services that address the needs of their real customers (i.e., the intended recipient) rather than being supply-led and based on needs perceived by others [and] aspirations of their funders and donors.'*

In other words, the foundation wants to avoid the poor simply receiving what somebody else decides they need, a situation which the separation can cause. It says:

'Many things happen as pro-poor enterprises become financially viable. First, they rely less on scarce aid money, which is a good thing. Second, they can grow, thus impacting more poor people. Third, through innovation and problem-solving, they are able to provide more of their customers – poor people – with more appropriate and more affordable goods and services.'

Notice that working with businesses which, as Shell Foundation puts it, are 'designed to exit from subsidy completely, secure earned income and achieve scale', is quite different from adopting a business-like approach when giving to charities which are inherently reliant on subsidy. There is a popular notion that a 'business-like approach' to charities is helpful, though in fact it can be pretty misleading – even dangerous – because charities are so fundamentally different to businesses, as we've established. Not for nothing does Jim Collins' book *Good to Great and the Social Sectors* bear the subtitle *Why Business Thinking Is Not the Answer*.

Working through fully for-profit businesses

This option might be a surprise but some problems are best addressed through commercial entities.

The Gates Foundation aims to eradicate malaria. Clearly, developing, testing and marketing pharmaceuticals are the domain of commercial companies, so to develop and trial drugs, the Gates Foundation has, in effect, hired GlaxoSmithKline (GSK). The foundation subsidises the work to a point where it is financially viable for GSK. Gates has contributed over $200m to the partnership which is making strong progress on a vaccine.

The Siebel Foundation viewed the usage of methamphetamine in Montana as 'a consumer products marketing problem. Meth is a consumer product. It is readily available. It is affordably priced.' The foundation ran a campaign to reduce usage using standard tools of consumer marketing: it hired ad agencies to do research and create adverts, which ran on broadcast, print, online media and billboards. They were highly effective: usage by teens and adults both declined by nearly two-thirds.

It's worth dwelling on these examples because sometimes a notion that businesses are 'bad' whereas charities are 'good' makes donors squeamish about working with businesses. We don't have to take a moral view, we can be pragmatic: if your goal requires ad agencies or pharmaceutical research centres, it may be impractical to confine yourself to charities.

Not 'giving money away' at all

Founded with the modest sum of £4m, the Beth Johnson Foundation has made a positive difference to older people's lives for almost 40 years. This UK foundation uses interest from its trust to fund research, innovative thinking and pilots of practical schemes that directly enhance the lives of older people and the wider community. These pilot schemes are then developed with external partner-funders, and many have been adopted as standard practice at local, national and international levels. The Beth Johnson Foundation's impressive list of achievements includes leading on the development of advocacy for older people, pioneering programmes of mid-life behavioural change and developing a UK-wide programme to support intergenerational relationships. The Beth Johnson Foundation is therefore neither a grant-maker, service provider nor a thinktank. It describes itself as a 'thinking organisation', and shows beautifully how a relatively small amount of money can dramatically influence an entire sector.

Working with government

Local or central government dominates many areas in which charities and foundations operate – such as health and education – and therefore government departments and agencies can make attractive partners. The Wolfson Foundation, for example, has partnered with central government in a number of fields: a fund for museums and galleries across England has been run jointly with the Department for Culture, Media and Sport for many years; and with the Department for Business, Innovation and Skills, it jointly funds the Royal Society Wolfson Research Merit Awards which provide universities with support to attract or retain respected scientists of outstanding achievement or potential.

The Paul Hamlyn Foundation partners with local and central government in supporting music education as children transition from primary to secondary school, and in a programme around supplementary education which tackles school exclusion and truancy.

The NHS can be a crucial partner too. A surprising amount of hospital equipment is funded charitably, and most hospitals have a group of 'friends' who raise money. Equally if you wanted to support the work described in Section 1 to force better disclosure of the effects of drug trials, you might partner with health professionals in the NHS who are working on it.

Partnering with private individuals and other types of non-profit

Potentially any entity can be useful in improving the world, and it's worth being creative. The Alfred P. Sloan Foundation supports original research and education in science, technology, engineering, mathematics and economic performance, and one of its aims is improving the public understanding of science. To that end, it supports the commissioning and production of plays about scientists, engineers and mathematicians, including a New York staging of the fantastic play *Copenhagen* by

The local council in Dharamsala, North India, has an unexpected partner for its refuse collection

the fantastic Michael Frayn (about physicists Bohr and Heisenberg meeting during the Second World War to discuss the bomb).

Impact investing (also called social investing)

The F.B. Heron Foundation in New York benefits low-income families in urban and rural communities in the United States by supporting work around wealth-creation, such as advancing home ownership, creating small businesses, improving financial literacy and helping low-income people to build savings.

It is the most famous example of a donor investing right across the investment spectrum we saw in Section 2. On the left of that spectrum, it makes grants; in the middle, it makes equity-like investments or 'soft' loans to non-profit or for-profit organisations whose work closely corresponds with its goals; moving to the right, it invests in credit unions, community development banks; and on the far right, it will invest in private equity and bonds which offer 'substantial social benefits to low-income families and communities'.

Panahpur, a family trust, also invests across the spectrum – indeed it produced the spectrum diagram in Chapter 9. For example, on one side it has given a grant to Cambodia Rural Church Pastors, who presumably have no mechanism for generating revenue from which to pay a return; whereas on the other side, it has invested in a fund set up by the Big Issue to invest in other social enterprises.

Being an operator yourself

You may be able to achieve a goal more rapidly as an operator yourself than by supporting other organisations. This could involve direct practical action, publicising a cause or representing other people. An example is McKenzie Steiner, the six-year-old girl we met in Section 2, whose beach cleanups Bill Clinton cites: she just gets on with what needs to be done.

Clinton himself follows suit. Though he isn't a major cash donor, he uses his personal brand to inspire and encourage others to give. The glitzy invite-only events of the Clinton Global Initiative convene hundreds of the world's leaders, and it's no accident that they take place in New York City to coincide with meetings of the U.N. General Assembly. 'All the people that you hope you will someday meet... you meet them here,' says Muhammad Yunus, who himself scooped a Nobel Prize for his work on microfinance. The Clinton Global Initiative claims to have raised an astonishing $46 billion in its six year life. Its offspring include several programmes largely funded by a less well-known people but carrying the Clinton brand, such as the Clinton-Hunter Development Initiative with Scottish entrepreneur Tom Hunter, and the Clinton Giustra Sustainable Growth Initiative with Frank Giustra, a Canadian mining businessman.

Diana, Princess of Wales was an operator, using her newsworthiness to address the stigma and fear of HIV/AIDS. In 1987, she opened the first HIV ward in a UK hospital and held the hand of a patient with AIDS in front of national media, and she used the same tactic to raise awareness of landmines and landmine victims a decade later. The way she gave her time was highly effective: she created much greater influence by generating press coverage herself than if she had, say, hosted dinners to raise funds for charities to do conventional media work.

Selecting recipients based on attainment rather than application: prizes

In some circumstances, prizes are a great way of getting work done and seem to bring significant additional funding to winners. There are broadly two types of prize.

Prizes for a specific development. In the nineteenth century, it was remarkably difficult to deliver fresh food to the front-line of an advancing army. So Napoleon offered a prize for a mechanism for preserving food. It spurred various innovations, eventually leading to vacuum-packing and tin cans. (Ideas also included putting vegetables in old champagne bottles... Gotta love the French!) The founder of the modern-day X Prize, which offers cash prizes for specific developments such as privately-funded space flight and putting solar technology into pavements, thinks that prizes encourage competitors to spend about ten times the value of the prize on solving the problem – in other words, this way of giving unlocks ten times as much work as would be enabled by a grant of the same value.

Prizes recognising achievement in a particular field. For example, the Nobel Prizes recognise achievements in medicine, literature, physics, peace-building and so on, and the Ashden Awards for Sustainable Energy root out and laud developments in production of clean energy in the UK and internationally. Sometimes likened to the Oscars, the Ashden Awards ceremony is presented by the likes of Al Gore, Sir David Attenborough and HRH Prince of Wales. Ashden Award founder Sarah Butler-Sloss reckons that winners of the international awards receive on average about six times as much money from other sources as a result of the prize as they do from the prize itself. Meanwhile Nobel Prizes bring the gift of life itself! Winning, as opposed to merely being nominated, has been found to extend people's lives by about two years, as well as, of course, highlighting their research findings.

To conclude

Be open to using all or any of these tools, alongside (or instead of) supporting charities and non-profits. The Kramer Diagram will guide you to which one(s) to use, based on the state of supply and demand in the issues in which you're interested, what is already being done, and your passions, team and resources. Whichever tool(s) you select, you're likely to achieve most by partnering, to which we'll turn now.

Chapter 12

Take your partner by the hand...

'If you want to go fast, go alone. If you want to go far, go together.'
– African proverb

'I sat down and thought about who could do a better job of dispersing wealth than myself. I came to realise that there was a terrific foundation already scaled up – that I wouldn't have to go through the real grind...
'[Bill and Melinda Gates] do a much better job than I could. What can be more logical in whatever you want done, than finding somebody better equipped than you are to do it?'
– Warren Buffett on the logic of giving his $31 billion through the Gates Foundation

Many causes and issues are already covered by at least one donor, and putting your resources through their existing 'machines' will be more cost-effective than building your own machine. If you are supporting other organisations, it also saves time and money for them by reducing the number of donors they have to deal with. Again, below are some ideas and models to spur and inspire.

Starting out

After a decade of giving grants for innovation in sustainable energy, Sarah Butler-Sloss wanted her foundation, the Ashden Trust, to set up an award programme. She began by partnering with the established Whitley Awards. Emboldened by the experience, she expanded the programme, establishing the Ashden Awards for Sustainable Energy in 2001. The Awards now, in turn, attract other partners, including the foundation established by Skype-founder Niklas Zennström.

Eurostar also teamed up with the Ashden Awards to create a prize for local sustainable transport initiatives. In principle, Eurostar could have created an infrastructure of its own – promoting the award, going out to find charities, getting some judges together, figuring out criteria, judging entries, creating some kind of award ceremony, getting press coverage. The Ashden Awards already has all that. The partnership leaves Eurostar more time and money to help the great initiatives it finds, and avoids having to learn the (sometimes not so obvious) lessons about how to run an awards programme, of which Ashden has over a decade's experience. As Eurostar Chief Executive, Richard Brown puts it:

> *'At Eurostar, we recently re-focused our 'Tread Lightly' environmental programme and began to look at supporting charities in the sustainability field. We were keen to develop an awards scheme which would enable us to recognise and celebrate organisations which share our vision. We quickly recognised the value of partnering, rather than creating our own programme and when introduced to the Ashden Awards for Sustainable Energy, we saw a great fit. The Ashden Awards already has the infrastructure, reputation and expertise.'*

Another example of effective partnering is provided by pop star Cheryl Cole. Her foundation is spending its first year working solely with The Prince's Trust to help disadvantaged young people in North East England. The 35 years of learning and networking by The Prince's Trust will enable Cheryl Cole's foundation to learn in an accelerated way about the issues and how best to help.

Outsourcing

Microsoft, Cisco and Symantec all donate their products to charities. Rather than each building separate 'giving machines', all three outsource the process to Tech-Soup, an international network of organisations which distribute software in their respective countries. This is cheaper for the donating companies, as well as more convenient for charities to whom TechSoup provides a single point of contact, avoiding duplicate application processes.

Robbie Williams' charity Give It Sum helps young people in his hometown of Stoke-on-Trent. He outsources all the mechanics to Comic Relief's powerful machine. In the ten years to 2010, it distributed over £5m on behalf of Give It Sum.

Robbie Williams' arrangement with Comic Relief is, I believe, unique, but several large foundations have specifically built capability to handle other donors' giving. The Pew Charitable Trusts, endowed with over $4 billion from the family behind Sun Oil, actively solicit funds from other donors, offering them the chance to use Pew's respected machine for generating social impact in many areas. Similarly, the

Rockefeller family's reputation for giving generated so many requests for advice about it that the family established Rockefeller Philanthropy Advisors. This now offers a full suite of services: advice on establishing a foundation or about issues and approaches, and fully outsourced management of grant-making, reviews and trustee meetings.

Reaching the parts you can't reach

If somebody else already specialises where you want to operate, they'll make a good partner. The Rufford Maurice Laing Foundation (RMLF) focuses primarily on nature conservation, so when it decided to allocate up to £250,000 per annum to HIV/AIDS projects in less developed countries, it had little relevant expertise. But the Elton John Aids Foundation (EJAF) focuses on precisely that. So RMLF puts its HIV/AIDS allocation through EJAF, effectively 'borrowing' its machine. Brilliant: RMLF's giving to HIV/AIDS rapidly becomes highly effective at little marginal cost to anybody.

The arrangement is particularly elegant because EJAF itself outsources a part of its own work. EJAF's machine was not designed to disburse small grants to grass-roots organisations, so it partners with the Firelight Foundation which specialises in this area.

Pooling resources

The Baring Foundation and John Ellerman Foundation, two endowed UK foundations, work together on their funding in sub-Saharan Africa. The various process stages are handled differently: the Baring Foundation does the initial assessment; a joint committee does the selection; support comprises a cheque from each foundation; and impact tracking is done by the Baring Foundation.

Similarly, several US funders have convened to scale-up charities which have proven successful. Edna McConnell Clark Foundation initiated a fund with $39m of its money, to which $88m has been added from other foundations and donors.

As with any good rule, there are caveats. Clearly you can only partner where another donor is willing to work on the same issues. If you're serving a need which is totally unserved by others – and one could easily argue the case for doing that – then you have no choice but to operate solo. But be open to letting other donors in on your machine. After all, if your machine is good enough for your money, it is good enough for theirs, and it it isn't good enough for theirs, perhaps it isn't fit for yours either.

Let's turn then to designing a machine which works well for your goals if the tool you choose involves supporting other organisations. The difference between a good machine and a bad one is, remember, a lot of children needlessly out in the fields.

Watch your language!

Half full, or half empty?	Nudge, or libertarian paternalism?
Inheritance tax, or death tax?	Free labour, or volunteering?
Steak, or dead cow?	Elizabeth Windsor, or Her Majesty the Queen?

The way that we describe something influences how we behave towards it:

> *'In an interesting experiment, participants played a prisoner's dilemma-type game in which they had the choice of cooperating or defecting. Those who were told that he exercise was called the "Wall Street game" were more likely to defect than those who were told it was called the "community game".'*
> – From *Money Well Spent*, by Hal Harvey and Paul Brest of the Hewlett Foundation

If you decide that the tool for you is supporting other organisations, be careful about how you refer to them. Terms such as 'partner', 'operating charity', 'delivery charity' or 'delivery partner' will entice you to respect them. They also reflect what the charities actually do.

'Grant seeker' must be the worst term. It implies that the charity exists solely to seek grants, like some kind of financial blood-sucker. It doesn't. It exists for some noble and commendable goal such as ridding the world of sexual violence or putting paedophiles behind bars. Sure, it needs subsidy to do that, which sometimes leads it to seek grants. But to refer to it as a 'grant seeker' is to trivialise its very purpose.

'Grantee' is probably the term most commonly used. I'm ambivalent about that. It implies that the organisation is defined by grants – which it isn't: it's defined by its goal – but at least it's not pejorative.

While we're on the subject of language, let's banish the term 'project'. Effective donors don't support a project because they know that the highest impact comes from supporting the entire organisation, that is, giving without restrictions. If you're supporting an organisation, you're supporting an organisation – not a 'project' at all. A charity is no more a project than BP or Intel or John Lewis are projects. They're institutions and need support to operate as such.

Chapter 13

Process: design around your goal

If the best tools for your goals include supporting other organisations – universities, hospitals, social enterprises, businesses or charities – you'll need a process which includes the following stages: sourcing organisations to consider, selecting which to support, supporting them, and tracking their impact. We'll look at those in this chapter. We'll cover tracking your own organisation's performance in the next chapter.

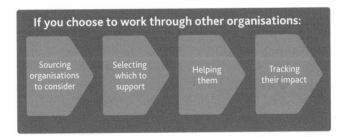

Again, there are myriad options at each stage, as well as clever tricks for the informed and traps for the unwary. The central principle is that each stage of the process should serve your goal and the organisations you support in pursuit of it.

Before we begin, let's take a moment to understand the process most commonly used by major donors, because I want to dissuade you from copying it. It goes something like this: define and publish some criteria for the types of charities you will support; invite applications on paper; consider applications at infrequent, closed meetings at which a few charities are selected; give cash to those few; request periodic reports on paper. Silent, solo, slow, reactive and unengaged, this process hardly looks like a recipe for achieving goals 'which have resisted great intellects and often great money'. The process appears to be organised for the convenience of the donor, which is clearly quite separate from the needs of the charities or beneficiaries.

How could we actually find out whether this process is any good? Ideally, we'd do an experiment. We'd change one feature of the process at a time whilst keeping everything else constant, and look at changes in impact. Sadly, to my knowledge, no such experiment has ever been carried out. However, one donor – the Shell Foundation – has run a kind of experiment: it has had the same goal for more than ten years, against which it has tried various processes and tracked its impact along the way.

Case study: the Shell Foundation

The findings are highly instructive. In short, the Shell Foundation discovered that restricted, small, short-term grants succeeded only 20 per cent of the time, whereas bigger grants over a longer time-span and with more engagement failed only 20 per cent of the time. The lessons are laid out in the remarkably candid self-assessment which the Shell Foundation published on its tenth birthday. It's not the most rigorous experiment imaginable, because several features are varied at once, but it is the best example of comparable performance data I've ever come across in philanthropy.

'We wasted loads of our money...'

Shell Foundation was founded by the Shell Group in 2000. It is funded by the energy company but operationally semi-independent, focusing on 'global development and environmental challenges linked to impact of energy and globalisation'. Its theory of change is to 'develop, scale-up and promote enterprise-based solutions to the challenges' in pursuit of which it has used three quite diverse processes:

Phase 1: 'Inception phase': '[During] our inception phase, an open Request for Proposal process was used as the main way of selecting grantees. It was the classic methodology: consulting widely, publicising our areas of interest and then reviewing proposals submitted. We largely provided short-term project-based support to multiple not-for-profit organisations.' It disbursed $17m in this phase (2000-2002).

Phase 2: Piloting strategic partnerships (larger, longer, more engaged). It disbursed $25m in this phase (2003-2005).

Phase 3: Focusing on a few, carefully selected partners into each of which it is putting $10-$15m over five to seven years. In the first two years (2006-2008), it disbursed $36m.

The graph opposite shows the success and failure of Shell Foundation's grants in each phase. (The report was published too early to tell whether grants made after 2008 have succeeded.)

Performance of Shell Foundation grants

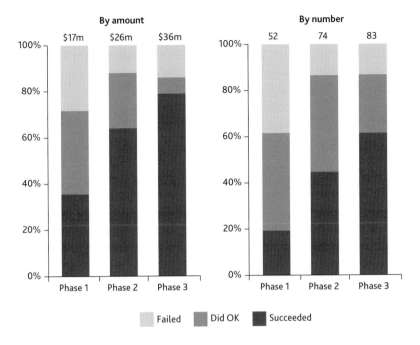

This graph is amazing, in my view. It's amazing that Shell Foundation has these data, and even more that it's willing to admit to such a high failure rate. There's no reason to think that Shell Foundation's hit rate is particularly bad: what is rare is its effort to collect and publish these data – which implies that donors are sitting on lots of unpublished data about what works and what doesn't which could prevent others making the same mistakes. Hats off to Shell Foundation for its rigour and candour. (Remember GiveWell's lovely view that 'information about how to help people should never be secret'?) And what an impressive turn-around, from which we can learn no fewer than six valuable lessons. First a lesson in how to fail, and then a clutch of ideas about how to succeed.

First lesson: 'Spray and pray' doesn't work. You'll remember that 'spray and pray' is the industry term for selecting so many charities that it's impossible to do reliable assessment on each or to provide each with much support. In the inception phase when Shell Foundation sprayed and prayed – and funded only 'projects' – 80 per cent of the projects 'failed to achieve scale or sustainability.' Even with considerable trial and error and a substantial budget to play with, Shell Foundation couldn't get the silent, solo, slow, reactive and unengaged model to work. Notice that it was only in a position to move away from that model because it had gone to the trouble of collecting the data.

Second lesson: Careful choice and focus pay off. By the third phase, Shell Foundation had changed its approach significantly, taking much more care over assessment, selecting just a few great organisations into which to invest substantial amounts of time and money. The figures were reversed: 'We now find that 80% of our grants achieve scale or sustainability.'

Third lesson: Provide what's needed, stay the course, build the organisation. The $10-15m provided to each recipient is, by standards of the charity sector, enormous. The Shell Foundation report notes that:

> 'Building sustainable enterprises requires investing in core capacity, slick operational systems and a robust infrastructure. This means recruiting the best staff and developing efficient operating systems. It also requires input over and above grant finance – [such as] business advice, market access and appropriate governance support. Few development problems of any kind are solved permanently by money alone. We believe that this 'more than money' approach serves to significantly reduce risk. Building sustainable enterprises takes time, patience and considerable investment.'

Fourth lesson: Be willing to go it alone if nobody else is interested. In all cases of success in Phase 3 Shell Foundation was 'the sole partner and subsidy provider'. In general, donors achieve more by working together. But if nobody else shares your goal or your flexibility about choice of tools, don't be scared to operate alone.

Fifth lesson: Get the data – track your own performance. Shell Foundation was able to make these changes (and thus we're able to learn the lessons) only because it collected data throughout. This is basic management information – any commercial investor, supermarket, barrister or cake company will know which types of activity work and which don't. Curiously few donors collect it systematically, normally under the misplaced notion that their own administration is invariably wasting money. It isn't: this example shows how a small spend on data-gathering enabled a donor to reverse its fortunes.

Sixth lesson: Admin costs tell you nothing. In the first phase, Shell Foundation probably had low admin costs because it had few staff reviewing applications and few (if any) staff supporting grantees. And, lo and behold, failure dominated. Further evidence that admin costs indicate nothing about effectiveness.

Bearing these lessons in mind, let's look through the options for each stage of the process.

Options at each stage for supporting charities

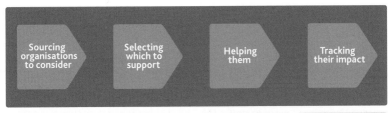

Sourcing organisations to consider	Selecting which to support	Helping them	Tracking their impact
• Partner/outsource	• Partner/outsource	• Partner/outsource	• Partner/outsource
• Leverage somebody else's list	• Select solely on merit: avoid irrelevant criteria	• Amount of ££ (not necessarily what is requested)	• Purpose: learning and/or accountability
• Let charities find you (responsive)	• Who decides? Staff, trustees and/or advisors	• Duration of support	• Performance relative to expectation
• Go find them (proactive)	• Select based on past performance	• Renewing support	• Form & frequency of data collected, e.g., paper, audio, video, collective learning
• Source from your own portfolio		• Restrictions	
• Type of data		• Practical & nonfinancial support	• Independent evaluation
• Form of data, e.g., paper, audio, video		• Introductions/ networks	

Sourcing organisations to consider

The Philanthropic Ventures Foundation (PVF) in Oakland, California created a Teacher Resource Grants programme, described in a seminal paper by Mark Kramer and Harvard Business School Professor Michael Porter:

> 'PVF provides [money to buy] inexpensive but badly needed classroom materials to teachers in its region – materials that are useless if they don't arrive quickly, when the teacher needs them. PVF notified more than 6,000 teachers that grants up to $1,500 would be available for teaching materials, field trips or teacher training. Teachers refer to the program as the "fax grant program" because the foundation takes requests by fax and then sends an answer within one hour of receipt and a cheque within 24 hours.'

Notice how beautifully this sourcing process is designed around the needs of the intended recipients: the foundation went out of its way to alert eligible recipients to the programme's existence and invite applications, and makes decisions in a relevant time-frame. Though your goals may differ markedly from PVF's, you may need the same level of creativity and willingness to depart from the standard silent, solo, slow, reactive and unengaged models you may see other donors using.

Donors often don't need applications at all, despite their ubiquity. For example, a family foundation wanted to encourage agricultural colleges to teach traditional techniques to their students. The foundation didn't wait for applications because agricultural colleges wouldn't know that it exists. Rather, the foundation proactively contacted the relevant agricultural colleges, gauged their interest, and worked collaboratively with them to create courses, for which the foundation provides the funding. Again, because the process is organised around particular goals, it's a little unusual.

You may not need to go outside at all: you can consider organisations which you are already supporting. For example, the Paul Hamlyn Foundation supports organisations in India which have the potential to be leaders in their field. Members of its well-networked team in India trot around visiting small community organisations. The foundation uses a 'nursery' arrangement: organisations first get a grant of around $5,000 for one year, which of course has considerable purchasing power in India. If they succeed, they graduate to larger grants for three years, and possibly a further three years after that. Donors often find these longer-term relationships are not only more effective but also more rewarding than short-term funding arrangements. The relationship evolves from 'ask/give' into a partnership for solving a problem wherein the two partners happen to have different roles.

Equally, you could source in partnership with another donor, or by using the recommendations of other donors and independent analysts (as we saw in Section 2).

Some circumstances require an open process. Just like democratic involvement in defining a focus, this will reveal what other people think needs doing - it's like doing your market research as you go along. However, being responsive relies on organisations being able to find you, so you it is incumbent on you to make yourself findable. Have good search engine optimisation (Google gives free AdWords to non-profits, which includes donors), get listed in catalogues of funders, go to conferences which attract the types of organisation you want to support. Because this can be expensive, new donors may do well to partner with somebody else in the first instance.

And get on Twitter! Along with other social media (i.e., media where people can talk to each other, such as Facebook, MySpace, blogs, forums), it's invaluable for you to find organisations and for organisations to find you. Use lots of hashtags[17]. You might want to search on relevant hashtags (e.g., #cancer, #Kenya, #philanthropy, #charity, #mentalhealth, #socent (social enterprise), #impinv (impact investing)) to see who else is active and interested in those topics, and include those hashtags in your own tweets to make yourself visible to those people.

---

17 Hashtags are Twitter's opt-in indexing system. For example, I'm writing this on the day that Apple founder Steve Jobs has died, so masses of people globally are including #stevejobs and #ThankYouSteve in their tweets (the short messages people broadcast on Twitter) to ensure that their thoughts are visible in the discussion about his life and work. Tweets about Stuff We Don't Want use #SWEDOW. Many conferences use hashtags (for example #giveandtech, a recent conference about the role of technology in philanthropy), so delegates can see the whole Twitter conversation about the conference. Start at www.twitter.com/search

If you're going to request applications – either from an open process or by invitation – please don't invent your own form. Completing masses of bespoke forms wastes loads of charities' time, reducing your 'net grants'. You may not need a form at all: you may do better with conversations or audio or video files, especially if you're looking for organisations where written English may be a problem. If you need an application form, use the one in the appendix, and only add questions if you really must.

Lastly, beware the silent witness – the applications you don't receive. Perhaps important groups can't find you, or are deterred by your application process or by the reporting you require. By definition you won't know about them. A little research – or possibly just a little imagination – is needed to discover them.

Selecting organisations to support

Make sure to select the most effective organisations. As you'll remember, impact relies on strong implementation of a robust idea (impact = idea x implementation), and you can get a good indication from a charity's answers to six crucial questions we met earlier:

Idea
- What's the problem you're trying to solve?
- What activities does the organisation do?
- What do those activities achieve? (i.e., how do they help solve the problem?)

Implementation
- How do you find out whether you are achieving anything? (i.e., what is the research process?)
- What are you achieving? (i.e., what results does that process produce?)
- How are you learning and improving? What examples do you have of learning and improving?

A good start is to check that the charity is not using an 'idea' which has already been proven ineffective: check for relevant evaluations, for example on the public databases of IPA and J-PAL. Beyond that, impact is the paramount criterion. Though, like motherhood-and-apple-pie, this seems an unarguably good idea, it gets lost or drowned out all too frequently by unrelated considerations. A handful of examples will illustrate the damage done by criteria unrelated to effectiveness. Utterly ridiculous, they're sadly all true.

An endowed foundation supports 'national initiatives (in the UK) which promote sustainable living' but will only support charities with incomes below £300,000.

Now, heaven knows, transitioning our society to sustainable living is a difficult task. Think for a second about the forces promoting 'unsustainable living' against which those charities battle: the fact that economic growth generally needs people to consume more whereas sustainability requires us to consume less; population expansion; the facts that practically anything we do involves consuming energy and virtually all energy production emits carbon, and so on. You'd think, therefore, that the task of getting adults to live sustainably would require organisations with significant resource. For comparison, Nissan thinks it takes £1,200 to decisively influence somebody's behaviour in relation to the single issue of buying a car. Yet this foundation seems to think that £300,000 is adequate. Now, there are just over 50m adults in the UK, so that's a penny per person (£300,000 ÷ 50m). Pardon? Surely if that were sufficient we wouldn't still have a problem. Even if the charity concentrates in a small town, of say a few hundred thousand people, it's still only got about £1 per person with which it can achieve practically nothing.

The foundation can't even argue that there is a particular shortage of funding for *small* organisations working in sustainability since there's hardly any funding for sustainability at all. Criteria which are don't relate to effectiveness don't encourage effectiveness.

Narrow Fields of vision

Though there are Nobel Prizes for physics, chemistry, medicine and economics (among others), there is none for maths. The gap would be filled by the Fields Medal – the 'International Medal for Outstanding Discoveries in Mathematics' – were it not for the fact that the Fields Medal can only be awarded to people aged below 40. Normally this is fine (mathematicians typically have done their best work by their mid-thirties). However, a solution to the riddle of Fermat's last theorem[18] – which had baffled people for centuries – was eventually provided by Andrew Wiles in 1995, when he was ... wouldn't you just know it ... 42. So by dint of its own rule which has nothing to do with outstanding discoveries in mathematics, the Fields Medal was unable to recognise this historic and outstanding discovery in mathematics.

---

18 You remember the one. It says that though you can find pairs of square numbers which add up to another square number (e.g., $3^2+4^2=5^2$), there are no pairs which, when cubed, add up to another number cubed, nor which when raised to fourth (or any other) power add up to the fourth (or other) power: $a^n + b^n = c^n$. It's taunted mathematicians because it's so easy to understand yet unbelievably complicated to prove. The 17th century mathematician Fermat – who proved many things – claimed in a margin: 'I have discovered a truly marvellous proof of this proposition which this margin is too narrow to contain'. Though Wiles produced a proof, it is still not known whether this claim could have been true, i.e., whether it can be proven using maths available during Fermat's life.

Also irrelevant is whether a donor has supported a charity before. Whereas in business, investors tend to stick to companies which are performing well, charitable donors are sometimes reluctant to sit still. This is borne of a sense of 'fairness' – sharing the funding around. But having seen the damage, I feel it's misplaced. Because charities by definition need subsidy, a donor who pulls out simply creates a gap which the charity must fill with a replacement donor, normally at some cost. This 'fairness' just creates a wasteful merry-go-round.

Stick with a winner

Warren Buffett's company Berkshire Hathaway has owned shares in The Coca-Cola Company for 23 years. A good call: even after inflation, Coca-Cola's value has grown by a fizzy 14 per cent per year over that period.

And lastly, oddly enough the charity's plan can be irrelevant – or at least, doesn't warrant the emphasis it often receives. 'The best indicator of future behaviour is past behaviour' as recruitment agencies are fond of saying, so look at the organisation's historic performance. Donors sometimes look almost solely at an organisation's idea and plan. These only really indicate whether the charity can put together a good plan, quite unrelated to its ability to implement anything. Remember too the point about how basic research and innovation are much-needed in relation to problems which have already 'resisted great intellects and often great money': though the plan may be rather sketchy, it may yield spectacular rewards, and charitable money is uniquely liberated to take the risks.

On the decision-making process itself, scrimping will preclude success. I once worked with a well-known couple who were concerned to reduce 'admin' in their foundation. Their foundation received lots of unsolicited applications which were handled by the foundation manager, whom we'll call Cathy, as was all other administration. She was processing about 100 applications a week. Even if that had been her sole task, she would have had about 20 minutes per application, leaving her no choice but to 'spray and pray'. In fact, Cathy had other roles too, such as doing the accounts, keeping up with developments in the foundation's areas of interest, dealing with existing grantees, fielding enquiries, and trying to learn what was working and what wasn't. She therefore spent less than 10 minutes assessing each application and was painfully aware that she probably got it wrong quite frequently. For donors just as for charities, impact relies on having both a good idea and good implementation, and starved 'giving machines' can't implement well.

Though donors' teams need to be properly resourced, this doesn't excuse wasting charitable money on excessive luxury for them. So where's the balance? Well, we can refer to the overall goal of improving the world as much as possible. One of the principles which flow from that goal is 'making good decisions'. That requires time, information and expertise, for which the donor may need to pay enough to attract and retain good staff. But on the other hand, there's also the principle of 'minimising waste' – clearly salaries and office rents eat into the resource which can be given. In situations like this where the principles seem to collide, we need the balance which maximises the improvement to the world.

Which brings us to mechanisms for involving your team, whether they be family, colleagues or community members. One partnership company based in Frankfurt has a charitable foundation, and since part of the objective is to build the culture in the firm, all selection decisions are made by the whole set of partners. However, rather cleverly, although any partner can nominate a charity, he must get first that nomination seconded by another partner. This avoids the risk of a partner taking personally the rejection of a charity he has nominated.

By contrast, an international family which has been giving for many generations has a charitable foundation in each of the several countries where it has businesses. The giving needs to be effective, which implies a degree of centralisation and tenacity, but also needs to allow participation by many individuals. To manage that tension, each foundation is overseen by a few family members, elected by the whole family for a determined period.

Thinking back to the Kramer Diagram, you need to involve people on both sides. 'Your' side will include family, colleagues, staff members and so on. But they may not suffice. You also need people who understand the other side: the needs you're trying to serve and the other players involved with them (government, business, universities, etc.). I'm highlighting this because quite often donors involve in their giving solely their friends and family and thereby lack enough expertise about the needs and charities to make consistently great decisions and optimise their effectiveness.

And lastly, as the fax-back grant programme example illustrates, decisions about selection needn't wait for an arbitrary date such as a quarterly trustee meeting. Some goals are much better served by a totally different set-up.

Immediately after you decide to support an organisation, make a note of what you expect it to achieve. Though it quite possibly won't achieve that – it'll achieve less or more or something totally unexpected – that note will help you in future to track the accuracy of the expectations which influence your decisions.

The old one is the best

The City Bridge Trust is rare – possibly unique – in that its decision-making happens in public. Do go to a meeting: you get to see not only the extraordinary Guildhall in London, but also all the papers which the Committee discusses and hear its deliberations.

The City Bridge Trust has a remarkable and quirky history. It holds money collected from tolls and rents on Old London Bridge after its completion in 1209. Eight hundred years later, its first responsibility is still to maintain five of London's bridges, after which it disburses remaining funds to charities in London. Its Grants Committee is appointed to oversee the grant-giving by the Trust's sole trustee, the Corporation of London.

Supporting them

> *'Money alone is seldom the answer.'*
> – Dame Stephanie Shirley, UK Philanthropy Ambassador

Crucial to your effectiveness is the way that you structure financial and non-financial support. Some ways help considerably, whereas others hinder horribly. Here are three examples of good practice.

First, the charity Fairbridge, which supports young people living in inner cities and was considering merging with The Prince's Trust in 2010. Each needed to analyse and assess the other (a process known in business as 'due diligence'). Fairbridge is supported by the Private Equity Foundation, formed by a group of private equity companies, whose members constantly analyse and assess companies with a view to acquiring them. One of the Private Equity Foundation's members therefore carried out the due diligence analysis for Fairbridge. Not only was the assessment done by very experienced people, but the additional burden on Fairbridge's management was minimised.

Second, a well-known UK foundation discovered that several grantees were struggling with a particular government policy. The foundation could have simply given the charities money to collaborate on the problem. However, the foundation has better access and influence than individual charities, so the foundation itself got involved. When it invited the relevant government minister to come and hear the charities, the minister turned up (this is the kind of foundation for which anybody would show up) which rapidly got the problem solved.

And third, the Northern Rock Foundation which found that many charities in its area (it operates in the North of England) had weak financial management. Again, rather than giving charities money to solve the problem individually, it commissioned and hosted a training programme for them, drawing on its own expertise and extensive network amongst experts in the charity sector.

The danger of foisting arises with large donors just as with small donors – more so, of course, because of the size of the incentive for the charity to put up with it. There is danger too in donors 'suggesting' improvements. This can be very helpful, not least because donors typically see more situations and solutions than charities do, but it must be done without any hint of the funding being dependent upon taking the suggestion. Speak softly because you carry a big stick.

Even with money alone, the way that you give is enormously important. The benefits of the guidance in Section 2 – giving a lot, giving without strings, giving without fuss and giving again – are amplified when donors are giving larger amounts, as are the problems of not doing so.

Let's look first at 'giving a lot' and 'giving again'. These are effectively equivalent because you won't need to give again to a charity for a while if you give it a lot in the first place. Research from the US shows that, as we saw in our illustration about wasting an entire donation, small grants are much more expensive than larger ones. Raising and managing a series of small grants costs nearly six times as much time (i.e., money) as would one large grant of the same total value:

Grant size	Average time spent on grant application & monitoring	Average amount raised per hour spent	Time necessary to raise $100,000
$10,000	7 hours	$1,500/hour	70 hours (nearly two person-weeks)
$100,000	12 hours	$8,500/hour	12 hours (only a day and a half)

As we've seen, the problems that charities address are some of the hardest known to mankind – if they weren't, they'd have been solved by now. Thomas Tierney, Co-founder and Chairman of The Bridgespan Group again: 'The median grant made by America's larger foundations is less than $50,000, while the average duration is less than 18 months (although many are renewed). How many social problems can be solved with $50,000 over 18 months? Not many, I would venture to say.'

Be aware that charities tend to ask for less than they truly need in order to increase their chances of getting something. After all, something – even an expensive something – seems better than nothing. You may do well to give more than they request if that's what would really make them effective. There's a love-ly story of John D. Rockefeller receiving a request for $500 from a young scientist named Albert Einstein. Rockefeller gave him $1,000 on the basis that 'he may be onto something'.

Moving then to giving without strings, donors sometimes think that restrictions will improve a charity's honesty or transparency. It's nonsense: overwhelmingly, charities are not on the fiddle and unrestricted donations do not magically mutate into shoes and handbags. Spotting any misuse is the job of the auditor and/or regu-lator. Even if they fail, it wouldn't be possible to say that it was 'your' money which had mutated because money is all the same colour anyway. Rather, you're inter-ested in the charity being effective, for which giving it flexibility and time to think and learn are invaluable. In a survey of nearly 2,000 non-profit executives in the US, unrestricted and multi-year support came out as the two actions by funders that would most help their work.

Sometimes donors restrict money because they are, in effect, 'buying' a service – 'deliver this programme in the Sudan', 'run these training courses in Northern Ire-land'. In those cases, better than restricting the funding is just having a service con-tract which stipulates what is to be delivered. The value of those contracts should cover the relevant pieces of the organisation's overhead costs. Donors sometimes allow a charity to add some arbitrary percentage for overheads – 10 or 15 per cent is not uncommon – although these percentages frequently bear no relation to real-ity, often being inadequate and thus starving organisations. There is a decent and widely-endorsed toolkit for organisations to calculate the accurate figure (of which I happen to be a co-author).

Outside those circumstances, donors should be 'building' great institutions with the flexibility and capability to use all of mankind's best tools on these difficult so-cial and environmental problems. This echoes the experience of the Shell Founda-tion, for whom success has come with giving $10-15m to each of its partners.

Finally, plan for fluctuations in the economy. When the economy is doing well, investment returns are high and people have jobs. If you invest your charitable as-sets and spend the returns soon after receiving them, you'll be flush and bountiful in the boom years, when people have jobs. But when the economy tanks, you'll have less to give, just when people are losing jobs and homes and when the need for your support rises. Donors do well to organise their investments to make money avail-able when it is most needed – for example, retaining some for rainy days or invest-ing in assets which run counter to the cycles in the needs that you're addressing. To maximise your effectiveness, it might be not just where and how you give, but also *when* you give.

Tracking them

> *'Why conduct rigorous evaluation?*
> *Because when you don't, children die.'*
> – Howard White, Executive Director for the
> International Initiative for Impact Evaluation

Remember when I said that donors can create substantial problems for charities without realising it because the pain isn't felt by the donor and the charities won't tell you? Tracking is a great example. Avoidable wastage from reporting could be as high as £250m, every penny of which could have been supporting people or pandas or buildings or deployed against other tricky problems. And yet tracking can be literally vital.

It's worth being precise about its role. Tom Kern at the Annie E. Casey Foundation views it as 'learning with a purpose – what works and what doesn't – grounded in evidence. And we need to act on what it tells us'. Gayle Williams, CEO of the Mary Reynolds Babcock Foundation, frames the central question as, 'What do we need to know to make good decisions about investing the resources of the foundation?' Which ideas seem to be best, which organisations are good at implementing them, and so where should you deploy resources in future?

Notice that the objective is essentially to gather management information which will be useful in guiding decisions. It isn't an exercise in omniscience – testing the limits of what is possible to know and gathering up evidence of every last jot of the charity's impact.

The charity sector distinguishes between 'monitoring' and 'evaluation'. Monitoring is an on-going process, managed by the charity, involving records of expenditure, activities (e.g., number of workshops held), numbers and types of beneficiaries, and other operational data. It will typically look only at one charity's activities, and normally takes only a historical view. In terms of our formula for impact (=idea x implementation), roughly speaking monitoring looks at implementation: is the charity doing what it's supposed to be doing? Evaluation is a periodic process which gauges the effectiveness of the idea. It is often managed by a third party and may well compare organisations and ideas.

From the formula, we can see that we need both monitoring and evaluation. Yet experience suggests that donors often rely solely on monitoring. This is necessary but insufficient to establish what the impact was, let alone what the impact of another programme would have been. Hence The Bridgespan Group reports a staff member at one leading evaluation firm recently saying that 'across his firm's evaluations historically, he did not see a correlation between the outcomes from performance monitoring and the outcomes [which] the evaluation firm finds when it does a rigorous study'.

Donors need evaluation to establish whether the idea is any good, and ideally also comparative evaluation to establish whether the idea is better than the alternatives. Great implementation doesn't help much if there are much better ideas around. To illustrate Howard White's startling view that without evaluation 'children die', a randomised control trial looking at primary health care in Uganda found an 'idea' which reduced child mortality by a third. A third! Just take a second to reflect on that from the perspective of those families and communities.

The types of useful evidence and nature of results are discussed in Section 4; in this section, we'll confine ourselves to the processes. With that £250m in mind, I'd suggest that you don't get an organisation to do any bespoke work for you (for example, no reports written just for you) at all, and certainly not if you're giving it less than about £20,000, in cash or in-kind. Vanessa Kirsch, the founder of New Profit Inc., a US venture philanthropy fund, laments that:

> 'Non-profit CEOs spend huge amounts of time – sometimes as much as half their time – dealing with funders. What's unfortunate here is that these leaders have incredible ideas about solving fundamentally important issues such as child literacy…but they can't focus on their work because of the constant demands of fundraising.'

From a commercial perspective, this is bizarre: corporate CEOs don't have to write bespoke reports for each of their shareholders, whereas charities have to write bespoke reports all the time. This is why raising money costs charities between three and five times as much as it costs companies. It's egregious and unnecessary: if you give on an unrestricted basis, the charity's standard annual report for its entire operation will suffice and create zero marginal work.

An easily avoidable problem arises when donors' rhythms don't fit the charities' rhythms. For instance, a donor requesting reports each calendar quarter demands the impossible from charities working in schools because schools don't work in quarters. Those charities can't report on results for July/Aug/September because most of that is holiday, and equally the charities can't report on achievements in Oct/Nov/Dec because their unit of time is the Autumn term (which includes September). I know what you're thinking: yes, it is bonkers. It can all be avoided by fitting the tracking process to the goal and the intended recipients.

Rather like application processes, the reporting process tends to be silent and written. And like application processes, there are many better alternatives, which are those designed around the goals and organisations which the donor is supporting. Visits, phone conversations or video-conference, audio files or videos files, surveys, interviews, or focus groups may be better.

> **Futurebuilders**, an innovative fund set up in 2003 with £125m of government money to make loans and other investments in charities to enable them to deliver more public services, very much saw itself as an experiment. To learn about it own effectiveness, it convened and consulted the charities it supported. The meetings were lively and honest, largely because Futurebuilders was quite open about its own hunger and need to learn. It published research into its own performance, and held conferences to share the findings.

Given that the goal is to learn, donors need to make it possible for charities to admit their mistakes. When a charity reports to a donor, it – surprise! – wants to impress. We've amply established that charities are reliant on donors for their existence. I'm not saying that charities lie. But I am noticing that people respond to incentives and that charities have every incentive to portray their performance as a resounding success.

Donors can themselves track changes at a macro level by using the wide range of available data: other charities you support, charities you don't support, academics, beneficiaries, the public sector, and commercial sources may have revealing data about progress towards an organisation's goals (e.g., whether healthy eating is increasing, or species loss slowing). If relevant data pertaining to several organisations you support are only available commercially, buy them once rather than having each organisation buy them separately.

Encourage the charity to report publicly about what it is doing and its results. (We'll talk in detail in Section 4 about what it should report about.) This is normally cheap for a charity to provide, and can be invaluable for co-ordination and for other charities to benefit from the learning.

If you are selecting and/or supporting work in less developed countries, please encourage charities to report publicly using the International Aid Transparency Initiative format. Here's why. After the tsunami on Boxing Day 2004, many aid agencies worked in Indonesia to prevent diseases including measles, so there was much concern in 2005 when measles appeared to be making a come-back there. It transpired that this was because some children had been vaccinated multiple times by different aid agencies because of poor co-ordination. At the time, there was no common standard through which the charities could report publicly and find out what other agencies had been doing and where. The International Aid Transparency Initiative

(IATI) was designed precisely to make information easily to find and usable, and thereby avoid these situations.

Some donors feel that they need to track charities' expenditure for purposes of accountability. This particularly applies to donors who raise money from somebody else, such as fundraising foundations or government. This is fine, but it's no substitute for forward-looking learning. Perhaps there's a concern about fraud. Well, a charity with an income above £500,000 will be audited, which should suffice for reassurance. The real risk is of hindering, by asking for excessive detail. There are examples of charities receiving grants of several thousand of pounds, and having to report on every item over £5 – literally shipping shoe-boxes of receipts to their funders. It's hardly commensurate with the importance of the roles entrusted to the charities, and brings to mind this letter attributed to the Duke of Wellington:

Gentlemen,

Whilst marching from Portugal to a position which commands the approach to Madrid and the French forces, my officers have been diligently complying with your requests which have been sent by H.M. ship from London to Lisbon and thence by dispatch to our headquarters. We have enumerated our saddles, bridles, tents and tent poles, and all manner of sundry items for which His Majesty's Government holds me accountable. I have dispatched reports on the character, wit, and spleen of every officer. Each item and every farthing has been accounted for, with two regrettable exceptions for which I beg your indulgence.

Unfortunately the sum of one shilling and ninepence remains unaccounted for in one infantry battalion's petty cash and there has been a hideous confusion as the number of jars of raspberry jam issued to one cavalry regiment during a sandstorm in western Spain. This reprehensible carelessness may be related to the pressure of circumstance, since we are war with France, a fact which may come as a bit of a surprise to you gentlemen in Whitehall.

This brings me to my present purpose, which is to request elucidation of my instructions from His Majesty's Government so that I may better understand why I am dragging an army over these barren plains. I construe that perforce it must be one of two alternative duties, as given below. I shall pursue either one with the best of my ability, but I cannot do both:

1. To train an army of uniformed British clerks in Spain for the benefit of the accountants and copy-boys in London or, perchance,

2. To see to it that the forces of Napoleon are driven out of Spain.

Your most obedient servant,

Wellington

How not to learn anything

There is a medium-sized, well-connected grant-making foundation in the UK, which for the sake of its modesty we'll call the Pepper Trust. It gives small, restricted grants, typified in its support to a charity which we'll call the Garlic Charity. The project went pretty badly wrong: Garlic's partners pulled out, as did the volunteer project manager, and the charity had to scramble to deliver anything at all. With hindsight, some of the problems looked predictable, and certainly the team at Garlic learnt what to look for in future. At the end of the year, the Pepper Trust asked Garlic to complete a simple one-page form about its results. It was clear that the trust considered itself progressive for having such a light-touch system. Garlic suspected that its form might get passed to other donors, creating potentially limitless reputational damage if it recounted the full tale, and the Pepper Trust did nothing to invite a dialogue. Therefore Garlic could not risk telling its story honestly. It wrote an account which, though the truth, was certainly not the whole truth. The Pepper Trust missed out on learning which could well have helped with future grants. What was the purpose of this form? Nothing, beyond producing a form. This (true) story illustrates the common phenomenon of donors asking for reports because they think they ought to have reports, rather than in the interests of learning.

To conclude, don't just copy

Having seen some options for each process stage, you can probably see some which fit your goals and interests, and others which don't. As we said at the beginning of this section, the important principle is to **design your process to fit your goals** – to maximise the improvement which your giving brings to the world.

Don't just copy other donors. For one thing, another donor may have designed their process for a goal very different from yours. (It's a bit like saying, 'I'm teaching some people. Sue over there is teaching some people. Can't I just copy what she does?' If she's teaching history to undergraduates, then it's fine for her to have 200 students in a lecture theatre for an hour at a time, to talk at them, and to ask for written work once a week. But if you're teaching struggling primary school children, this approach is likely to be a disaster.) And for another, their process may just not be very good. But donors, unlike teachers, may well not know that. If the process is silent, reactive, slow and/or unengaged, I'd be sceptical.

The greatest 'hurt' comes when the process itself takes over. Too often, donors' role becomes soliciting and processing applications, making decisions about who to support and who to decline, possibly meeting a few grateful recipients, soliciting and processing reports about progress. What do you notice here? These donors have become machines for sourcing and selecting charities. Minimal effort is going to understanding the problem they're trying to solve, looking for partners, helping charities, learning about their effectiveness, tracking their own impact, sharing lessons. This is quite different from being a machine for improving the world.

Be nice

Considering that their sole purpose is dishing out money, grant-making foundations are, in general, remarkably unpopular. The following (real, published) feedback from charities is not atypical:

'...is consistently arrogant and disrespectful...'
'...was impossible to reach. She rarely returned phone calls and was unable to clearly articulate [the process for] grant proposal[s] and funding...'
'...they are not easy to communicate with – and staff is often curt...'
'...the foundation... conducts itself in an ivory-tower-like fashion...'

You see why I keep suggesting that you don't just copy.

Why do charities have such low opinions of people who give them money? Largely because foundations waste so much of charities' time and therefore money (to which they often appear oblivious), and because in their everyday dealings with charities they sometimes behave rather like medieval royalty. And, just like medieval royalty, a charity proffering its opinion risks its head. Hence Paul Brest's experience that when he became president of the Hewlett Foundation, he 'by all external signals, achieved perfection'.

Consequently, a great deal of what charities report about donors' helpfulness is based not on the support or money itself but simply on the courteousness and responsiveness of the donors (and/or their staff).

As a result, good people to involve in your team are those who are humble enough to avoid conflating distributing money with being important, and who are knowledgeable about the areas in which you're specialising. Jack Welch's view that 'the team with the best players wins' applies to donors just as it does to charities and other organisations.

If you keep your eyes on your goal and design everything around that, you'll avoid all this and become truly effective. Now comes the moment of truth: is it working?

Chapter 14

Tracking your own impact

'It is amazing what you can accomplish if you do not care who gets the credit.'
— Attributed to various people, including
Harry S. Truman, 33rd President of the United States

Since the aim of everything we've discussed is improving the world as much as possible, we're not looking here at just whether there is *some* improvement but whether there could be more. So establishing whether you are doing that is in many ways the most important stage of all, despite the fact that we come to it last.

We'll divide our discussion into four elements. First, do no harm: could you be wasting your entire donation and/or could you waste less? Second, is there evidence of progress towards your goals? Third, do the charities you support – if you choose that tool – like you, and feel that you help and don't hinder? And finally, can other people learn from your experiences?

We're not going to worry much about whether improvements in the world are due to you. Perhaps this is a surprise because it seems so crucial. The issue of attributing change is tricky (as we'll see in Section 4 when we explore results in detail): it's hard enough to attribute changes to charities, and it's worse for donors because they're a stage removed from 'the action'. This means that in practice it's often simply impossible to attribute a change to a particular donor, and we could squander much time obsessing about it. In the words of Paul Brest and Hal Harvey, who worked together as senior directors at the Hewlett Foundation, 'you and your grantee will seldom, if ever, be able to take credit for success; all you can hope is to be part of the winning team'.

So does your team seem to be winning, and does it feel that you are helping?

Do no harm: the costs you create for other organisations

Donors create costs for charities and/or other organisations primarily through application and reporting processes, as discussed. The costs are real and hurt somebody. Guess who? The poor or buildings or pandas. And whose money is being wasted? Yours, since most charity money comes from a donor somewhere. Since we're aiming to improve the world – not just a bit but a lot – we'd better monitor this.

The diagram below shows the work created by a donor who supports one quarter of all applicants, and then asks for bespoke reports. If we drew the equivalent diagram for the NatWest Community Force programme, there would be nearly 14 fruitless application processes for every success.

Costs created by donor borne by charities

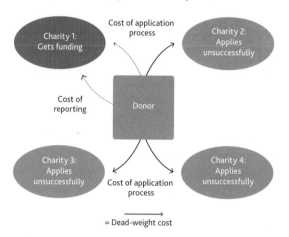

These costs are dumped by donors on the charities. But as a donor, you won't see them: they don't show up on your accounts, and since charities are unlikely to moan to the hand that feeds them, you may not realise they're there. These costs can be so large that they make the donor a net drain on the charity sector. So periodically estimate the costs you create for other organisations, say every couple of years. The maths is given in the appendices and isn't hard. The cost should fall over time.

BBC Children in Need currently funds one in four of its applicants: though that is quite high for the industry, it means that three quarters of applications are wasted. BBC Children in Need Strategy Director Sheila-Jane Malley says: 'We're painfully aware that every application which doesn't get through was work for somebody. As a responsible organisation interested in children, we've begun to look systematically at how we can prevent as much of that work as possible.' To reduce the cost of its application process, it's working to cut the number of unsuccessful applications by being still clearer about what it will and won't fund.

BBC Children in Need

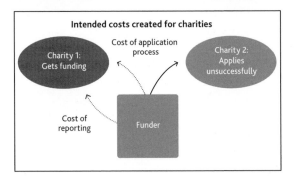

Are you making progress?

The easiest metric to track is the proportion of your grants which achieved what was expected. You might call this your 'hit rate'. It was only because the Shell Foundation consistently tracked this that it noticed the problem which it then remedied so spectacularly. Hence, the suggestion to note your expectations when you make a decision. Classify as a success any grant which produces something valuable even if not what you envisaged, and feed the insight back into the selection process in future.

If your giving involves a team, you'll need to deliberately make it easy to discuss failures and problems. This is normally hard, just as it is with grantees. Harvard University's Chris Argyris has been researching effective communication for thirty years and laments 'the inability of organisations to discuss risky and threatening issues, especially if these issues question underlying organisational assumptions and policies. The curious feature is that in most cases the information required is available (albeit scattered) in the organisation. The problem is that discussing or writing up risky issues is unacceptable'. The Hewlett Foundation has a great solution: an annual prize for the worst grant, awarded to the team member responsible. (Remember the Pepper Trust whose form only elicits positive news: it would have no clue which was its worst grant because its grants appear to be invariably faultless.)

If your hit-rate is low, there are three main suspects:

- Poor idea. For example, the Gates Foundation found that its programme of reducing the size of US high schools in order to improve attendance – on which it had spent the tidy sum of $2 billion – was not working. 'Many of the small schools that we invested in did not improve students' achievement in any significant way… Based on what the Foundation has learned so far, we have refined our strategy.' If you are supporting innovative work (as Gates was here), it may fail – which is fine, so long as we learn the lessons and let others learn them too.
- Good idea but wrong charities. That is to say, there are better charities or projects 'out there' but your sourcing and selection process somehow misses them.
- Good idea but bad support. You're finding charities with good potential but are somehow 'making them bad' or at least failing to make them good.

In general, your hit-rate within any area of focus should increase over time. The only exceptions are if you are supporting increasingly difficult or innovative work. Beyond hit rate, donors can evaluate their own progress in the same way as they would evaluate a charity. Once you've read Section 4, you'll have a good idea of how this works. In brief: is there change in the right direction, and does it appear to be connected to your work? If you are expecting results which are quantifiable and evident relatively rapidly (for instance, falling numbers of polio cases, or more children showing up to school), you can use various public data – from charities, from other funders, and from public or commercial sources. It will be easier to judge progress if you have noted the 'baseline' (e.g., the number of polio cases) when your activities started (though beware that changes in the number of cases may have other causes too).

For results which aren't quantifiable and evident relatively rapidly, you will probably need to look at:

- Whether the goal is being achieved (leaving aside the question about causes for now). You might find this out by polling your recipients – if, for example, your goal is strengthening charities in a particular area such as the arts or Northumberland. Or you might poll other organisations, if for example you're aiming to improve governance in African countries, or societal attitudes to people with facial disfigurements, or preservation of cultural heritage.

- The scale of the charity's activities. For example, the number of training courses held or people who attend conferences you enable.
- Whether the evidence supporting your theory of change is strengthening or weakening over time, i.e., whether it looks more or less likely that the results you observe are caused by the activities which you are enabling.

Frequency and helpfulness of management assistance activities

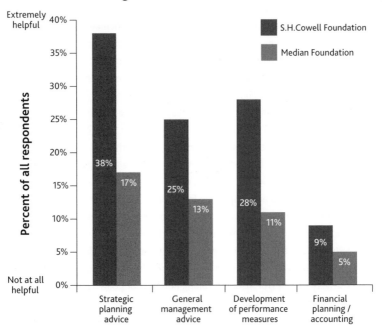

What charities think of you

The 'gold standard' for gathering views from charities is the Grantee Perception Report created by the US-based Center for Effective Philanthropy. It is a confidential, third-party survey of charities which collects views about donors' processes, their use of non-financial support, clarity and timeliness of communications, the quality of the relationship, the administrative burden they create, and their impact. Over 190 funders have commissioned Grantee Perception Reports, and the Center has over 52,000 responses from charities. The great beauty of Grantee Perception Reports is that the Center can compare a donor's performance to that of many peers. If you're keen to avoid settling for average, it's helpful to know what the average actually is.

The chart above is from the Grantee Perception Report for the S. H. Cowell

Foundation, which 'works to improve the lives of children living in poverty in Northern and Central California by providing support to strengthen families and communities', and is one of many donors which publishes its report. The chart covers one aspect of performance, the management assistance provided to grantees, and compares the S.H. Cowell Foundation with the median score for all the foundations in the Center's data-set.

Grantee Perception Reports also contain detailed qualitative feedback. These quotes are taken from reports about various funders:

'I'm not aware of any impact the Foundation is having in the field or community.'

'They have been approachable, practical and direct in their suggestions.'

'Foundation was at times unreasonable in the demands it made for data that we could not collect or just was not available asking us to collect data up to a year after the project funding has finished. We have no money to pay anyone to do this work.'

'They are one of very few funders that understands the importance of supporting basic research in the field. They are essential in the field.'

'The Foundation's work has resulted in major policy improvements.'

'We were very sorry to read that [our program officer] had left the Foundation. We had no contact in the course of the ensuing months... So to be honest, we do not know who our project officer is... since we have received no communications from them at all.'

'The Foundation provides opportunities for us to increase our knowledge and gives us the support needed to be successful.'

'The Foundation has assisted the large organizations but has left the medium and small organizations to fend for themselves in difficult times.'

The insight and learning from these reports can be invaluable for donors ambitious about improving the world. For one thing, they reveal a perspective which, for reasons we've seen, donors don't naturally see.

For large foundations, the Center for Effective Philanthropy can evaluate staff members separately. This is important because there can be surprising variation in performance of staff members within a single funding organisation. Tellingly, the Center's report on this issue is entitled *The Luck of the Draw*.

Can other organisations learn from your experience?

'We were being too passive in not sharing our grantmaking portfolio, experience, and strategies with other foundations,' says Stewart Hudson, President of the Emily Hall Tremaine Foundation, a $100m family foundation in Connecticut. 'We thought that if our grantees are doing good stuff, people would hear about it, and that's enough… But we found that we needed to be more proactive.'

Your information – about the state of the field, what is working, what isn't and about great organisations – may be invaluable to other charitable donors, legislators and policy-makers, other charities or beneficiaries themselves. Though nobody likes to admit failure in public, this is a powerful contribution to the field: it prevents mistakes being repeated, at real cost to beneficiaries, and accelerates the development of better solutions. It's analogous to the problems which arise for doctors when pharmaceutical companies withhold results of trials. In a survey at the beginning of 2011, over three-quarters of US foundations thought they would benefit from hearing more stories about foundations' failures.

Your learnings about failures may be your most valuable assets so make them public – put them on your website (and make them findable by employing likely search terms), put them into journals, and share them through donor networks and conferences. Fish where the fish are: if your information is useful to policy-makers or big businesses, you'll probably need to take it to them. Yes, the effect of this sharing is hard to measure, but the work is pretty cheap so don't obsess about impact: just make it available and celebrate anecdotal evidence of its value.

Finally comes your opportunity to make use of everything you've learned. (Remember the little dotted line marked 'learning' in the process diagram?) Like the Shell Foundation, feed what you've learned back into each stage from choosing a focus, partner and tools, and sourcing, selecting, supporting and tracking. Make time and space to think about your hard-won evidence. All these processes are dynamic, and if something isn't working, it's time to change the way that you're giving it.

Drilling for data

The Shell Foundation on the report on its impact during its first ten years:
'This report was triggered by a simple question: "Has our performance to date in achieving scale been good, average or poor when compared with our peers?" Given the lack of other published information around performance – including both success and failure – from peer organisations, this proved to be a very difficult question to answer. That is surprising given the billions of dollars managed by foundations.'

Chapter 15

Corporate giving

'Few phrases are as overused and poorly defined as "strategic philanthropy". The terms is used to cover virtually any kind of charitable activity that has some definable theme, goal, approach or focus. In the corporate context, it generally means that there is some connection, however vague or tenuous, between the charitable contribution and the company's business. Often this connection is only semantic, enabling the company to rationalize its contribution in public reports and press releases. What passes for "strategic philanthropy" is almost never truly strategic, and often it isn't even particularly effective as philanthropy.'
– Mark Kramer and Michael Porter[19]

Climbing Borneo's Mount Kinabalu is hard work. Climbers are legally required to hire a guide. Not that it always helps: guides sometimes just abandon the tourists and climb with each other. Why wouldn't they? – there'll be a fresh batch of tourists tomorrow who will be obliged to give them money.

When I went up the mountain, I was lucky: the guides supporting my group stuck with us, even on our incompetently slow descent. They even missed their village football match for us. Why did they care?

Probably because I was travelling with Intrepid Travel, a global 'adventure tour' organiser which takes loads of groups to Borneo. Intrepid Travel has given generously to the guides' village, supporting teaching programmes and providing learning resources. Clever: the villagers value their good relationship with Intrepid, and consequently the guides look after Intrepid's clients assiduously.

Is Intrepid's work in that village 'charity' or is it 'investing in the business'?

---

19 This chapter is much informed by the work of Mark Kramer, Professor Michael Porter and FSG Social Impact Advisors, which they founded.

Great corporate giving

When corporations engage with social or environmental goals, the results can be very powerful. So when they engage badly, they miss sizable opportunities and at worst, simply waste somebody else's money.

When Goldman Sachs engaged with the issue of financing immunisations, it turned a relatively small amount of staff time into a remarkable increase in speed and scale of delivery of vaccinations through structuring the IFFIm. Why is this such a great way of giving? Because it uses resources which the bank is particularly well-placed to give, in such a way that they amplify the impact of some 'supply' already committed (governments' financial commitments) in order to meet a searing need. It's what the Kramer Diagram suggests.

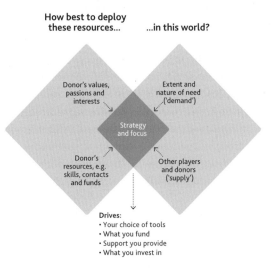

Let's revisit the left-hand side of the diagram in the specific context of corporate giving because it creates some peculiarities.

First, the resources. A company's **resources include a lot more than money**: staff, offices, brands, teams, distribution systems, warehouses, training programmes, relationships with accountants, systems, information, knowledge of government, and so on. It would therefore be surprising if a company's best option for improving the world were simply to give cash to another organisation. As Kurt Hoffman, then Director of the Shell Foundation observed, 'Money is the least valuable social change asset'. Better surely to use those non-cash resources, just as Goldman Sachs did in helping to create the IFFIm. A glorious example is Google, which worked with the Samaritans to ensure that if you search for 'suicide', you see this at the top of the page, ahead of the search results themselves:

Need help? In the United Kingdom, call 08457 90 90 90
Samaritans

This probably cost Google very little to arrange, yet probably has a huge impact, and in a way which Google alone could generate. Mark Kramer and Michael Porter noticed this more generally: from their extensive work on corporate giving, they conclude that 'when a well-run business applies its vast resources, expertise and management talent to problems that it understands and in which it has a stake, it can have a greater impact on social good than any other institution or philanthropic organisation'.

Second, **a company's interests include those of its shareholders.** Put another way, the resources in the company don't belong to the people giving them (except in private companies[20] which we'll address specifically later). Shareholders are within their right to be interested solely in capital growth and dividends, and to be unimpressed at a company giving away *their* money.

So should a public company give at all, and if so, when? (Again, for simplicity, we'll refer to 'deploying resources for social or environmental goals' as 'giving' even though the resources may not in fact be given to another organisation.) Two criteria seem sensible:

If the giving creates value for the company. It might increase sales, decrease costs, drive brand value resulting in greater sales, improve customer service by getting tired clients down the mountain safely, improve skills in the pool from which the company hires staff, improve morale. Given that companies are spending somebody else's money, it's hard to see why they'd be shy or apologetic about gaining commercial value from it.

At a more sophisticated level, a company's giving may create value by bringing about a social change which is beneficial for the company. Coca-Cola in Africa used the trucks and network which form its legendary logistical operation to combat the spread of HIV and AIDS. It distributed condoms and attractive informational materials to all those dusty villages in the back of beyond where, astonishingly, you can always get a Coke. Not just serving a major need, but creating value for the company because, by 2002, Coca-Cola was Africa's largest private sector employer and stood to lose a great deal by declining physical and economic health of the population. You probably didn't know about this: there wasn't a massive PR campaign about this work in 'the West' because the goal wasn't reputation but rather keeping staff and customers alive in Africa. 'The acid test of good corporate philanthropy is

---

20 'Public companies' are ones in which anybody can buy shares. 'Private companies' do not allow for this. (To be clear, we're not using 'public company' to mean companies owned by the government, such as Russia's Gazprom or the UK water companies were before they were privatised in the 1980s.)

whether the desired social change is so beneficial to the company that the organisation would pursue the change even if no-one ever knew about it,' say Kramer and Porter.

If the giving achieves more than individual shareholders could achieve themselves. After all, shareholders put commercial money into the company to achieve a financial return which they could not achieve themselves (a parallel of how wise donors give through charities only if that achieves a social or environmental return they could not achieve themselves). Corporations meet this criterion if they deploy their unique sets of assets and market positioning in some useful way which only that company could do. That is, the giving should relate deeply to a company's strategy.

Goldman Sachs has skills in structuring bonds, whereas its shareholders collectively don't, so that meets the test. Similarly Coca-Cola has trucks all over Africa, whereas its shareholders don't, so it is well-positioned to distribute condoms.

Let's apply these criteria to a couple more examples. Take Booz & Co.'s work with the British Red Cross. On the first criterion, does the company gain value from giving its time and expertise to the British Red Cross? Yes: amongst other benefits, it gains insights which Booz & Co. can use with other clients. And on the second, does it achieve more than the shareholders (here the company's senior managers, since it's a partnership) could achieve individually? Yes: the partners, and more junior people they employ, achieve more for large and complex organisations collectively than separately, which is precisely why they configure themselves that way for commercial clients.

Or take Sony's Open Planet Ideas competition in which anybody can submit ideas for how Sony technology can help address major environmental challenges. Sony and its partner, the international environmental charity WWF, collate good ideas, work up the winning suggestions into technical abstracts or working prototypes, and then makes the intellectual property available publicly on an open source basis. Does this add value for the company? Yes, in several ways. Sony gains innovative ideas, entices a large community to think about uses for Sony technology, and quite possibly develops a viable product which spurs sales of Sony kit. Oh, and reducing environmental degradation is handy for technology companies who are on the hook for proper disposal of electronic waste. Does the competition deliver value which individual shareholders could not have created themselves? Absolutely, because it uses Sony's unique fame, reach, design, manufacturing and technological capabilities.

Clearly in these examples, the companies have chosen the tool of being 'operators themselves', using the 'machinery' of their businesses rather than supporting other organisations. We'll look at two further fabulous examples before turning to the tool of supporting charities.

Iodine Deficiency Disorder is the world's most prevalent cause of brain damage, affecting over 740m people, 13 per cent of the world population. Yet it is easily prevented, simply by including iodine in diet. Unilever created a brand of iodine-enriched salt for sale in India and has since taken it to Ghana. By working with Ghana's Ministry of Health and UNICEF, Unilever converted 35 per cent of the population to iodine-enriched salt within two years, becoming profitable within 18 months.

Timpson, the shoe-repairer and key-cutter chain (mentioned earlier), also makes positive use of its own training and recruitment processes to help resettle prisoners on their release. James Timpson, Managing Director of Timpson, describes how he visited a young offenders institution, and met a lad who 'was a really good guy. I slipped him a business card and said, "when you get out, give me a ring and I'll give you a job". Now he manages one of our shops in Warrington.' Encouraged by the success, Timpson now works with prisons to train inmates, some of whom go on to work for the company. They've had over 120 recruits this way, half of whom stay on and don't reoffend.

Even more successful has been employing prisoners Released on Temporary Licence (ROTL), who work for the company whilst still serving their sentences. 'We've had 100 per cent success with this approach. They already understand how to work, and have confidence. Every time someone's come out on ROTL, they've stayed with us.' (This programme is even more remarkable considering that Timpson gives unusually high autonomy to staff in its shops. For example, its cash-registers aren't electronically linked to head office, and any shop assistant has discretion to spend up to £500 dealing with a staff complaint.)

A particularly striking feature of the Goldman Sachs, Coca-Cola, Unilever and Timpson examples is that the work costs very little – the latter two may be cost-neutral or even attractive financially.

A word about giving by private companies

Because the owners of private companies are not beholden to external shareholders, they can choose whether they mind if their giving creates commercial value for the company or not. However, they and their companies will still improve the world most through using the companies' unique assets in a strategic manner. Several of the examples of good giving we've encountered come from private companies: the consultancies Booz & Co. and the Monitor Group, as well as Timpson and Intrepid Travel.

What then of companies which use the tool of giving money to charity?

Straightaway it's clear that simply looking at how much they give (whether money or staff time or anything else) will tell us nothing. It's a measure of input, and, like most measures of input, is irrelevant to impact. There used to be rankings of companies based on how much cash they give, which mercifully have disappeared now: not only did they ignore non-cash donations but simply looking at what is given indicates nothing about what is achieved.

From the analysis above, you may have figured that I'm sceptical about corporations giving solely money. If 'money is the least valuable social change asset' and companies have a dazzling array of more valuable assets they can deploy, why are they giving money at all? Is that really the best option they can think of? Think of it different way. Suppose that a company has £10,000 to deploy socially or environmentally. If the company creates some 'bad' thing, such as carbon emissions, it could put that money towards reducing its emissions, towards developing technologies which reduce emissions, or into developing products or services which will reduce its customers' emissions. That money may well improve the world more than would a cheque to another organisation. Or the converse: perhaps the company could put the money towards developing or delivering products or services which are 'good' socially or environmentally: subsidising delivery to the poor (as Goldman Sachs was, in effect, with the IFFIm bonds), subsidising R&D of products or services which might not be economical on their own (perhaps inspired by the Unilever example), or giving their staff time to teach their skills to charities which need them.

If a company is to give money, then, like any donor, it should use all the advice we've seen: have a clear goal which relates to all elements on the Kramer Diagram; partner if possible; use that goal to design its processes for sourcing charities to consider, selecting them solely on merit, supporting them with all available skills, and tracking them; and track its own performance and share its learnings.

Dismal corporate giving

There is an insurance company in Edinburgh which gives six-figure grants to a demonstrably effective international children's charity. How nice, you say. Actually, this philanthropy is rubbish.

Does it add value to the company? No: the insurance company does not work with children, serve children, hire those children's parents, serve those children's parents as clients, need to know about children, meet anybody useful to the business through the charity. This makes the giving vulnerable: spending which doesn't benefit the business is an easy target when the chips are down. And does the giving deliver anything which the shareholders couldn't deliver on their own? No: the insurance company gives nothing more than money – despite, obviously, having considerable skills in all sorts of things – and therefore the charity gains only the company's lowest-value resource.

So what's wrong with that? The missed opportunity, that's what. The money which that company is contributing could deliver so much more. People miss out because these resources are given in the wrong way. Even given to effective charities, money alone is lower value than other resources which could be given at the same cost to the company. We're supposed to applaud the generosity of the insurance company (though it's giving somebody else's money) but in fact we should deplore its carelessness.

Perhaps this is harsh. Perhaps it's enough to look at whether the charity is effective. I don't think so: we should always strive for our giving to achieve not just something but everything possible. Goldman Sachs could have made money from those bankers' time and simply given it to the vaccine programme, but it would never have created anything like the impact of the bond. Intrepid Travel could have supported an effective charity anywhere. But by supporting a village from which it draws guides, it not only does work worthwhile in its own right, but enhances the customer experience which is good for the company, and thus makes more revenue available for good works in future.

Furthermore, if you're a shareholder of the insurance company – which, through your pension, you may well be – you're within your rights to be mighty cross that it's giving away your money without asking. (Oddly shareholder revolts about dismal corporate giving are rare, presumably because the amounts involved are negligible compared to those affected by other corporate decisions.)

So why do companies give like this? PR and 'brand building' are often cited. But giving is patently not essential for building brands: people left candles and flowers outsides Apple stores around the world as tributes after the passing of Steve Jobs – whose company, beloved of so many, has given barely a pip to charity. It's even been criticised[21] for making it difficult for customers to donate to charity through its phones and other products.

This isn't to say that all corporate involvement with charities is dismal. Far from it: we've seen several examples of the converse: Booz & Co. and the British Red Cross, various technology companies donating product, Timpson and ChildLine, Sony and WWF, the banks giving free services to the Disasters and Emergency Committee. Notice that each of these examples involves the company using more than money.

There are other ways that companies can support charities. In addition to the 'machine' of the company's core business, they can help by raising money from their staff and customers, by encouraging employee giving, and by organising

---

21 Along with Gap, American Express, Starbucks and others, Apple has products in the (RED) range, created by U2 frontman Bono, a portion of the revenue of which goes to the Global Fund to Fight AIDS, Tuberculosis and Malaria. For most (RED) products, the companies state the portion donated to the Global Fund. For the (RED) iPod, Apple does not disclose the amount it donates. Hmm.

volunteering opportunities for staff. Just one little practical tip if you're taking a group of staff to volunteer for a charity for a day. Offer to pay. Yes, pay the charity you're helping. The charity will incur costs in managing you: sending you maps, insuring you on site, probably offering you lunch. Though this may seem obvious, sometimes charities are treated as cost-free providers of team-building exercises or jolly days out. Offer to cover (at least) any costs that you create: don't create waste.

To conclude

In terms of this book being a driving course, you should now be safe driving big trucks in most circumstances. If you're to give excellently – and even if you're just curious – you'll need some theory more advanced than we've covered so far about results, sizes and mergers, and government. We'll turn to that now, and draw it all together in the full set of principles of good giving.

Section Four

Advanced theory

Chapter 16

Charities' results

'Everything should be as simple as possible, but no simpler…
'Not everything that counts can be counted. Not
everything that can be counted counts.'
– Albert Einstein

As we've seen throughout this book, charities vary significantly in their effectiveness, as do giving strategies ('ways to give it'), and therefore it's important to choose the good ones. We'll now look in detail at how to tell whether any particular organisation or giving strategy is any good. It's complicated (and this chapter is easily the most complicated in the book), so let's first be clear about why precisely this matters. It matters because we need to decide what to do in future.

Whether you are choosing a charity, choosing a strategy, or evaluating work which is already underway, results will show whether you should (continue to) support a particular type of work or to swap to something else, whether you as a donor should (continue to) operate in a particular way, and what lessons your work in future can learn from work in the past.

The aim of the game is not to demonstrate every last drop of impact. For one thing, as we'll see, that would often be ludicrously laborious and costly, and for another, it doesn't actually help unless we extract the lessons for the future. I'm spelling this out because sometimes donors get distracted by rather forensic examinations of charities' histories.

Now, results are unavoidably complex because we live in a complex world. One response is to simplify. This is helpful up to a point, but we must avoid measures which are simple but don't actually matter. Admin and fundraising ratios are the most common culprits: counting something which doesn't count. Another misplaced response is to restrict funding. Not only does this reduce the funding's impact but it also doesn't actually make measurement simpler. A third response is to retreat into activities which are simple to measure. These are typically at the top of the triangle, and therefore this response can exclude work which might be more substantial. Where there is a trade-off between scale of impact and certainty of impact, surely we should veer towards the options with bigger scale. Sometimes donors seem to behave as if the aim were to produce impact reports which are as detailed as possible.

To cut through the complexity, we need to know three things. First, what happened? Second, to what extent was that due to the charity and/or us – in other words, what would have happened anyway? And third, since we will be making choices between goals, theories of change and individual charities, how do the results compare to other charities? We'll look at the complexities in each of those questions in turn, before turning to what is possible. Figuring out what happened and why is the fundamental purpose of the scientific method, so it's no accident that we'll borrow from that, as well as relying on clear theories of change.

1. What happened?
Sometimes ascertaining this is as easy as falling off a log. How many people attended the training about supporting disabled colleagues? Do their disabled colleagues now feel better supported at work? Are the children to whom we've given deworming pills now free of worms? And so on. We don't need to dwell on the easy cases, but will look at four complexities which can arise in establishing 'what happened'.

First, in many cases, *you can't ask* the beneficiaries: work with animals, or for the benefit of future generations, for the glory of God or gods, or to honour our ancestors are examples. Sometimes, the difficulty isn't solely practical: the charities' work may involve influencing people who have good reason not to reveal that they were influenced, such as legislators, corporate leaders, and prison guards persuaded or pressured to stop torturing people. Or conversely the beneficiaries may have good reason to overstate the benefit they received: they may reason that if they are derogatory about a poor service, it might disappear completely. They may be right.

Second, it's common for charities to have *diffuse impact* across many people or institutions. In these cases – which include much work at the base of the triangle – it's often prohibitively difficult (or expensive) to see everything which happened.

Remember the climate change charity TippingPoint we came across in Section 1? It held an event in Spring 2011 to brief artists about climate change and various cultural responses, at which one of the delegates was a puppeteer. He was totally new to environmental issues but fascinated by what he learnt, and inspired to integrate issues around climate change into a show he was taking to Beirut the following year. What happened? It's pretty easy to establish the most proximate effect: whether the puppeteer did adapt his show. But finding out what happened beyond that is rather harder. His audience might have been dozens, or even hundreds, of people in Lebanon, making it expensive and arduous to investigate whether each of them changed their attitudes or behaviour after seeing the show. Add in the fact that perhaps 20 or so such artists attended that particular TippingPoint event, and that TippingPoint runs numerous events a year, and it becomes impractical to track the total impact of TippingPoint's work.

Third, charities' results can be totally unexpected. Hugh Montgomery, a wonderful polymath medical professor, founded Project Genie which educates young children about climate change. He recounts that children write to him about what they've done as a result: 'Some persuaded their parents to drive less or use less water, and some report *ectopic results* like "it got my dad to stop smoking"'. These 'ectopic results' – a particularly pleasing term meaning results in unexpected places – can be positive or negative, and are hard to spot precisely because nobody's looking in those places.

And fourth, the results *may not have happened yet*. For instance, extracurricular activities generally increase children's life-chances by increasing their confidence. On this basis, you send your eight-year-old child to ballet or karate not only because it's fun but because it may give them self-confidence which might get them through a difficult juncture in their career in their 30s or 40s. Is it working? Well, if your child is only 12, you've no idea. Similarly if a charity is lobbying for a change to the law, there may be scant demonstrable progress until the decision is actually made.

In some instances, you will not live to see 'what happens'. Think about the £10,000 given to the University of Manchester which is still producing Nobel Prize winners 130 years later. Or the Wellcome Trust's work on the human genome which will facilitate discoveries for generations hence. These can be the most productive uses of resources but witnessing the results requires a long time.

The good news is that you have a long time. Whereas companies (at least the public ones) must report results every quarter and politicians go to the electorate every few years, charitable donors aren't answerable to anybody. They're perfectly at liberty to undertake work which will take ages to bear fruit, precisely because companies and government can't.

What a charity can do. At a minimum, a charity can monitor the scale of its activities (e.g., attendance at its events, downloads of its information materials). This is of course tracking 'what happened' at the beginning (left-hand side) of its theory of change. If possible, it should also track what is happening on its goal, e.g., whether the rate of rainforest loss is falling or whether disabled people feel less excluded (at the right-hand side of the theory of change). Now we need to investigate whether the two are connected.

2. What would have happened without the charity?

In 1994, the Getty Museum in California offered $12m for Antonio Canova's famous statue *The Three Graces*. There was a public campaign to keep the statue in Britain, but despite attracting substantial sums from the Art Fund and the National Heritage Memorial Fund, it didn't raise enough. At the last minute, John Paul Getty II, the London-based son of the oil baron who founded the Getty Museum, rode to the rescue, offering the campaign $1.5m, enough to swing the deal. In this case, it's very clear 'what happened': the statue remains in Britain (it is owned by the Victoria and Albert Museum and the National Galleries of Scotland), and it's clear what would have happened otherwise – it would have left the country. If only it were always that simple.

Imagine a city with poor air quality. Suppose that a charity works there, trying to persuade residents to turn off their car engines when idling at traffic lights or waiting to pick people up. The charity reports that at the beginning of the year, the air was clean 10 per cent of the time ('clean' meaning graded as low health risk on the national air quality measures), whereas by the end of the year, the air was clean 20 per cent of the time. Great! Really? Actually this indicates precisely nothing about whether the charity is doing a good job: perhaps the improvement was due to the charity; but perhaps it would have happened anyway; and perhaps *more* improvement would have happened without the charity. It's not unknown for irritating campaigns to provoke people to 'rebel' and do precisely what the campaign is trying to curb. We also discussed how social programmes can exacerbate problems, such as short-term mentoring harming the children it tries to help.

Which scenario are you in?

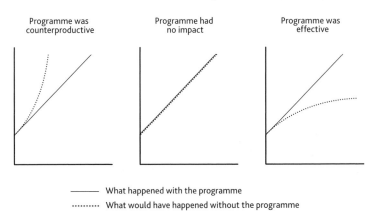

| Programme was counterproductive | Programme had no impact | Programme was effective |

——— What happened with the programme

·········· What would have happened without the programme

The air quality work has the **attribution problem**: we know what happened but we don't know why. Before we look at resolving this, please notice that these kinds of 'before/after' data are very common (amongst charities and elsewhere) and all have the attribution problem. Statements like these are typical: 'awareness of HIV transmission is much higher than when we started'; 'following our campaign, the law was changed'; 'at the beginning of the year, the children had a reading age of seven; now they have a reading age of eight'. Well, you'd expect a child's reading age to increase during a year irrespective of whether a charity is involved. This is no more impressive than saying that 'before our work, the average height of a child was 1.2 metres whereas afterwards it was 1.3 metres'! We can't infer causation from simple before/after statements.

To resolve the attribution problem, we need a **control**, that is, a situation in which everything is the same apart from the charity's work. This will show what would have happened without the charity's work, i.e., which of the scenarios above applies and therefore whether the programme is actually doing anything useful. (Control groups show a counterfactual: what would have happened in a different set of circumstances.)

Testing a programme against a control is not some optional technicality. Without a control situation, we have literally no clue about causes. Professor Esther Duflo of J-PAL says that without setting up control situations for our social or charitable programmes, we're no better than medieval doctors 'treating' patients with leeches. It is only through proper comparisons of ailing people treated with and without leeches that mankind learnt that the slimy bugs weren't helping much and could move to more effective treatments. Many of us literally owe our lives to experiments with proper controls. Charities too need controls to test whether their programmes are working.

What would constitute a control for the air quality programme? Suppose that the charity runs the programme during some months and not during others, and air quality improves in the months when it runs the programme and doesn't improve when it doesn't. The months without the programme are 'control months', and the finding implies that the improvement is due to the programme.

Is that a good control? Well, a good control is, as we said above, a situation in which everything is the same except the charity's work. Perhaps the control months are the same in every respect. But they might not be. Perhaps the charity uses volunteers to persuade motorists to switch off, and that the easiest source of volunteers is non-working parents of school-age children. The programme only runs when there are enough volunteers. The charity will have more volunteers during school terms: during school holidays, the parents are unavailable. However, also during school holidays, traffic decreases because there's no school run. Oh dear:

now if we look at the difference in air quality when the programme runs (i.e., during school terms) and when it doesn't (i.e., school holidays), we can't tell whether any difference is due to the lack of school run traffic or to the programme itself. We've got multiple possible causes, so we're back to the attribution problem. To identify the precise cause, we need to vary just one factor at once, which you'll probably remember is integral to decent experiments in science[22].

One easy way round this problem is to not run the programme for a month during term-time. The charity could compare 'term-time, no programme' air quality with 'term-time, with programme' air quality. That would 'control for' (i.e., annul the effect of) the school-run, and isolate (i.e., show just the effect of) the impact of the programme itself. Bingo[23]. The important point is that the control group and the other group need to be actually equivalent, differing only in the factor we're investigating.

Let's look at a real example. Goldman Sachs has a programme called 10,000 Women which supports female entrepreneurs. Apparently '70% of [its] graduates surveyed have increased their revenues, and 50% have added new jobs.' Goldman Sachs obviously thinks this is impressive because it took out full-page adverts in magazines to tell us this. Should we be impressed?

You can now see that this is pretty hopeless. For one thing, this isn't even before/after data: it's just 'after' data. It doesn't say that '30% of them were growing their revenues before, whereas 70% are now'. For another, no control or comparator is given. We're not told that '70% of graduates increased their revenues, whereas only 20% of other businesses did in the same period.'

And there's a third major problem which is also pretty ubiquitous. Let's wonder for a second what those women would have achieved anyway. It's not hard to imagine that the kind of women who get themselves onto a Goldman Sachs programme are just the kind of go-getters who would do well in virtually any circumstance. That is, this programme may well attract and select people who are atypically entrepreneurial. This **selection bias** also creates the attribution problem: we don't know whether the results are due to the programme itself or to systematically unusual characteristics in the women it selects. Returning to the triptych of graphs we saw a couple of pages ago, it's conceivable that the women might have been helped by

---

22 Sometimes it's impossible to isolate causes experimentally. Statistical methods can sometimes be used to identify the contribution of each cause, including regression analysis, for which we sadly don't have space in this book.

23 Technically speaking, this is not a brilliant control because it only compares one month with one other month. There may be other unpredictable changes in those two months (perhaps the ring-road outside the town is blocked off, or petrol prices rise, or building work on a new shopping centre starts), any of which are possible causes of changes in air quality. Rigorous control experiments compare groups large enough for differences to be statistically significant.

the programme, or that it made no difference, or even that they would have done better without it occupying their time.

To 'isolate' the effect of the programme, an experiment would have to 'control for' selection bias. A researcher would need two sets of female entrepreneurs who are identical in every respect. She would put one set through the 10,000 Women programme and see how much better they do in their careers than a set which doesn't (this latter set is the control group, which will show what those women would have achieved anyway).

Irritatingly though, we can't create groups this way because people don't come in handy matching pairs: they have all manner of quirks and experiences and attitudes and individual traits which might affect their performance (introducing other possible causes). However, if the researcher takes a large enough group of women all of whom are eligible for the programme and divides them randomly, it's reasonable to expect those quirks and individualities to even out between the two groups. The randomness of the division removes the selection bias, leaving the programme itself as the sole difference between the groups. It isolates the effect of the programme and therefore comparing the groups' results will show the effect of the programme. Voilà.

The experiment we've just created is a **randomised control trial**. Executed properly, they do succeed in isolating the programme from all other possible causes and thereby show what would have happened without it[24]. This is why they're the 'gold standard' of evaluations, developed for pharmaceutical drugs trials and now increasingly used to provide robust and reliable insight elsewhere. For example, it was randomised control trials (by Innovations for Poverty Action and J-PAL) which showed the cost-effectiveness of deworming in improving school attendance, the usefulness of lentils in getting children immunised in India, and the relative cost-effectiveness of various programmes to decontaminate water in Kenya. IPA and J-PAL also use them to test programmes around improving sexual health, reducing corruption and even post-conflict peace-building. This is why I said earlier that they're a revolution, essentially deploying proper scientific method – the great intellectual achievement of the modern era – onto the most pressing social problems of our modern era. Randomised control trials (RCTs) have also been used to study the effect of work to counter disadvantage among children in the US which is currently creating interest in the UK, and the example of reducing child mortality in Uganda.

I said 'executed properly' because it's also not trivial to ensure that the division is actually random and doesn't introduce some other bias. Flipping a coin? Nope: people

---

[24] The trial described here would test the impact of the programme relative to doing nothing. In fact, we're generally not choosing between *doing something* and *doing nothing*, but rather seeing whether a new/proposed programme is an improvement on what is already being done. So more useful is for one group to do the new/proposed programme and the other to do the best programme already available.

pretend not to have seen the answer if they didn't like it. Getting the receptionist to allocate people based on their birthday? No: again, too much potential for influencing the allocation. This too is not some point of minor, technical, academic detail which can safely be ignored. It's been studied in medicine (which is much more studied than charities are) where, according to Dr Ben Goldacre, an epidemiologist, it swings the data wildly: 'People have studied the effect of randomisation in large numbers of trials and found that the ones with dodgy methods of randomisation overestimate treatments effects by 41%.' That's a lot of children out in the fields.

Should all charities do randomised control trials? Ideally then, all charities would demonstrate their results via control trials, and any charities where selection bias might be a problem (which is most of them: virtually anything involving people is open to selection bias) would have randomised control trials. A good move for a donor is to find out whether a charity you're considering supporting has done such a trial, and/or whether its 'idea' (its theory of change) has been tested in this way by other organisations.

Several practical considerations limit the use of randomised control trials. Sometimes it's impossible to get a sample large enough for the quirks and other factors to even out between the two groups. Imagine a charity which isn't primarily focused on government policy but which occasionally weighs in on policy matters (the charity Changing Faces might be a reasonable example). Ideally, such a charity would compare what happens when it gets involved with issues versus when it doesn't. But if it only gets involved a couple of times per year, there may not be enough relevant instances for the results to be statistically meaningful. And if the charity can only engage in policy infrequently, it will choose the issues on which it feels it can have greatest impact, which is perfectly reasonable but does create a good dose of selection bias. There are occasions when charities can get around this problem by pooling data with each other, or collecting data over a long enough period to accumulate sufficient cases.

At other times, there's no possibility of a control group. Suppose a charity is trying to prevent nuclear warfare, or reform the UN, or understand the effect of the Fukushima nuclear meltdown on attitudes to nuclear power. These are each single instances without useful comparators: it's inconceivable that any faintly informed person would be unaware of Fukushima and thereby eligible for a control group.

People often ask about the ethics of control experiments, because they necessarily involve excluding some people from the programme. The point is that we only do control experiments when we don't know whether a programme works or not – or which of two possible programmes works best. In those cases, surely it's unethical to subject some people to a programme *without* finding out whether it works, that is, without doing a control trial. And people sometimes ask about the ethics of randomising. Much the same logic applies. Charities often can't serve all the people who they would like to serve so they have to choose somehow. If they don't know which groups will benefit the most, randomising enables them to find out.

What a charity can do. Any charity should report a good deal of detail about its work and impact research[25]. This enables anybody to see the validity of its results (e.g., whether they're a statistical fluke), the reliability of its control (which will show whether it's better than the leech-bearers), as well as integrate the data into broader studies. The truth is in the details. For instance, the following data should be public:

- Clarity about what the charity did and what happened. Again this sounds rather obvious but often the published details are surprisingly sketchy. Since we're here trying to understand what happened and why – and furthermore to compare it to what happens in other programmes, since we're not interested just in whether the programme does *some* good but in whether there are others which are better – the detail matters. Precisely what type of beneficiaries were served, how were they selected, and what was done, how and when, to how many of them, at what cost, what was the drop-out rate and so on.

- Clarity about the research: when and where the research was done. If a survey was used, how were respondents chosen, how was the survey done (online surveys get different types of respondents to street surveys or phone surveys), the sample size (small sample sizes produce results indistinguishable from no result), the precise questions used (wording and sequence matter, as we shall see).

- Clarity about any control used: how were members of the control group chosen, what happened to them, how were they measured. (Despite the difficulties mentioned, my strong suspicion is that charities could use – or even simulate – controls much more frequently than they do. We'll come to an example in a minute.)

The attribution problem in everyday life

Now that you know about multiple possible causes, selection bias, and distinguishing causation from correlation and random chance, you'll spot any number of occasions when they get conflated.

Lack of control

The US inaugurated a Republican President in 2001 and then suffered a major

---

25 There is no peer review process for charities' results, nor any requirement – or even convention – about disclosing these kinds of details. Beyond integrity, there's nothing to stop charities publishing total fiction, or facts which are methodologically weak. (Don't blame the charities. If donors started demanding a peer review process, one would appear in a flash.)

terrorist attack. It elected Democrat President in 2008 and the banks promptly collapsed. The US had a massive budget deficit in 2011 and there was a hurricane on its East Coast, where the government sits. Were those causal? Republican presidential candidate Michele Bachmann seemed to think the last one was, saying that it was God's way of getting the politicians' attention. The Fields Medal for maths is awarded every four years, in the same years as the Winter Olympics. Maybe the medal causes the Olympics...

Selection bias?
Oxford University churns out more UK Prime Ministers than does Cambridge. (You'll have your own views of whether they're any good!) Does Oxford disproportionately select people who could become Prime Minister or does it turn them into Prime Ministers?

Members of environmental charities tend to live greener lives than non-members. Is this selection bias (only greenies sign up) or is it because members are influenced by the charities' campaigns around greener living of which they see more than non-members do?

The MELMAC Education Foundation in Maine found that graduation rates improved more in the schools which ran its programmes than in those which didn't. Maybe the programme was responsible or maybe the programme only ran in better managed schools.

Private schools tend to get better exam results than state schools do. Do private schools make children better exam-takers, or do they only admit good exam-takers? Before you start paying thousands of pounds, it would surely be worth finding out. (The fact that most good private schools have entrance exams might be a bit of a clue.)

People who study statistics tend to understand them better than those who don't. Could that be selection bias too?

Events, dear boy, events
In the real world, sometimes controls just get messed up by events.
Global Cool Foundation is a climate change charity. In early 2010, when I was Executive Director, it ran an innovative campaign to get people in the UK to fly less. Success would ultimately mean fewer people taking flights. For several days of the campaign, the number of flights into, from and within the whole country fell to precisely zero.

What a fantastically successful campaign! In fact, a volcanic ash cloud had arrived from Iceland for those few days, closing British airspace.

Even at a more subtle level, our results were messed up by events. The campaign's theory of change involved influencing public attitudes to air travel by highlighting the fun and adventure of rail travel, making it more attractive than air travel. The ash cloud together with the strike by British Airways staff at around the same time produced significant media coverage of passengers camping out at airports – which clearly also influenced public attitudes.

This example rather nicely illustrates that, at the end of the day, charities are doing real work in the real world in which loads of other unpredictable stuff happens, which also influences the observed results.

3. How does that compare to other charities / types of work?

The easiest comparison of all is between a charity and itself, in other words, looking at its performance over time. We'll return to this.

Next easiest is comparing charities which produce quantifiable, readily-attributable results relatively rapidly. For example, Age Concern Swansea helps older people claim their welfare benefits. It's pretty easy to measure the results because they're in this category. As it happens, for every pound spent providing benefits advice, Age Concern Swansea helps secure £26. This 'return on investment' of 2,500 per cent appears pretty high (we're here using the term 'return on investment' figuratively, since the money doesn't go to the donor or to Age Concern Swansea but rather to the beneficiary), and we can easily compare it with the results of other organisations doing similar work, such as other Age Concerns. Most of the randomised control trials we've seen in this book have been designed to produce quantifiable, rapid and readily-attributable results for several types of programme, precisely so that the programmes can be compared: the various programmes to chlorinate household water in Kenya, and the various programmes to improve school attendance in India and so on.

However, comparisons are complicated by several factors, which we'll look at now.

Picking the high-hanging fruit

Building trades offer good employment options for women: they suit part-time work which can be fitted around other commitments; pay is much better than in comparable industries dominated by women such as hospitality; and tradeswomen are preferred by organisations such as housing associations with Muslim tenants, many single women, and women at home with families during the day. Yet the building trades are overwhelmingly male – when did you last see a woman working on a building site? Andy Walder, Director of the National Construction College points out that women make up half the UK population but only 13 per cent of the construction workforce.

Several organisations support women into the building and construction trades. Agenda Construction Skills for Women, a charity, focused on women who had been out of the workplace for a while and needed support to be 'job-ready'. So the best metric of success for Agenda was the number of women helped into jobs. Right?

Wrong.

Women vary in the levels of support that they need before they are 'job-ready': from practical help with child-care to emotional support, from job-specific skills to basic literacy and numeracy.

Support needed from Agenda Construction Skills for Women

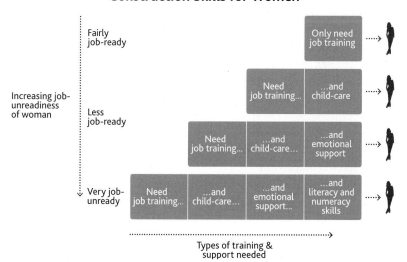

Suppose that Agenda gets fewer women into work than another similar organisation does. That metric would imply that Agenda was less effective that its peer. But that might not be true: perhaps Agenda's 'in-take' is women who – for whatever reason – are less job-ready than the other organisation's in-take. Similarly, suppose that Agenda is getting fewer women into work than it used to. Again, that metric would imply that it was doing a less good job now. But again that might not be true because perhaps its in-take is – for some reason – becoming less job-ready. The measure of simply counting successes is misleading because it assumes that the 'starting point' of the beneficiaries is always the same (at least on average) which is often untrue. It's is an example of where oversimplifying becomes dangerous. For example, a hospital ward may have an unusually high mortality rate, not because its physicians are murderous or incompetent but because they deliberate select or receive the most difficult cases.

It's therefore important to donors to be clear about whether charities are serving what we might call the low-hanging fruit or the high-hanging fruit. Consider the Gates Foundation's work to eradicate polio. It's reasonable to suppose that the easily preventable cases (that is, the cheaply preventable cases) will be dealt with first. So over time, the cost of preventing cases will rise – not because the Foundation becomes less efficient but because it's reaching for progressively more difficult cases. The work in India to improve school attendance is similar. Lots of children's attendance will be improved very cheaply by deworming treatment. But that won't suffice for others – for children who don't attend despite being worm-free, or who have worms and also can't afford a uniform. They are higher-hanging, requiring other solutions which are more expensive.

Whether serving the low-hanging fruit or the high-hanging fruit is the 'right answer' will depend on the specifics of the situation. In some cases (perhaps, an emergency famine situation), perhaps the scarce resources should be deployed to maximise the number of successes, which would mean favouring the low-hanging fruit. In other situations, one can argue that charitable resources should be focused on those most in need, who are least likely to be helped by the commercial market. This seems to be Warren Buffett's view: 'You look for easy things in business. Philanthropy is just the opposite'.

Clarity is the key. And not just for ease of measuring, but also because metrics create powerful incentives which drive how charities operate – and it's worth making sure we're calling the tune that we really want. For example, measuring Agenda solely on the number of women it got into work would incentivise it to select the women it can get into work with least effort – the low-hanging fruit. That is, that metric would encourage Agenda to abandon the tough cases. In education, these kinds of metrics encourage organisations to focus on students most likely to succeed anyway; in drug rehabilitation, to select the most easily treated patients. We can't say here which is 'right' – that depends on what the donor and charity are best equipped to do and the state of supply and demand – but we can see that the donor should be careful to choose metrics which incentivise the behaviour she intends.

Above and beyond

Caring for a patient for one night costs less at Hospice A than at Hospice B. Does that mean Hospice A is more cost-effective? Maybe, maybe not. We need to understand the detail of what it provides. Perhaps it's like this:

Hospice A	Hospice B
• Board & lodging for patient	• Board & lodging for patient
• Basic nursing care	• 'Full-service' nursing care
	• Emotional support for patient
	• Activities during the day for patient
	• Emotional support for the family

Crudely comparing unit costs assumes that the services are identical, ignoring the possibility that one hospice may go above and beyond the others, providing additional services which might make all the difference in the world to the patient or their family. (As with admin costs, this comparison fails because it doesn't ask 'cost *of what?*') Furthermore, it assumes that the patients are roughly identical in each hospice, which we know may not be true: one hospice might be serving patients whose conditions require more expensive treatments. These situations arise in many sectors in which charities operate. For example, dealing with high-hanging fruit may require more services than does dealing with low-hanging fruit (as the diagram for Agenda illustrates).

Qualitative results

Plenty of charities aim to improve quality of life in some way which is not readily expressed in numbers: broadening children's world-view by giving them access to the arts, improving family relationships, supporting vulnerable children for example. This work is enormously important but tough to compare. Tough, but not impossible: there are sometimes ways to quantify even these 'soft' results.

When children are happy, they can learn and their educational chances are high. When parents are confident and able to cope with their lives, they make better parents, which improves their children's lives. On this basis, The Place2Be works in schools across the UK, often in deprived areas, providing counselling to children, parents and teachers in order to improve the emotional well-being of children, their families and the whole school community.

We'll take the work with parents as an example. Typical issues which parents raise with The Place2Be's counsellors are lack of self-confidence or self-esteem, doubts about being a 'good enough' parent, bereavement, domestic violence, drinking problems and mental health issues such as depression. Though these issues don't immediately translate into numbers, The Place2Be quantifies its impact by using a third-party tool to assess each parent's 'level of distress' before and after the counselling. On the graph below, each vertical line represents a parent: the black dot shows their level of distress before The Place2Be's support, and the grey dot is that same adult afterwards. (The horizontal arrangement of lines is irrelevant: the chart simply show parents in decreasing order of initial distress. So the drop from left to right is incidental: the significant point is that the grey 'after' dots are predominantly lower than the black 'before' dots):

Results of parent work, 2009-10 academic year

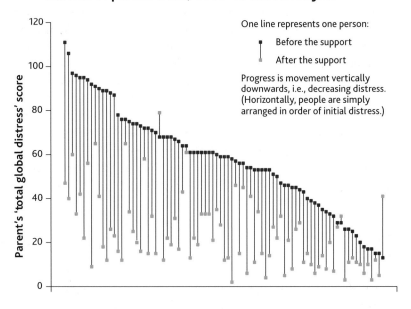

These quantified results enable The Place2Be to compare results between schools, between counsellors and between time-periods. They allow donors and others to compare The Place2Be's results and effectiveness with those of other organisations who do similar work and use the same measurement tool.

Different measures

Charities normally choose what they measure. Consequently, even if several charities have broadly similar goals, they may use quite different measures, which makes it hard to compare them. To understand why this happens, suppose that several charities run campaigns to encourage the public to eat more healthily. Charity A makes informative and funny videos about food which it posts online, following a theory of change that people will be inspired by the videos to change their lifestyles. It quite sensibly measures the number of times those videos are seen. Charity B runs events in public spaces to give people ideas and inspiration, so it measures the number of people who attend its events. Charity C offers a weekly email with ideas and tips, and monitors the number of people who receive it and who open it.

Each charity chooses measures based on its theory of change, and they're all sensible. However this doesn't enable direct comparison because there's no obvious exchange rate: how many video-views are equivalent to one event attendance? It's simply not clear.

Work with reasonably similar goals

The world of healthcare has solved this problem by developing a formula which, in effect, squashes numerous factors into a single number which allows comparison.

Suppose we have two patients. They have different conditions which require different treatments with different costs. We cannot afford to treat both so must choose which patient will benefit most. The treatment for Patient A will make his life pretty nasty but will extend it a lot, whereas the treatment for Patient B will make her life reasonable but extend it relatively little. Health economists assess the length of life which each treatment adds, recognising also the resulting quality of life. Quality-Adjusted Life Years (QALYs) 'measure a person's length of life weighted by a valuation of their health and related quality of life'. Each year of life is assigned a score of quality, based on a wide range of criteria. A year of full health scores one, poor health scores less than one, death counts as zero, and some dreadful conditions score below zero.

The effect of treatments can therefore be compared, even if the treatments and results are dissimilar. The first step is to look at the Quality-Adjusted Life Years the person gains. In our example:

Treatment for Patient A	Effect is four additional years in health state 0.5	QALYs added = 2 (4 x 0.5)
Treatment for Patient B	Effect is two additional years in health state 0.75	QALYs added = 1.5 (2 x 0.75)

If the two treatments cost the same, this analysis has provided a rational way of choosing between them: we'd treat Patient A[26]. If they have different costs, we can get to a rational basis with a further step, of comparing cost-effectiveness:

Treatment for Patient A	QALYs added = 2	Cost of intervention = £18,000	Cost per QALY added = £9,000
Treatment for Patient B	QALYs added = 1.5	Cost of intervention = £12,000	Cost per QALY added = £8,000

Based on cost-effectiveness of each additional QALY, we'd choose the treatment for Patient B.

QALYs are helpful because although patients, conditions, treatments and costs vary hugely, the various treatments share the same goal – giving patients quality and quantity of life. QALYs have their detractors, not least because people disagree with the weightings with which they squash diverse variables into one single number. In the absence of an alternative, QALYs are widely used and helpful for medical practitioners and donors. The analogous Disability-Adjusted Life Year (DALY) is used in work in less developed countries. It considers the total years of life which are lost because of disease, combined with the reduction in quality of life for people with disability or ill-health. It therefore also squashes multiple factors into a single number which can be used to allocate resources methodically.

Different goals

What about comparing activities with radically different goals? This is rather harder. In fact, it is often simply impossible to make a comparison analytically, and thus the donor's own taste and preference are major factors. Suppose you're choosing between preserving archaeological remains and supporting bereaved people. These are so different that it's hard to imagine a single meaningful metric which captures them both. You might think that you can use the fact that both activities aim to increase human happiness. Let's try.

It's pretty clear how supporting bereaved people increases human happiness. But to quantify the incremental happiness created by the archaeological remains, you'd need to deal with the fact that the effect will be diffused over many people, over a long time, and intermingled with numerous other factors. Then you'd need a meaningful method of comparison, and good luck with that: happiness is a complicated concept and the human brain computes it very strangely. To take just one

---

26 This analysis is also used for choosing between multiple possible treatments for an individual patient.

example, when young people are asked how happy they are and then asked when they last went on a date, their happiness rates totally differently than if they are asked the exact same questions just in the opposite order! (This isn't just the craziness of youth: older people do the same thing, though the question might be about love-making with their spouse rather than dating.)

Even once you've navigated all that, you still have the issues of risk, return and timescale. Consider, for example, supporting one bereaved person today versus researching to improve bereavement counselling techniques which might affect countless people in future. It's not at all obvious which is best for human happiness, hence my suspicion that the right level of risk and return for you is determined largely by your own taste.

Even if you did have some über-measure of human happiness which resolves all of this, it wouldn't help much in comparisons involving work which hasn't yet produced (all its) results, or which aids religion or animals – which is not unlikely since these are popular uses of charitable money. It therefore seems unlikely that there is a single metric for choosing analytically between work with very different goals. By analogy, consumer guides (such as *Which?*) compare types of washing machine, types of camera and types of car, but when an individual selects which gadget to buy, he or she must make a subjective judgement because cameras and cars have fundamentally different purposes. This is why, when we started out in Section 1, we said that to choose between causes (that is, work with different goals), start with your own heart. It also explains why rankings of diverse charities are necessarily subjective (except ones based on admin or fundraising costs which are just hopeless).

The fact that results from very different types of work can't be squashed into a single metric creates a practical problem for donors who support diverse work. It prevents them aggregating their total impact. If they support, say, work with bereaved people, work on child literacy and work to preserve archaeological remains, they must use a range of metrics. This may seem a rather obvious point but donors sometimes try to find a single metric. Normally a good range includes numerical data and qualitative data such as stories or perceptions – in fact, just like the range of data most of us use to form an opinion about other issues, from the quality of a hotel to the state of the economy.

What a charity can do, and what you can do

So, for lots of reasons, understanding charities' results is tricky. What can be done to gather useful results of some kind?

The best option is a proper randomised control trial (RCT), conducted independently, for the reasons we've seen: by dealing with selection bias, they provide high quality of evidence about the charity's effect. They can be used to compare programmes, and thereby provide clear guidance on what to support.

If the idea which a charity uses has already been robustly proven somewhere (e.g., using an RCT), it doesn't need proving again. Returning to our formula for impact (= idea x implementation), all that is needed in this situation is to assess the charity's implementation. (In the language of tracking results, an evaluation has proven the idea; monitoring will look at implementation.) There's a caveat here because things work differently in different places as we've seen. The more similar the situations in which that idea has been used, the more valid the comparison.

If other reasons prevent an RCT being used, a charity should collate information in three areas:

1. Is its goal being achieved? (Is biodiversity increasing around the lake? Is air quality improving? This is looking at 'what happening' at the end of the theory of change, leave aside the attribution problem.)

2. The scale of its activities. ('What happened' at the beginning of the theory of change.) How many events has it held, or people has it served, or MPs has it contacted? As discussed, the more detail the charity can give about this, the better, since it enables others to use its methods and data.

3. Is evidence for its theory of change strengthening or weakening over time? A control will help hugely with this, as will evidence from other circumstances and relevant interim results.

Let's walk through each of those in turn. We'll again use TippingPoint as an example because its results are diffuse, unattributable and slow to materialise, and therefore it raises most of the complications you'll encounter.

Is its goal being achieved? TippingPoint's ultimate goal is preventing/reducing damage from climate change. This is too long-term and diffuse to attribute, but TippingPoint can – and should – track evidence about whether climate change is slowing, and whether members of the public are acting to reduce their carbon emissions and/or creating political pressure around climate. This is information about changes towards the end of TippingPoint's long theory of change. TippingPoint itself won't need to undertake primary research here because it can draw on studies by meteorologists, polling agencies and so on. It's quite common for data about a charity's ultimate goal to be available from other agencies: issues such as health, education, biodiversity, economic development, literacy rates, voter turn-out are widely studied.

TippingPoint can also use interim measures specific to its theory of change. Good examples might be the number of artistic events created by its attendees which relate to climate change and the collective size of their audience. A spurious interim measure for TippingPoint would be the range of artistic disciplines represented at its events. We can see that this is irrelevant because it doesn't feature in the theory of change.

The scale of its activities. What is happening at the beginning of the chain? In TippingPoint's case, how many events does it host, how many artists attend, and how many artists cite TippingPoint as an influence on specific pieces of work? Clearly this is simply a matter of keeping track of the charity's activities, which should be pretty straightforward.

A charity should monitor the unit cost of its activities (or of its results, if it can see them), and can compare its performance with itself, over time. Normally, those costs will fall as the charity becomes more cost-effective, though they will legitimately rise if it progressively takes higher-hanging fruit.

Is the evidence supporting the theory of change improving or weakening over time? Over time, there should be a growth in evidence supporting each link in the theory of change. When the results are diffuse, it may be possible for a charity to sample the people affected: TippingPoint might survey audience members at *some* of the events produced by *some* of the people who attended TippingPoint's events (taking care to avoid biasing the sample).

How can TippingPoint set up a control to see whether its events increase the amount of representation or influence of climate change in art? Well, it could look at representations of climate in art produced by artists who don't come. Is that a good control? You don't need me to point out that that's not great, because we'd expect the artists who show up to a TippingPoint event to have an atypical interest in climate (i.e., we would expect some selection bias). One way of controlling for that would be to compare the work of artists who *do* come with that of those who *ask* to come but for some reason can't attend. Another way is to simulate a control by looking at the work of artists who are already members of other environmental groups, i.e., who've already self-selected for an environmental interest but haven't been through TippingPoint's particular activities.

TippingPoint can also assemble evidence from analogous circumstances. For example, evidence for the third link in its chain – that public awareness drives action – might come from research into whether people drive more safely after being informed about the dangers of drink-driving. If interim measures or data from analogous circumstances make you disbelieve a charity's theory of change – that is, you don't believe that success in the intermediate steps will lead to its ultimate goal – this is not great work to support.

Donors: ask, think and pay

The donor's role in all this could be summarised as **ask, think and pay**. Though these three steps are relevant to all donors, they are particularly crucial for donors giving a lot because their effect on charities is amplified – positively or negatively.

Ask for results. Amazingly often, donors just ask *about* results but not *for* the results. They commonly ask 'how do you measure your results?' Though this question is not mad of itself, it is pretty mad if it is asked by itself. It's a question about process, so elicits an answer about process: 'We run some surveys, count attendees, run such-and-such type of trial, use the Blah-de-Blah measurement tool'. Surely a donor ought also to inquire what the results actually are.

Ask for, and look for, relevant evaluations from other organisations. For instance, if the charity doesn't yet have a formal evaluation of its work, ask (or look) for whether its theory of change (its 'idea') has been evaluated by another organisation in similar circumstances.

Ask about the charity's research method (if it's not clear). 'Garbage in leads to garbage out' as the computer scientists put it, and to see whether the results are statistically distinguishable from garbage, make sure you understand the detail. For instance, the word 'would' normally has no place in surveys. 'If organic baby food were priced the same as normal baby food, would you buy it?' is a pointless question, because what people say in answer to these hypothetical questions (what market researchers call 'expressed preferences') bears scant relation to what they actually do ('revealed preferences'). Because there is no peer review process for charities' results, any 'garbage' may not have been removed from the research before you see it.

Ask for recent results, for the good results and the bad ones, for results of all the charity's research. The charity is selling, remember. It relies on subsidy by definition, so it needs cash (and other things) and has every incentive to put a rosy gloss on its data, to select the data which look good, to not bother collecting data for a while if it suspects its impact is falling. It's called **publication bias** and we'll come back to the reasons for it in a page or two.

Think about what the data really say and what they don't say. For example, if there's no control group, then they don't give much indication about what the programme actually achieved as opposed to what would have happened anyway. If the sample was small, they may not say much that's significant.

Be aware that research itself is only one of three stages of investigating results. The first stage is defining a question to investigate, then comes the research process itself, and finally the data get interpreted. We've seen how selection bias affects the research stage, and there's also masses of scope for bias in the first and last stages. To take an example in the first stage, suppose that you're running a training programme in several countries and have funding to evaluate just one. Which do you choose? Well, if it's your programme, you'll probably – subconsciously – choose the one you reckon is best. This isn't born out of malign intent, but occurs consistently. (This phenomenon is well-documented in medicine.) Even if the research itself is fabulously rigorous, there's a bias before it's even begun. Nobel Prize winning physicist Werner Heisenberg surmised that 'What we observe is not nature itself, but nature exposed to our method of questioning'.

At the interpretation stage, a pile of psychology influences what we think we see. To select just one phenomenon, people give greater weight to information which reinforces their existing world views than to information which doesn't. It's called **confirmation bias**. An example is a study reported recently in the scientific journal *Nature* which found that people presented with neutral data – about nanotechnology, environmental risk, public health and crime control – 'splintered into highly polarised factions consistent with their cultural predispositions' towards, on the one hand, egalitarian and communitarian values and suspicion of commerce and, on the other hand, values which prize individualism and personal initiative. This psychology makes it genuinely difficult for human beings to interpret data objectively, and an interpretation which is 'obvious' to one person might seem quite far-fetched to another.

> *'A man hears what he wants to hear and disregards the rest'*
> – "The Boxer", Simon and Garfunkel

Before we go any further, please watch this video: www.youtube.com/embed/vJG698U2Mvo If you're not near a computer now, then watch it when you can, AFTER which, read the piece on page 198.

Think about the incentives you set up. It has to be 'safe' for a charity to share data about what isn't working. You need that – and so does everybody else – because after all we're looking at problems which urgently need innovative approaches because they have already resisted great intellects and great money. Charitable money is well-placed to support innovation, some of which won't work, and we need to know which those are and why, in order to move rapidly to those which do. Incentivise openness: don't inadvertently encourage charities to hide bad data and prevent others learning (i.e., don't incentivise publication bias). This point bears repeating, because many donors give results a rather cursory look and penalise charities whose data 'look bad'. Since sharing self-denigrating data is nobody's top priority, charities need to know that they won't be punished for bothering to collect and share it.

And lastly, *pay*. If donors want charities to measure their results, to share their learning – victories, failures and all – then donors need to ask for those data and pay for the studies. Proper studies can be expensive – getting an adequate sample, randomising it properly, eliminating all the other biases. But the alternative is to carry on handing out leeches in the hope that they're alleviating something. Charities often struggle to afford robust studies, not least because good results don't necessarily bring in more money: that, as we have seen, relies on success in the entirely separate operation of hosting lovely dinners or organising fun-runs. Donors – uniquely – can change that by paying for studies, and making decisions based on what they say. (Conversely, if there isn't enough funding to do an evaluation properly, perhaps don't do one at all. For example, it's pointless to waste money collecting detailed before/after data since that on its own proves nothing.)

A peculiarity of the charity sector is that most of the research into results is done by the charities themselves. While in one sense, they're well-placed for the job because they understand the work, in another sense they're the worst people imaginable because they're the protagonists. They're selling. They're conflicted. I'm not saying that they're corrupt or evil: it's just unreasonable – possibly to the point of foolishness – to expect people to be impartial about their own work, their own salaries, their own reputations. To my knowledge, nobody's ever examined this amongst charities but as we've seen, they have in medicine – where independent studies produce rather different results to those produced by the protagonists. Again, donors can change this, by paying for independent evaluations.

In short, make sure your money follows the *value*: not the pretty pictures which are irrelevant nor some graphs which look plausible but actually aren't terribly robust. Back charities which are doing a good job of figuring out what works and are willing to admit their mistakes in public. (Admit yours too.)

A donor's results

Assessing a donor's results is even harder than assessing a charity's results (if the donor supports other organisations as opposed to being an operator themselves). Since donors' impact is vicarious, assessment would involve working out what to attribute to the charity, and then how much of that is attributable to each donor. If your giving is unrestricted (as it should be: and as it is, in reality, even if you think it isn't, because money is all the same colour), its effect is intermingled with that of all other donations, and it'll be impossible to disaggregate. This is particularly pronounced for small contributions.

Don't obsess about it because it will paralyse you. To return to where we began, the first goal is *getting* results rather than *proving* a link to them, and the second goal is having a good basis for decisions in future. Your goal isn't documenting every jot of your diffuse impact and/or proving it beyond doubt. If you can see the evidence building – about things which work and/or things which don't work – then you're on the right track. Tom Ross, CEO of the Z. Smith Reynolds Foundation in the US, articulates a pragmatic view: 'We care about whether [charities we support] have reached their goal, not whether they have reached their goal because of us. We will never be able to take credit for that movement, but we want to know if things are improving.'

Why is this all so complicated, when comparing companies is pretty simple?

At the end of this chapter, you may feel like throwing up your hands and asking, 'But why isn't it as easy to compare charities as it is to compare companies?' Let's be precise. Companies' impacts are just as diffuse, diverse, ectopic and long-term as charities'. For instance, companies variously:

- improve the happiness of customers by providing products which are fun, handy, labour-saving and beautiful
- decrease the happiness of customers by making products which are bad for them, by, for example, giving them cancer or making them fat
- extend and improve people's lives by developing and distributing medicines
- shorten and worsen people's lives by creating air pollution, water pollution, noise and stress
- increase autonomy and meaning in lives of their workforces through creating employment and professional development
- decrease the happiness of non-customers who become jealous of other people's possessions, driving dissatisfaction, social division and exclusion
- improve governments' accountability by reducing the role of the state
- decrease governments' accountability by paying bribes and exerting influence on policy-makers despite having no democratic mandate
- increase demand for goods from less developed countries by giving access to markets elsewhere
- reduce demand for goods from less developed countries by swamping them with cheaper, more heavily branded international goods
  ...and so on.

So comparing companies' total effects would be complicated. Comparing them only *appears* easy because their reported results are almost exclusively about their financial performance. With charities, the complications arise partly because we're trying to understanding their total effect on the world. It's not weird that that's complicated: what is weird is that when we analyse companies – the most influential machines on the planet – we ignore every single type of effect bar one, including the effects on the longevity, health and well-being of every single one of us[27].

This, ladies and gentlemen, is why we have an environmental problem – and hence most of the 'biggest problems facing humanity' we saw in Section 1. The environment doesn't belong to anybody, so it can't charge a factory for providing water nor fine a company which pollutes it. Companies' damage to the environment, and the environment's services to companies are invisible to the financial machine. As a result, water gets used up and the air gets polluted and so on as though that didn't matter. John Conant, director of the Center for Economic Education at Indiana State University, wrote recently that if we were really running out of trees, the price of trees would rise. It's patently not true for all environmental resources: the air doesn't belong to anybody so there's nobody to set a price or issue an invoice to polluters[28]. Collectively, we've created a giant machine blind to almost every effect on us. I could go on about this for a long time.

If we really tried to understand a company's total effect, the analysis would be similar to that for charities. There would be lots of factors which are tough to quantify, effects diffuse over many people and long time periods, lots of long causal chains, and plenty of ectopic effects.

Once you've seen the video:

Did you spot it?

About half of us miss the gorilla because we're distracted by counting catches. Amazing, isn't it? You probably thought your gorilla-noticing skills were pretty good. The experiment's creators, Christopher Chabris and Daniel Simons, think it reveals two things: 'that we are missing a lot of what goes on around us, and that we have no idea that we are missing so much.' Philosophers of science know this important phenomenon and say that observation is theory-laden: what we see is heavily influenced by we're expecting to see – catches, not ectopic apes. Simon and Garfunkel were only half right: not only is what we hear influenced by what we *want* to hear, but also by what we're *expecting* to hear.

It's important for donors and charities to know this. Suppose you have a programme to improve children's literacy. Children come, maybe with their parents,

---

27 Yes, some evaluations of companies do include environmental, social and governance issues as noted in Section 2. But even there, 'ESG' issues are often only considered as risk factors, i.e., only relevant *insofar as they affect financial performance.*

28 This is well articulated by the Dr Seuss book *The Lorax*. Amusing for children, who don't really understand it, it's terrifying for adults.

to an after-school club each week and volunteers help them with their reading. So you measure children's reading ability. Fantastic. What you're not expecting – and therefore don't notice – is that the parents' literacy is improving too; or maybe that the children's relationship with their parents is improving because they now have that time together; or maybe their health is better because they're not at home for that time eating junk; or less cheerily, maybe the parents have additional financial strain because they're having to buy child-care for their other children while they take one to literacy club. In the complex world in which charities operate, these ectopic results can be very significant. Let's go back to where we were, on page 195.

Chapter 17

Size, growth and mergers

In Section 2, we established that large charities are not consistently better than small ones, nor vice versa. Now we'll revisit the issues of size, and will see how neither size, growth, fragmentation nor mergers has the implications you might expect.

Sizes of charities: giants and dwarfs

The charity world is dominated by dwarfs. Of the 171,000 charities registered in England and Wales, about half have an annual income below £10,000. They're tiny.

To put that in context, a company counts as a 'small or medium enterprise' (SME) if its annual income is less than about £44m (it's defined as EUR 50m). That is to say, £44m is a useful cut-off when analysing companies because an appreciable number of them have income above that. But that cut-off would be hopeless for charities because hardly any are bigger than even a quarter of that: 99.5 per cent of charities have income below £10m.

Right at the top end, the UK's largest charity, the Wellcome Trust, spends £600m per year. By comparison, Marks & Spencer is 15 times greater, with annual revenue of £9,500m, and even that is nowhere near the biggest company nationally. (For example, BP's global annual income in 2010 was £308,928m.)

---

29 The domination of the big players is much more pronounced in many commercial industries. For example, in food retailing, the top five players in the US control about one-third of the market, and in the UK the figure is about 50%, in Germany 60% and France 90%. In soft drinks in the UK, the top five players have 65%. And in the market for auditing the largest listed 350 UK firms, the top four firms control about 99%.

Distribution of incomes of charities, England and Wales, 2007/8

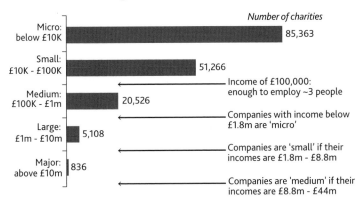

Number of charities

Micro: below £10K — 85,363

Small: £10K - £100K — 51,266

Medium: £100K - £1m — 20,526

Large: £1m - £10m — 5,108

Major: above £10m — 836

Income of £100,000: enough to employ ~3 people

Companies with income below £1.8m are 'micro'

Companies are 'small' if their incomes are £1.8m - £8.8m

Companies are 'medium' if their incomes are £8.8m - £44m

The money, however, is dominated by giants. About half the total income of the charity sector goes to just over 400 charities, with the biggest ten charities accounting for 8 per cent of the total income[29]. (They're listed in the appendices.) The other half is split amongst 170,500 organisations.

How the income is distributed among charities, England and Wales, 2007/8

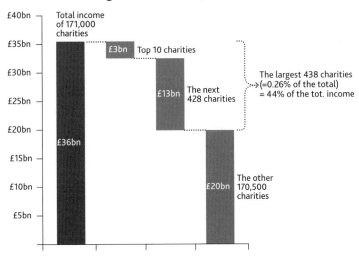

Total income of 171,000 charities — £36bn

£3bn — Top 10 charities

£13bn — The next 428 charities

The largest 438 charities (=0.26% of the total) = 44% of the tot. income

£20bn — The other 170,500 charities

Why are there so many charities, and why are so many of them small?

The UK has about 190,000 registered charities. People sometimes think that is a lot, but is it really? The UK has more than ten times that many companies.

There are a few reasons for the proliferation of small charities. First, charities tend to be 'service businesses' – running drop-in centres or training or breakfast clubs. These don't need large amounts of capital to get started, meaning that the barriers to entry are lower than in many commercial sectors: you and I could probably start a drop-in centre next month (leaving aside whether we'd be any good at it!) whereas we'd have a much harder time getting together the money to start a factory.

Secondly, because of the separation between donors and beneficiaries, charities which fail to serve their beneficiaries don't always get their money cut off in the way that companies which fail to serve their customers do. As one donor put it, 'there is no death in this sector'. That overstates it – charities can die – but the mechanism isn't as strong as in business which makes death rather rarer.

The third reason is all those volunteers. In the corporate world, if your operation requires 20 people, then you'd better pay 20 people. By contrast, it's perfectly normal for charities to have loads of volunteers – people beavering away but who don't need to be covered by revenue. So the revenue chart we saw earlier is deceptive: the fact that a charity only has enough revenue to employ three people indicates nothing about the number of people it needs to run its operations.

Shouldn't there be more mergers?

Possibly.

People often conclude from the fragmentation of the charity sector that charities should merge more. In fact, charities do merge as frequently as companies, according to a sizable study which looked at 3,400 charities in the US over 10 years. High-profile mergers in the UK include Imperial Cancer Research Fund joining with the Cancer Research Campaign in 2002 'out of a shared vision to cure cancer faster through closer collaboration and partnership'; Age Concern and Help the Aged merging into Age UK; and the two climate campaigns 350.org and 1SKY merging in early 2011. Partnering is also common but generally less visible than merging: The Sutton Trust and Impetus Trust are partnering to boost the educational attainment of disadvantaged children; the large aid agencies collaborate frequently (and not just around emergencies); and the 'the big five' children's charities (Barnardo's, The Children's Society, Action for Children (formerly NCH), NSPCC and Save the Children) also collaborate.

However, it's worth being cautious about mergers because they're hardly failsafe in the commercial world:

'Mergers have failure rates of more than 50%. One recent study found that
83% of all mergers fail to create value and half actually destroy value.'
– Robert W. Holthausen, Professor of Accounting and Finance and Management,
Wharton Business School, University of Pennsylvania

'Most [mergers] fail to add shareholder value – indeed, post-merger, two-thirds
of the newly formed companies perform well below the industry average.'
– Harvard Management Update

While we're on the subject of businesses, why are there so many banks, so many bike manufacturers, so many publishers? Wouldn't it be better if they all merged with each other? No. We know that customers generally get better service and price when companies compete and specialise. Both Aldi and Fortnum & Mason are grocers, and they both do well precisely because they are configured around the particular needs of their very different customer-bases. We're so convinced of the value of specialisation in businesses, and the dangers of domination, that we have specific legislation and a taxpayer-funded body to prevent excessive merging.

Broadly the same logic applies with charities. The 'customers' of charities may get better service at a better cost if charities specialise. Let's take the cancer 'industry' as an example. Cancer Research UK primarily works on medical research and providing information to the public. Macmillan Cancer Support provides care and support for cancer patients and their families at home. Maggie's Cancer Care Centres give advice and support to patients and anyone affected by cancer in specially-designed centres adjacent to hospitals. The Teenage Cancer Trust provides specialist care and units in hospitals for teenage inpatients (who don't feel comfortable in either adult or children's wards). There's no particular reason to think that an organisation which does amazing medical research is the one you want coming to your home in the middle of the night. Personally, when a member of my family was diagnosed with an unusual form of cancer, I was mighty thankful for the Rarer Cancers Foundation which had heard of this particular form, unlike the larger cancer charities I contacted first which have a broader focus and didn't know about it.[30]

There are real barriers to mergers which are peculiar to charities. The lack of personal incentives is one. Entrepreneurs who merge their businesses into bigger companies can get paid off very nicely, which offsets the loss of income or of a job. This doesn't happen in charities. It's legally difficult to provide a pay-off so one set of managers simply faces redundancy. This is nobody's fault, it's a consequence of charity law, but does disincentivise charity staff from pursuing mergers.

---

30 There are so many rare forms of cancer that although each affects only a small number of people, collectively many are affected. It's estimated that 30-50 per cent of all cancers are rarer forms.

Merging can also be unattractive to trustees. If a charity merges, the existing trustees may not be needed. Conversely, they may become trustees of a much larger organisation, involving more responsibility and/or more work than they want.

And then there's our old friend, the person who pays the piper, because he also inadvertently discourages mergers between charities. Many donors will only give a charity one grant at once. If my charity has a grant from a donor with this rule and yours doesn't, yours could apply for one if it remains on its own, but not if it merges with mine. That is, separate, we're eligible for two grants, but if we merge, we're only eligible for one, irrespective of the quality of our work and the value of the merger. (I have seen sensible mergers disintegrate for exactly this reason.) Even worse are some donors' insistence on supporting charities with revenue below a stated ceiling (as with the trust discussed in Section 3 will only support charities below £300,000). If two charities under that ceiling merge, they may well have combined revenue above the ceiling and therefore automatically forfeit their eligibility. When they're separate, the charities are eligible for two grants, but if they merge, they're eligible for none at all, again irrespective of the merit of their work or of the merger. These are further examples of selection criteria unrelated to effectiveness fail to encourage effectiveness.

The question of whether more charities should merge is often a question about charities' admin costs in disguise. Administrative costs, as amply discussed, are often a total red herring. Mergers between charities are desirable if – but only if – they improve impact.

Costs are a better indication of size than revenues are

When you're assessing a charity, its costs are a more reliable guide to its size than its revenues. Here's why. Costs relate to what the charity has been doing: the number of people it employs, the size of premises it needs to accommodate them, and its spending on medical research equipment or children's play equipment.

Revenue is separate from all this because it depends entirely on what donors do. Consider legacies. Suppose you're running a charity with annual revenue of about £200,000. One sunny day, you get a legacy of £200,000, bringing your revenue that year to £400,000. Your organisation hasn't instantaneously doubled in size, though its revenue has. For obvious reasons, legacies are hard to predict, as is income from fun-runs, people donating their bonuses, and unsolicited large gifts. Therefore charities' revenues can fluctuate independently of what's happening in the organisation itself. (This doesn't usually happen in companies because their revenue comes from their operations: they only increase their revenue by selling more or better cake.)

But even costs don't tell the whole story. For a start, they don't include the value of volunteers' time or donated goods, which can be highly significant.

They also indicate nothing about the size of the charity's impact. Changing Faces' website gives advice about dealing with facial disfigurements. Suppose there's a huge increase in people using the site and taking the advice. Great. That would substantially increase Changing Faces' impact, but it wouldn't affect its size, and wouldn't be at all evident from its financial statements. The same happens when charities move from delivering services themselves to teaching others how to do it (moving downwards on the triangle): the organisations themselves may not grow – they may even shrink – though their impact probably rises dramatically. If you're trying to understand impact, you need to look at impact: looking at income and costs are no substitute.

Lastly, shrinking may be a sign of success, which is counterintuitive. If we consider causes such as homelessness, deforestation, people-trafficking, drug abuse or polio, it's clear that many charities work on problems which we'd rather weren't there, and which they aim to eradicate. Their primary indicator of success is a falling number of 'cases' to deal with and, ultimately, being able to shut up shop and go home. Clearly this is the opposite of the corporate world, in which success is growth. Since we all have so much experience of companies, the 'growth is good' paradigm runs deep in us and we need to guard against applying it inappropriately to charities.

A disability charity supported people with a particular medical condition which impaired their mobility. Its revenue came largely from specialist hotels for people with this condition, and from fees people paid to join their local support group where they could meet other people with the condition.

Both types of revenue were falling.

Fantastic. They were falling because – happily – medical advances made living with this condition much easier, so sufferers no longer felt the need for mutual support, and new disability laws ensure that *all* hotels are adapted for people with impaired mobility.

Chapter 18

Charities and government

Charities often work in close proximity to government: in areas dominated by government, in areas where government has legal obligations, and in areas which you might believe ought to be government's responsibility. It's helpful to understand why they undertake that work.

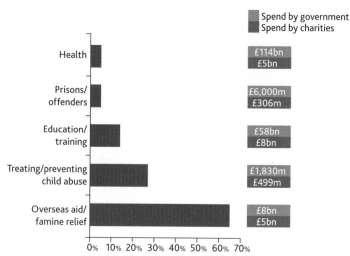

Charity spend as percentage of government spend for a sample of issues (UK)

Charities and non-profits play two basic roles relative to government. First, they deliver work which supplements the role of government. And second, they are often 'hired' by government to provide services which are statutory[31] responsibilities of national or local government.

Supplementing the government

Pioneering. Charities often play a pioneering role, identifying and meeting needs which later become the responsibility of government. In the UK, schools, hospitals and even fire brigades were first developed by private or charitable bodies. As the population saw the value of these services, legislation was brought in to make them available universally, funded by taxation.

> Teaching Leaders (which we mentioned in Section 3) was co-founded by Absolute Return for Kids using charitable money. Now that Teaching Leaders has developed and proven its model, it is being funded by government to scale up. It has received £8.9m from government to extend the programme into over 400 disadvantaged schools in the UK.

You may well be asked to support activity which you think should be the responsibility of government, but isn't – at least not yet. This has historically been an important role for charitable money. Lord (David) Sainsbury agrees with the point we saw about charitable money being 'the research and development arm of society': 'Private charitable foundations can try out things, take risks and move the agenda forward, in ways that is very difficult for government to do.'

> In China, 100m people carry the hepatitis B virus and suffer discrimination as a result: by one estimate, in 2011, 60 per cent of state-owned enterprises were requiring applicants for jobs to be tested for it. The Hong Kong-based ZeShan Foundation has been working to eliminate the disease. ZeShan began work in the Hainanzhou District in Qinghai Province, partnering with Stanford University's Asian Liver Center to vaccinate 56,000 children there during in 2007. It then enlisted other donors to expand the programme to the whole of Qinghai Province. The success of the programme helped prove the value and feasibility of vaccination against hepatitis B to the Chinese government, which it announced in 2009 that it would vaccinate all children under 15 across the country. Furthermore, in 2010 the Chinese government formally outlawed discrimination against people carrying the virus.

---

31 i.e., defined by statute, that is, law.

ZeShan Foundation is a lot smaller than Bill Gates' 'tiny, tiny little organization', yet has created giant impact – vaccinating all the 267m children in China currently and the others who will follow them. Pioneering, risk-taking and influencing larger organisations are powerful tools for donors to magnify their impact.

Making government deliver. A common role for charities is helping individuals to get the support to which they're entitled. The UK benefits system is notoriously complicated, and the charity IncomeMAX provides one-on-one support to help people navigate it. For every £1 spent on IncomeMAX's service, it can obtain £10 of extra income for low income customers, a pretty impressive 'return on investment' of 900 per cent.

Charities also help people obtain non-financial support. Independent Parental Special Education Advice works with local authorities and central government to ensure that children with special educational needs get the help to which they're entitled. The 'returns' on this work are also highly attractive: it costs £300 on average to take an appeal to tribunal, which typically secures support for the child worth an additional £3,000: coincidentally also a 900 per cent return.

The extra mile. In sectors such as health and education, charities often do work which goes beyond what the state can provide. Maggie's Cancer Caring Centres is an example. It provides practical and emotional help for anyone affected by cancer, in warm, welcoming and beautifully-designed centres adjacent to hospitals. The state provides the medical care, but charitable money allows Maggie's to provide information, support groups, benefits advice and courses on all aspects of living with cancer. For people nervous before or after appointments with doctors, Maggie's are friendly places, with sofas, a cup of tea and professional staff to talk with.

Where government doesn't help. Many noble and important activities have surprisingly little involvement from government. National monuments such as the Tower of London and Hampton Court Palace are managed entirely by Historic Royal Palaces, a charity which receives zero funds from either the government or the Crown. The 22 air ambulance services in England and Wales, which collectively undertake over 19,000 missions every year, pay for their helicopters, fuel, pilots and so on entirely from charitable donations – the NHS funds only the cost of the paramedic crews.

Lobbying to change laws and policies. We've seen several examples of voluntary action fuelled by donors' money which have prompted changes in the law. Examples include outlawing discrimination on the basis of physical disability, ending slavery in 1833 which is often cited as an iconic achievement of charitable activity, and the introduction in 1944 of school meals and milk in the UK following research and lobbying by Save the Children.

Though charities may (and do) campaign around particular laws which pertain to their charitable objects, they may not do overtly political work, such as supporting political campaigns or parties, or challenging entire governments. You can see the distinction in two organisations with quite similar aims set up by the same people. The Joseph Rowntree Reform Trust Ltd which funds 'political campaigns in the UK to promote democratic reform, civil liberties and social justice' is not a charity. By contrast, the Joseph Rowntree Foundation, which aims to 'understand the root causes of social problems, to identify ways of overcoming them, and to show how social needs can be met in practice' is a charity. During 2011, the Charity Commission took the rare step of ordering the closure of a charity because of political activity. It said that Atlantic Bridge, founded by (among others) Liam Fox MP, the now-former Defence Secretary, was 'promoting a political policy [that] is closely associated with the Conservative party...[and whose] activities have not furthered any of its other charitable purposes in any way'.

Delivering government obligations

Nearly three-quarters of the money which charities receive each year from government in all its guises (itself about a third of charities' total income) is payment for delivering services under contract. For example, the London Borough of Greenwich meets its obligation to provide leisure and sports facilities by buying services from Greenwich Leisure (a social enterprise). Similarly, government provides housing for people on low incomes: previously, this housing was built and maintained by local councils, whereas now much of it is outsourced under contract to independent non-profits such as housing associations and charities. There is vigorous debate about whether charities are better at providing these public services than government agencies.

This creates a complication for donors. If you're a UK tax-payer, you've already paid for these activities once, so paying for them again is a poor use of your charitable resources. However, it can be confusing because many charities which take on government contracts also do other work which isn't the responsibility of government and which therefore legitimately needs support from donors. Actually you can get round this complication by giving on an unrestricted basis: a good charity will have a decent cost-accounting system so that it knows the costs of its government work and doesn't inadvertently subsidise it with donors' money.

An aside related to the point about the separation between donors and beneficiaries. You might think that, when a charity provides a public service with funding from a government agency such as the NHS or local authority, the separation doesn't apply, because you might think that in those cases, charities compete for funding based solely on their ability to serve beneficiaries. I'd love to agree. In fact, the separation does still exist. The operation of running a leisure centre or supporting the terminally ill is pretty different from the operation of writing and winning government contracts, and therefore the money doesn't always follow the value, even here.

So charities working closely with government offer good uses for donors' money, such as doing work beyond the state's responsibility, and bad uses, such as for work already supposedly funded by taxes. There is also a recent innovation through which charities hope to improve government's ability to deliver.

Social impact bonds: an interesting recent development

Work done by charities often reduces the bill for government, and therefore for tax-payers. To take a simple example, helplines and websites run by health charities prevent many unnecessary and costly visits to hospitals. In a more complex example, savings can be made in the long-term by preventing young people truanting and being excluded from school: a child who is excluded from school will probably earn less than his or her peers and is more likely to commit offences. The costs in the criminal justice system and losses in income tax and contribution to the economy could be as high as £770,000 per individual. So should you support charities to prevent truanting since that may reduce the bill for government?

Until recently, it wasn't clear how a private donor should respond. On the one hand, this type of work can be attractively cost-effective. But on the other, perhaps government itself should invest to reduce its own future costs. However, governments don't often do that, for a range of understandable reasons: today's problems are prioritised over tomorrow's, preventative work is not certain to succeed, and preventative work often creates a bill for one governmental department but a saving for another. Many donors take a pragmatic view that the work won't happen without them so they get on with it.

Social Impact Bonds are a new mechanism through which individuals, grant-making foundations, companies and others fund work which should save the government money. If the work succeeds, some of the money saved is returned to the funders, repaying their investment and possibly more. The 'investors' take the risk and share in the upside.

The world's first Social Impact Bond was launched in the UK in September 2010. It focuses on reducing the number of prisoners (specifically male prisoners in Peterborough) who reoffend after they are released. Investors get their money back if re-offending falls by at least 7.5 per cent, and make money if reoffending falls by more than that.

When I wrote the first draft of this book, this was the sole Social Impact Bond in existence; now, a few months later, there are currently five in the UK with more planned, and there is considerable interest elsewhere. They can potentially succeed wherever work creates savings for the public purse fairly quickly and where results are readily attributable. They are not currently retail products.

Notice their relationship to the separation between funder and beneficiary. Social Impact Bonds are a way for investors to put their money into programmes which genuinely fix social problems and thereby do get the money to follow the value.

Chapter 19

The principles of good giving

Although this book has covered many issues and situations that arise in charitable giving, it can't cover them all. Before we finish, I want to equip you with the fundamental principles which will help with any decision you face in your giving. To my knowledge this is the first set of principles for charitable giving ever articulated, and I'm very interested in whether you find them helpful, complete and consistent.

These principles all flow from the core goal of **improving the world as much as possible**. Now, doesn't that sound blindingly obvious? Yes, but that doesn't matter because some unexpected advice follows from it and anyway, if improving the world really is our overriding goal, we'll do well to bear it in mind in all our charitable work.

Straight from that goal flow four principles. We'll examine them in turn.

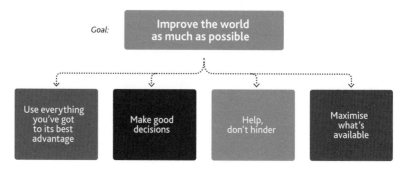

1. Use everything you've got, and to its best advantage

Improving the world is hard work, so we need to use everything available: talents, contacts, knowledge, cash, invested assets and passions. We've seen this principle in action when looking at how you can help charities by offering them use of meeting rooms or including them in orders with bulk discounts.

Furthermore, you want to use all of those resources to improve the world *as much as they can*. This principle gives rise to the advice to give without restrictions, which (among other benefits) builds skills within the charity. It also means finding where your skills are most valuable: for example, if you're a lawyer, you'd probably help a community centre more by streamlining its contracts than by painting a wall. Whether you work for an investment bank or a shoe-repair company, you have unique skills, opportunities and expertise to improve the world, and these will add more value than generic or cheaper skills.

Another important resource you have now is an ability to assess charities. You can use that to best advantage by recommending good charities you find to other donors. If you're giving a lot, that means making public the list of charities you support and your rationale in order that others can use it. If you are a charity, it means publishing your learnings and research in enough detail that others can use them.

How can this principle help in situations not covered in this book? Suppose you work for an aid agency and are charged with buying equipment to use in a less developed country. This principle will help. It implies that it's better to purchase equipment from in-country providers wherever possible because that builds skills, jobs and infrastructure in-country. This way, the procurement budget supports the charity's aims better than would buying from first world providers miles away.

Other implications of this principle are shown overleaf:

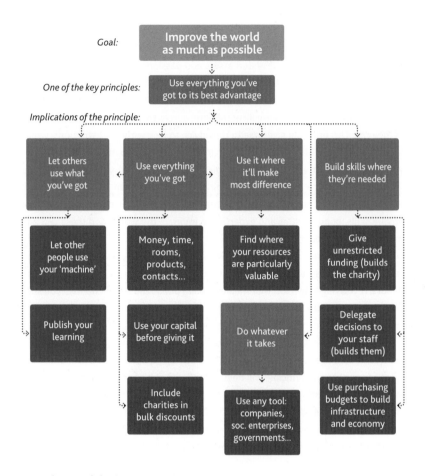

2. Make good decisions

The most obvious implication here is to find high-performing organisations (and yes, that is at the expense of lower-performing ones). Hence the advice in Section 2 that people in a rush follow somebody else reliable, such as J-PAL or a Community Foundation or The Funding Network. And hence too the suggestion of checking for research into whether a charity's approach has previously proven effective.

Right at the beginning we talked about the need to get proactive, and that was driven by this principle. The best options – complete with a valid control, good randomisation and statistically significant sample size – are unlikely to walk up to you in the street and so you need to go looking for them.

This principle also ties together other advice about finding good charities, such as focusing on merit rather than location, size, or spend on admin or fundraising. It was behind the advice to support strong organisations on a repeated basis: the instinct of some donors to 'spread the love' by continually moving their support around in-troduces a selection criterion ('Have I supported you before?') which is unrelated to effectiveness.

You will also make better decisions – about what to support and also how to sup-port it – by understanding the problem you're trying to solve. Hence the need to fo-cus, since it's clearly easier to understand a few problems than to understand many. This principle explains why partnering is a good idea: by partnering with the Prince's Trust, Cheryl Cole's foundation will learn to make good decisions more rapidly than if it were learning by itself.

Again, this principle has further implications for major donors. For instance, it shows why a process of waiting for applications may not be the best: there's zero guarantee that the best candidates will find you, so it may not enable decisions which reward merit.

OK, here's a little test.

> You notice a newspaper advert for a new foundation set up by elite athletes which is soliciting donations for a set of charities. What questions spring to mind?

One of the first questions is whether they have made good decisions about charities to support. After all, being a great hurdler or weight-lifter doesn't qualify somebody to assess social needs and charities' effectiveness. So I'd look for whether they've ar-ticulated the rationale for their choice of charities, and whether I agreed with it. And second, I'd wonder whether this is using the athletes' resources in the *best* way possi-ble. It's using their fame, which is great, but perhaps they could also use their ability to draw a crowd. Roger Federer did this after the Haiti earthquake: 'I had the idea that we could do something to help Haiti after the tragic earthquake. So I spoke to some other top players ... I have some connections.' What emerged was Hit for Haiti, a fundrais-ing tennis event the day before the Australian Open in 2010, which raised £114,000 in addition to the amounts various players had pledged already.

Another little test. What do you notice about this situation?

> A large family set up a foundation to work on three areas: sustainable devel-opment, cancer and higher education. Within the family were people who had worked in and around sustainable development for a while, and they also knew lots of people who had worked extensively in education. So they easily recruited trustees with expertise in those fields.

We've not talked much about the team which foundations need. But we can now see that this foundation can't yet reliably make good decisions unless it adds some people knowledgeable about cancer. (I know it sounds obvious, but this example is based on a real situation in which the board hadn't noticed this gap.) While we're on the subject of teams, for the same reason it's a good idea for large donors to include 'users' of relevant services, such as hospice patients and/or their relatives, in their boards and/or decision-making processes. Foundations often rely on friends and family, but omit people who know how charities work, who they need if they are to make consistently good decisions. A good move is to include somebody who really understands statistics, since charities' results often involves them and they can be vastly misleading. (For example, two hospices have very different incidences of accidents. Maybe one is very dangerous, or maybe the difference is just a statistical quirk related to its size).

Other implications of this principle include:

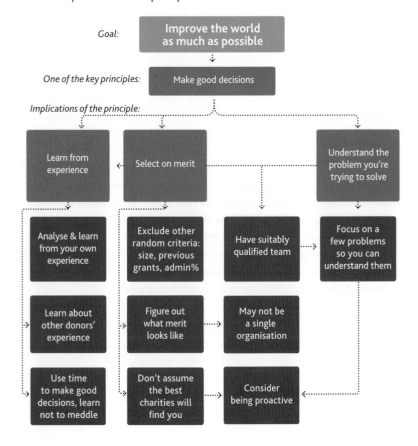

3. Maximise the amount available

One implication of this principle is that it's often better to make a few large gifts rather than several smaller ones because this creates less waste in the actual cash transfer process. Similarly, making repeat donations frees up your time (no need to do a whole new set of analysis), so you can get on with helping. This principle was behind the guidance that if you're making a bequest or other big gift, tell the charity in advance because it can then plan and may be able to use your gift to persuade somebody else to support it too.

This principle ties together the example of Fred Mulder averting a dispute with his neighbours and thereby making available money which nobody had allocated for charity with the discussion about investing money in charities and social enterprises before you give it away. Both make more money available for improving the world.

Excessive application forms and reporting requirements contravene this principle by reducing the amount available for a charity's important work (they reduce the 'net grant'). Hence there is a standard form in the appendices. This principle is helpful in situations like the following:

> Congratulations on your new job. You're now running a medium-sized foundation which is the sole funder of a programme run by an established charity to create jobs for the rural poor in part of Latin America. Your foundation has agreed quite a 'light-touch' template for the charity to report on its progress, which is appropriate for this particular situation.
>
> The charity now tells you that it's secured additional funding for that programme from a (non-UK) government agency. Great. The agency requires quite complicated reports at different times to the ones for your foundation. What do you do?

Based on this principle, the (real-life) foundation on which this example is based decided to slot in alongside the new funder. It agreed to receive the reports which the charity created for the government agency rather than having the charity collect two sets of data and produce two sets of reports – because this would have wasted a load of money, reducing the amount available for the work in Latin America. (I know this too sounds obvious, but this foundation's sensible behaviour is actually pretty unusual.)

Ensuring that resources are available for 'real' work rather than duplicating existing infrastructure is why Eurostar partnered with the already-established Ashden Awards when it was setting up a new charitable programme. And it's why we applaud BBC Children in Need for going out of its way to reduce the unsuccessful applications through increasingly clear guidelines.

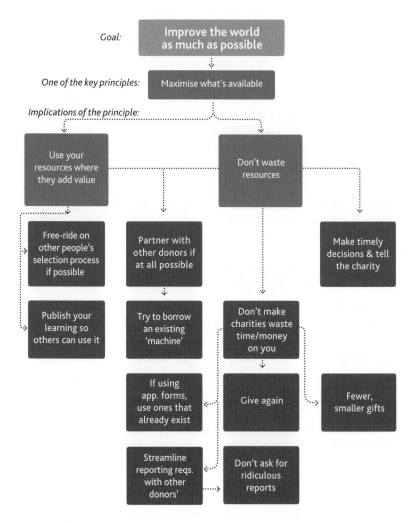

4. Help, don't hinder

Restricting your gift is a good way of hindering because it prevents a charity's management making decisions and being flexible, so this principle was behind the advice to avoid doing that.

It's from this principle that we see the importance of asking whether your 'help' is actually helping. Do they really want Pop-Tarts® raining down from the sky? Because the charity is unlikely to tell its donors, it's better still to get somebody independent to ask on your behalf in the way that the Grantee Perception Report does. (This will also help you make good decisions.)

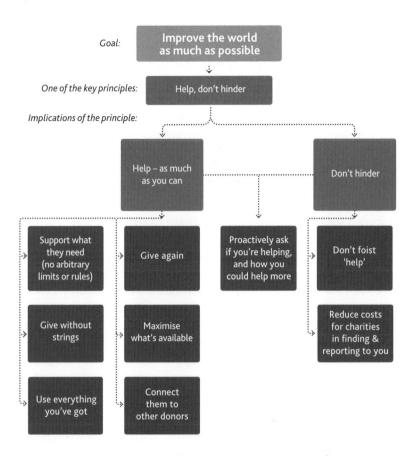

Remember the question of whether it's a good idea to give anonymously? We resolved that by reference to this principle: be covert if association with you would be a hindrance, but overt if your name would be helpful. 'Everything you've got' may include your ability to inspire and motivate others.

Let's pull all these principles together, and see how they help in some other situations.

You've joined The Funding Network in your area and got to know a few other people who give and representatives from a few charities. Great. But now someone from your son's school gets in touch because they know you know a bit about charities. The school wants some of its students to do some community service and is asking for your help in finding a suitable charity. How do these principles guide you?

One option is to call some charities whose recent applications to The Funding Network you've just read to see whether they'd like the help. Bad idea. The Funding Network primarily provides money so these charities are probably mainly interested in money. They may see your approach as an opportunity to build a relationship which may lead to money – thus they may say yes, even if they don't need the help. Therefore the help may not achieve as much as it might elsewhere, and those charities will let you hinder them quite a bit without complaining.

A better approach is this. First, figure out what you've got to deploy: how many children, staff, parents, how much time, when, and whether there's any money, equipment or other stuff coming too. Then you want to find some good charities (using the principle of making good selections) and to do so with minimal effort for yourself and for them (in accordance with the principle of minimising waste). So look for an existing 'machine' for matching volunteers to opportunities: perhaps other schools or the Scouts have ways of using volunteers, or you can find something through www.do-it.org. The local Community Foundation may know of opportunities – and since it will already be known to lots of charities, it may get a more honest sense of what they really need than you could. Next, using the principle of helping as much as possible, you want to assess where your resources will be *most* valuable. Check that the charities aren't just agreeing to all this because they're polite but they can actually really use the help. And finally, to avoid making them spend time or money on you, offer to reimburse any costs they may incur (such as additional insurance or teas). Here's another situation:

> Suppose you've just inherited or won £20m which you want to give to charity. Do you give it in your own lifetime, or set it up as an endowment in perpetuity? (In the US, foundations must give at least of 5 per cent of their assets each year and some other countries have similar rules – though the question of whether to give more than that still stands.)

The principles make pretty clear that you should give it relatively rapidly. We'll take here only two of the numerous arguments which point that way. First, it makes more money available, because the money is managed over fewer years. At a minimum, the endowment would have to be managed to ensure that returns exceed inflation to avoid the capital value declining, which is not always trivial. John Bothamley, founder of the Four Acre Trust noticed that the Trust was receiving income of around 5 per cent of its capital, and paying 1 per cent in management fees. It was therefore spending 20 per cent of its income on fees. 'It just seemed to me that this was a big chunk of income that wasn't actually doing any good.' Consequently, the Trust decided to 'spend out' (disburse its resources and then wind up), giving itself ten years to do so. Secondly, giving relatively rapidly probably produces better decisions. An endowed foundation is immortal and well-capitalised, with no incentive to perform. 'I think over time it would cease... taking forward change, bringing about improvements, taking risks', says Lord (David) Sainsbury, about why his Gatsby Charitable Trust is giving the bulk of its £1 billion during his lifetime.

Now imagine that your employer asks you to structure a programme to support domestic violence charities in towns where it operates. Should you ask those charities what they need? Yes, say the principles, because their knowledge will enable you to make better decisions, but not in such a way or in such laborious detail that your asking hinders them.

Consider whether and how a charity should involve beneficiaries in planning its work. On one hand, this will help to ensure good decisions by bringing them into the feedback loop; but on the other hand, involving too many beneficiaries will be a pain to coordinate and waste resources. So what's the right number? Where the principles present a trade-off, as in this case, look for the balance which maximises the improvement to the world.

Similarly, the robustness of charities' data can present a trade-off. On one hand, getting robust data improves decisions. But on the other hand, it takes time and effort, and thus reduces the resources available for the 'real' work itself. Where's the balance? (This applies to donors choosing between charities, but also to charities allocating resources between their own programmes and between potential new programmes.) Well, at a minimum, get data which show whether a programme creates harm: given that that is perfectly possible, we shouldn't commit a dime before establishing this. Beyond that, again, look for the balance which will maximise the improvement to the world. If the theory of change has already been proven in very similar circumstances, and evaluating it in these particular circumstances would be expensive, perhaps a new evaluation would be more wasteful than instructive. However, if it hasn't and the lessons of a new evaluation could be widely used, perhaps the evaluation's insights would have greater impact than would the additional implementation which that money could otherwise enable.

And finally, suppose that your daughter comes home from secondary school one day saying that they're participating in a giving programme and are asked to vote for charities to support. She and her friends are thinking of choosing some small charities and some local ones, because those are the same decisions as they see adults making. Well, are those adult decisions? Moreover, are they *good* decisions?

I hope that you now understand why giving effectively is too tough a game to just copy other people. I hope too that you can explain some rather better ways to choose charities, and know some tricks which will amplify the effect of their money, as well as other ways in which they can help and how they can avoid hindering.

I began this book in Hope. Literally: I was staying in the beautiful Derbyshire village of that poetic name when I had the idea to write. And I end it in hope – hope that has given you some ideas and inspiration and impetus, and hope that you will use *all* your resources, not just to do 'something' but to do everything that they can. To bring the children in from the fields, to pull more ship-wrecked people from the sea, to enrich our cultural life, to make our world safer.

I hope too that you have a great time in your giving, that you're achieving the goals you set and that people applaud your efforts as you go along. But in case nobody else says so – because you're keeping a low profile, or doing preventative work which nobody sees, or are doing work which will take ages to bear fruit – let me say here, on behalf of the human race:

Heartfelt thanks

Good luck. Stay in touch: www.giving-evidence.com

Appendices

1. Who does what in the charity world

Ownership, regulation and governance
Ownership. Charities aren't owned by anybody and therefore cannot have shareholders. A charity receives and uses resources for pursuing what are called its 'charitable objects'. These define the remit within which, by law, it must remain, and are stated publicly in the charity's governing document. The law defines certain areas as suitable for charitable work (e.g., sport, religion, education, health) and excludes other areas, notably party political activity.

Charities are regulated: by the **Charity Commission** in England and Wales, the Office of the Scottish Charity Regulator or the Charity Commission for Northern Ireland. Many other countries have similar regulators but not all: for instance, Singapore does but, at the time of writing, Hong Kong doesn't yet. These monitor against fraud and ensure that charities are operating wholly within their objects. Registered charities must abide by the regulator's rules about transparency, governance and reporting, and the regulator holds and publishes charities' accounts, lists of trustees and other basic data. New charities apply for registration, and changing objects or working outside objects requires the regulator's approval. (Social enterprises which are incorporated as Community Interest Companies are regulated: see 'Definitions' for details.)

Charities with annual income below £5,000 do not have to register with the regulator. This includes surprisingly many charities, which survive despite their financial smallness because they are run by volunteers.

The regulator does not monitor charities' effectiveness, just as Companies' House doesn't opine on the quality of a company's products or its financial performance. Hence the need for donors to do this themselves.

Charities exempt from registering. Certain genuine charities are exempt from registration and supervision by the charity regulator because they are considered adequately supervised by another authority. They therefore don't have registered charity numbers and normally cite that they are 'an exempt charity'. They include various museums (e.g., the Victoria and Albert Museum, the Science Museum, the Armouries), various universities (e.g., Bristol, Liverpool, Cambridge), housing associations and organisations which are Industrial and Provident Societies. Check with the Charity Commission or other regulator if in doubt.

Tax breaks are available to any charity, effectively in return for abiding by the regulator's rules and meeting its standards of transparency. They include: exemption from corporation tax (i.e., charities can take unspent revenue from one year to the next without penalty), sometimes exemption from rates, ability to reclaim income tax on gifts from individuals. Charities are sadly not exempt from VAT – which costs them over £1 billion per year.

The tax-payer therefore subsidises all of this. For example, if a charity claims Gift Aid on your donation it gets the income tax which you would have paid if you'd kept the money, so in effect, all the nation's tax-payers chip in. Foundations get other tax relief such as not paying corporation tax. Since part of the money which a donor gives isn't his, surely this amplifies his duty to use it well.

Politics. Charities may not do overtly political work. They are free to campaign around particular laws which pertain to their charitable objects which can be very valuable as in the examples we've seen. But they may not support political campaigns or parties or challenge entire governments.

People
Trustees collectively comprise a charity's board, and are legally responsible for ensuring that it uses its resources solely in pursuit of its objects. For the purposes of law, trustees are normally the charity's directors. By law, they cannot benefit financially from being trustees and are therefore unpaid. This has the rather odd consequence that the charity's Chief Executive, if paid, cannot be a trustee and therefore can't be board member. (By contrast, corporate CEOs are almost invariably directors of their companies and belong to the board.) Normally, the Chief Executive attends board meetings, as often do other senior staff. There are examples of charity boards who routinely meet without their Chief Executive: this is as bonkers for charities as it would be anywhere else.

Trustees are listed publicly. They have no obligation to give money to the charity of which they're trustees, though many do. Charity boards often have subcommittees, similar to those of corporate boards, for example, for finance, campaigns, foreign operations.

Staff are generally paid. Charities of significant size and complexity normally have a Chief Executive (who might be called CEO, Chief of Staff, or Managing Director or Executive Director, despite not legally being a director) who reports to the board through the Chair. The board can delegate virtually any responsibility to the CEO: best practice is to have a written Delegation Agreement.

Staff are paid whatever it takes to attract and retain them. Though research indicates that sometimes charity salaries sound high, they're often lower than equivalent roles elsewhere, that is, staff sacrifice some income in order to work on an issue they're passionate about. Panahpur, a family trust which has been working with charities in the UK for over a century:

> 'Our experience is that, by and large, people who work for charities are not paid an appropriate salary for the responsibility that they take or the skills that they bring to the job. It is not uncommon for someone expected to take senior management responsibilities, live in London and raise a family to be being paid less than quarter of what they might get in the state or corporate sectors. Often it is not really a viable wage.'

There is sometimes a notion that charity staff should all be volunteers in order to save money. How they are supposed to live is not clear! And since charities and their staff add value, minimising the money spent on them may be a false economy.

Fundraisers are sometimes employed by the charity and other times employed by specialist agencies, hired by charities. The tabard-wearing chuggers in the street and door-to-door fundraisers normally work for agencies. They work (partly) on commission to incentivise them to recruit donors who will give over a long period.

Volunteers are hugely important in augmenting the workforce in many charities. Roles vary widely: working as paramedics for St John Ambulance; stuffing envelopes; giving strategic advice; serving in the cathedral book shop. (All trustees are volunteers, since they're unpaid.)

Though by definition volunteers are not paid, there are normally costs associated with them, such as recruitment, reimbursement of travel and other expenses, and they may need resources like computers or uniforms. The RSPB, for example, spends over £500,000 managing its volunteers.

Some charities are entirely run by volunteers; others have staff.

2. Definitions

> *'It doesn't much matter what people call things, it's what they do.'*
> – Sir Ronald Cohen

Bequest. Gift of money or object(s) made in a person's Will (discussed in Section 2).

Charity. An organisation with purposes recognised in law as charitable (only a certain set of purposes is admissible) and registered with the relevant regulator (see 'Who does what').

Community Interest Companies. A legal form created for social enterprises and used by some of them. They allow for Directors (including founders) to be paid whilst also being board members (disallowed in charities), have an 'asset lock' to ensure that assets are retained for serving the CIC's social/environmental purposes. CICs do not enjoy all the tax benefits available to charities. They are regulated by the Office of the Regulator of Community Interest Companies (www.bis.gov.uk/cicregulator/about-us) and a list of CICs is at www.bis.gov.uk/cicregulator/cic-register

Donor. Used in this book to mean any person or organisation who/which is actively supporting charitable work – irrespective of whether they give money and/or other resources, and of whether they support other organisations or undertake activities themselves. The term 'funder' is reserved for people or organisations providing solely money.

Earned income. Some charities earn income by selling products and services. Revenue from charity shops normally counts as earned income, as do museum entrance fees. Many charities run training courses which carry a charge such as the (very good) facilitation training by the Environment Council. Income from government contracts can count as earned income.

Effectiveness. The charity's ability to make a difference. Note that this is often totally independent of efficiency and should not be mistaken for it. This book uses 'effect', 'results' and 'impact' interchangeably.

Endowment. If you sell your house and use the proceeds to set up a charitable foundation, you have endowed that foundation. If the intention is that the foundation does not spend the capital but rather invests it and donates just the investment returns, then the foundation has a 'permanent endowment'. If you instruct the foundation to spend the capital over some period (say, 20 years), it has an expendible endowment. Similarly if you give money to a university to generate income to fund a professorship, you have endowed that professorship.

Federations. The Age Concern which supports older people near your home – which since Age Concern merged with Help the Aged may now be called Age UK – is probably one of more than 300 free-standing charities within the Age UK federation.

They have common branding, activities and objectives but the independence enables each organisation to respond rapidly to local circumstances. It's a relatively common structure: other federations include Women's Aid (working on domestic violence), MIND (mental health), Relate (relationship support). Normally in federations, donors can give to a local branch or to the national body.

Grant. A financial donation. Normally used to refer to donations which are large and/or from grant-making foundations.

Grantee. An organisation in receipt of a grant.

Grant-making foundation / grant-making trust. A charitable organisation which gives grants, i.e., which achieves its charitable objectives by supporting other ('operating' or 'operational') charities. Many grant-making foundations are endowed and many give solely money, though increasingly many offer other types of support. This book uses 'foundation' and 'trust' interchangeably.

Impact investing: see social investment.

Intended impact. A charity's goal. Normally used in relation to theory of change, this is synonymous with objective or goal ('the theory of how to achieve the intended impact').

Non-governmental organisation (NGO). Normally used synonymously with non-profit (see below), though sometimes used more specifically to mean 'non-profit which works on development issues', i.e., in less developed countries. (Oddly the term is almost never used literally – in which it would mean anything which isn't government. One never hears Exxon described as an NGO.)

Non-profit. An organisation which does not distribute profits to shareholders. The term includes charities and some social enterprises, as well as many universities, museums, political parties and schools.

Philanthrocapitalism. Applying tools and principles from capitalism to philanthropy. A 'philanthrocapitalist' (a donor who uses these tools and principles) might look for high 'returns' (that is, high impact), monitor recipient organisations, be highly engaged in charities (just as venture capitalists are highly involved in companies in which they invest), make funding conditional upon performance. These tools and principles work well sometimes but not always. We've seen many fundamental differences between business and charity, corollaries of which include that capitalism would rarely applaud (or reward) a company shrinking or seeking its own obsolescence, though this can be highly appropriate for charities. The term was coined by *The Economist*, specifically the journalist Matthew Bishop, who later co-authored a book of this name with Michael Green, about the practices of new, major and often famous donors.

Philanthropy. From the Latin meaning 'love of people', philanthropy is usually taken to mean giving to charities – and not just to charities which support people, but also charities which work on the natural environment, built environment, religion, animals and so on. Though normally applied to giving money, the term is sometimes applied to giving other resources such as time or contacts. It is sometimes applied more broadly still, to include supporting any activity with a social or environmental purpose, such as supporting social enterprises or government, or campaigning. This book uses the terms 'charitable giving' or 'giving to charity' where others might use 'philanthropy'.

Social enterprise. A company which has explicit social and/or environmental goals in addition to financial goals. Social enterprises normally create social and/or environmental value through their business model, e.g., employing ex-prisoners, creating demand for fairtrade products, being employee-owned, creating products which are more environmentally-friendly than their competitors. Some are Community Interest Companies (see above). (Under some definitions, John Lewis Partnership classes as a social enterprise because it is employee owned.)

Socially-responsible investment / ethical investment. Investing on a for-profit basis using criteria around the investee's performance on social and environment issues and governance ('ESG criteria'). Normally taken to mean investing in mainstream assets such as stocks, bonds, shares.

Social investment / mission-related investment / programme-related investment/ impact investing. Putting money into businesses primarily to advance the donor's charitable objectives. For example, lending to social enterprises such as fair trade companies. Can include investing via debt or quasi-equity in charities' income-generating activities, such as shops.

Theory of change. The logical model about how the charity achieves its objective. For example, running a breakfast club represents one theory of change about improving educational attainment of primary school children in disadvantaged areas, because children who arrive hungry having had no breakfast are in no state to learn. Alternative theories of change include improving teaching techniques, supporting parents, or re-designing the curriculum. Discussed in detail in Section 1.

Umbrella groups. These support charities in a particular sector, in a particular region, or across the board. For example, Help the Hospices provides support for hospices, including advice, some funding, and championing in Whitehall. The Friends of Cathedral Music supports music in Anglican and Roman Catholic cathedrals through funding scholarships, supporting choir schools and increasing public awareness of church music.

VONNE (Voluntary Organisations Network North East) is an example of a regional umbrella body, supporting charities undertaking any type of work in England's North East with information, networking, advice and co-ordinating responses, e.g., to government proposals.

Support for the whole charity sector includes the National Council of Voluntary Organisations and membership bodies for various disciplines, such as the Association of Chief Executives of Voluntary Organisations, the Charity Finance Directors' Group and the Institute of Fundraising. Other organisations work to improve, study or resource the whole charity sector, such as nfpSynergy, a research consultancy, Charity Technology Trust and the Media Trust which helps charities communicate through media, and various university departments focus on charities and philanthropy.

Venture philanthropy. 'Venture philanthropy describes an activity that brings business approaches to achieve scale and sustainability to philanthropic service providers – which I find a useful definition,' says Sir Ronald Cohen, who practically invented venture capital in the UK and is now an active donor:

'I am not just being philanthropic in the sense of giving money away, I am investing time and effort in making sure that organisations actually develop scale and sustainability and social impact. In that sense the inspiration of venture philanthropy is indeed very deeply rooted in the hands-on approach of venture capitalists.'

Like venture capitalists, venture philanthropists often raise funds which they use to support several non-profits with high impact and high potential for growth. Though the term came to prominence with the considerable money entering the charity world from the dot.com entrepreneurs in the late 1990s, the practice is much older: Oxfam, for instance was borne of a grant-making foundation which invested time, effort and other resource to ensure its sustainability.

Voluntary organisations. Any organisation whose board is unpaid. Notice that this does not require that all staff are voluntary. It includes therefore: charities; some clubs, societies, faith groups, sports groups, private schools, co-operatives, mutuals, trade unions, social enterprises, industry membership bodies and universities. Many voluntary organisations are unincorporated. Voluntary organisations may depend on donations, in whole or in part.

3. The Fundraising Promise

The Fundraising Promise is a voluntary commitment which charities can make to the public. It is based on six key pledges around honesty, accountability and transparency, and is managed by the Fundraising Standards Board (FRSB), the self-regulatory body for fundraising in the UK. Charities pledge that:

We Are Committed to High Standards

We do all we can to ensure that fundraisers, volunteers and fundraising contractors working with us to raise funds comply with the Codes and with this Promise.

We comply with the law including those that apply to data protection, health and safety and the environment.

We Are Honest and Open

We tell the truth and do not exaggerate.

We do what we say we are going to do.

We answer all reasonable questions about our fundraising activities and costs.

We Are Clear

We are clear about who we are, what we do and how your gift is used.

Where we have a promotional agreement with a commercial company, we make clear how much of the purchase price we receive.

We give a clear explanation of how you can make a gift and amend a regular commitment.

We Are Respectful

We respect the rights, dignities and privacy of our supporters and beneficiaries.

We will not put undue pressure on you to make a gift and if you do not want to give or wish to cease giving, we will respect your decision.

If you tell us that you don't want us to contact you in a particular way we will not do so.

We Are Fair and Reasonable

We take care not to use any images or words that cause unjustifiable distress or offence.

We take care not to cause unreasonable nuisance or disruption.

We Are Accountable

If you are unhappy with anything we've done whilst fundraising, you can contact us to make a complaint. We have a complaints procedure, a copy of which is available on request. If we cannot resolve your complaint, we accept the authority of the Fundraising Standards Board to make a final adjudication.

4. The 10 largest voluntary organisations in the UK by total expenditure, 2007/08

Charity	Revenue	Area
Wellcome Trust	£597m	Medical research. Endowed
Cancer Research UK	£476m	Medical research
National Trust*	£351m	'Places of historic interest or natural beauty'
Gavi Fund Affiliate	£304m	Global health. ('GAVI' is the Global Alliance for Vaccines and Immunisation. It set up the International Finance Facility for Immunisation (IFFIm) and benefits from the bonds described in Section 3)
Oxfam	£298m	International development
The British Red Cross	£234m	Helping people in crisis
Barnardo's	£205m	Children in the UK
Action for Children	£200m	Children in the UK (formerly NCH, National Children's Homes)
British Heart Foundation	£195m	Medical research, information, campaigning and care
UFI Charitable Trust	£183m	Makes grants in education. The UFI Charitable Trust owns Ufi Ltd, which runs learndirect which delivers online adult learning

*This figure is for the National Trust, which operates in England, Wales and Northern Ireland. The National Trust for Scotland is a separate organisation, whose income in 2008 was £44m. The extent of the National Trust's clout is clear from the fact that its membership is seven times bigger than the combined membership of all political parties. See chart overleaf.

Membership of National Trust and political parties

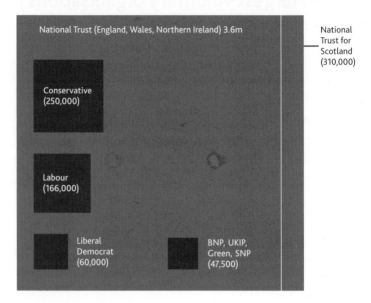

5. Sample application form

For donors giving a lot, asking organisations to make an application is only one mechanism to find them. Appropriate in some circumstances, this mechanism is highly inappropriate and/or wasteful sometimes, as discussed in Section 3.

If you do ask organisations to apply to you, please minimise the work created for them. You can do this by:

- using the form overleaf (which you can download from www.giving-evidence. com)
- being willing to accept any application the charity has previously written for any other donor, thereby creating zero new work for them
- accepting applications in any format, including video or audio files
- being very clear about what you will and won't support in order to reduce unfruitful applications, and/or
- teaming up with other donors to avoid duplication in the 'selection' processes

The form opposite is based on the six questions which any charity should be able to answer, and the Standard Information Return which is required of charities in England and Wales with income above £1m.

Basic information

Organisation's name	
Registered charity number (if applicable)	
Website	
Incorporation date	
Address	
Contact details	

Please provide 1-2 pages explaining the following:

Aims and work
- What is the problem you are trying to solve?
- What activities does the organisation do?
- What do those activities achieve, i.e., how do they help solve the problem, and who benefits from your charity's work?
- What is the evidence on which the charity's work is based?

Partnerships, collaboration
- Explain any partnerships or collaborative working. How do you endeavour to reduce duplication, and to learn from other organisation's learning?

Finances
- Revenue and costs for the last three years, and reserves at the end of each of the last three years (just attach your Annual Report and Accounts if you have them).
- How would you describe your charity's financial health?

Management and governance
- By whom is the organisation managed?
- What is the governance structure?
- Please provide biographies for the board and senior managers
- How does your charity ensure that its governance arrangements are appropriate and effective?

Results
- How do you find out what you are achieving? (What is the research process?)
- What are you achieving, i.e., what evidence is there that the intended beneficiaries do/will benefit from your work?
- How are you learning and improving? What examples do you have of learning and improving? What are the key elements of your charity's medium- to long-term strategy? How will your performance last year affect your charity's medium- to long-term strategy?
- What are your charity's main objectives for next year?

6. Calculating the costs you're creating

I suggest doing these calculations periodically (say, every two years) if you are operating by supporting other organisations.

i) Calculating the cost that you create for other organisations

There are two pieces to this. First, the costs created before giving a grant (through you and the organisation finding each other) and second, the costs once the grant is 'in play'.

Cost pre-grant (A)

Cost which each organisation incurs in finding you*	+	Cost which each organisation incurs in applying: your application form, meeting with you, presenting, chasing to find out about progress	x	Number of organisations which apply to you each year	= Total cost pre-grant (A)

Cost post-grant (B)

Cost which each organisation incurs in reporting to you/ being monitored by you	x	Number of organisations which report to you each year	= Total cost post-grant (B)

Total cost which you create (C)

Total costs pre-grant (A)	+	Total cost post-grant (B)	=	Total cost which you create for other organisations (C). This should fall over time

*Note that you will need to ask some of the organisations you support for this data: for their estimate of the time it took them to find you, to go through your application process, and which they spend with you once you are supporting them. I strongly recommend that you also ask some of the organisations which you declined to support: they are perhaps more likely to give you an accurate answer about the time spent applying to you than are those who you do support.

ii) Calculating whether you are adding or detracting money from the charity sector

Write down the amount that you give. If you're giving cash, this is straightforward. If you're giving non-financial help (and/or cash) then estimate a value for that and add it in.

Then calculate the costs of your own operation: all the costs of staff/freelancers/contractors, office, IT, back-office, recruiting and supporting trustees and volunteers (travel, insurance etc.), attracting applications (e.g., listings in relevant catalogues), running your websites and other communications, accountancy, lawyers' fees, fund managers' fees, and so on.

Then compare the amount that you're giving with the amount that you're consuming:

Total cost which you create for organisations (C)	+	Cost consumed in your own operation	vs.	Total amount that you give

Continued overleaf.

Summary of how to reduce costs you create
A) Pre-grant:

Cost which each organisation incurs in finding you	+	Cost which each organisation incurs in applying: your application form, meeting with you, presenting, chasing to find out about progress	x	Number of organisations which apply to you
Be findable. Use networks e.g., other donors already active in your area, be listed in the grant lists, be findable online (have good search engine optimisation), use social networks. Have an open process. Don't make people have to get to know you and become your friend – which takes ages		Make it quick and easy. Best is to enable applying organisations to reuse application forms they've already created – incurring zero marginal work (i.e., cost), e.g., allow them to send you a form which they've already created and sent to another funder. Make sure that the only bespoke work the organisations do for you is around specific information you need. Have a staged process: only ask for more information as it becomes more likely that you will support the organisation		Cut the number of unsuccessful applications by being very clear about what you do and don't support

B) Post-grant

See whether the organisation really needs to do any bespoke work for you. It may already be reporting for other donors, in which case you can just have that data and thus create zero marginal work. If you're funding on an unrestricted basis (as recommended), this is likely.

If it's not reporting to anybody in precisely the same way or on the same timescale as you would like, see whether you can co-ordinate with another donor and get one set of reports between you. Hurrah.

Acknowledgements

This book owes much to the many organisations and individuals with whom I've been privileged to work and who have generously shared their time, data and experience since I began writing. Errors in the book are entirely mine and will be corrected on my website. Though I have probably omitted many helpful people, through weakness not deliberate fault, they include, in no particular order:

Jo Rossi; New Profit Inc. and Vanessa Kirsch in particular; Foundation Strategy Group and Mark Kramer in particular; Deborah Churchill; Victoria Hornby; Bonny Landers; BBC Children in Need and Sheila-Jane Malley in particular; John Kingston; Chris West; Innovations for Poverty Action; Sarah Butler-Sloss; Monica Bartlett; The Synchronicity Foundation; Professor Dean Karlan; The Bridgespan Group and Tom Tierney in particular; David Carrington; Sarah Sandford; Isabel Kelly; Ernest, Jean and Ilse Newhouse; Fred Mulder; Hetan Shah, CEO, Royal Statistical Society; Shrupti Shah; Booz & Co.; New Philanthropy Capital; The Monitor Group and Katherine Fulton particularly; Comic Relief; Niamh Swords; Emma Cheshire; The Private Equity Foundation; Dr Rob John, European Venture Philanthropy Association; Nicola Bowyer, Wellcome Trust; Thomas Tallis; Ashley Goodall; Professor Mark Maslin; the Beth Johnson Foundation; John Oakey; Harvey Koh; Professor Hugh Montgomery; Philippa Ouvry; Roz Price; Rosie Wanjie; John Fiennes; Sharath Jeevan, Director of Global Giving; Jane Leek; Saree Rice; Maya Prabhu; Diana Barran MBE; Marcelle Speller, LocalGiving. com; Serena Wilson; Eurostar; Rebecca Griffiths; Will Crouch, Managing Director, Giving What We Can; Toby Ord; Emilie Goodall; Trevor Pears; Rebecca Eastmond; Dr Amrita Ahuja, Harvard University; Michael Green; Global Cool Foundation; The Place2Be; Elie Hassenfeld, co-founder of GiveWell; Rev'd Dr Martin Dudley; Robert Butler; Eleanor Margolies; Professor Joel Fleishman; David Emerson and Cheryl Chapman, Association of Charitable Foundations; and TippingPoint, for not minding being vivisected.

I'm particularly grateful to Dr Stephen Fisher, the University Lecturer in Political Sociology at the University of Oxford, and to John Lloyd, the Professor of Ignorance at the University of Buckingham, for pointing out that the first drafts they reviewed were rubbish. They were right.

Notes

pvii 'It is more difficult to give money away intelligently': Philanthropy UK, 2009, A Framework for Effective Giving. Available from www.philanthropyuk.org/publications/guide-giving/framework-effective-giving.

pvii 'To give away money is an easy matter ': Chapman, C., 2010, 'What is a philanthropist?', Philanthropy UK (www.philanthropyuk.org/quarterly/articles/what-philanthropist, accessed 28 October 2011).

pvii 'In business, you look for the easy things': Stein, G., 2006, 'Buffett Makes $30.7 Bln Donation to Gates Foundation', Update8, Bloomberg www.bloomberg.com/apps/news?pid=newsarchive&sid=axbiyJ8O.yKk, accessed 28 November 2011.

pvii 'It's a chilling thought': Goldacre, B., 2008, Bad Science, London: 4th Estate, p. 108.

pvii 'Deeply ingrained "best practices"': National Committee on Responsive Philanthropy, 2009, Criteria for Philanthropy at Its Best: Benchmarks to Assess and Enhance Grantmaker Impact, Washington DC, p. 44.

p3 'one in four people globally has some form of worms': Karlan, D., Appel, J., 2010, More Than Good Intentions: How A New Economics is Helping to Solve Global Poverty, New York: Dutton, p. 205.

p3 'Some deworming programmes add a year of education for just $4': The numbers are so huge partly because of a magical-sounding effect. If you deworm children in one school in the village, you get better attendance not only there, but also in other schools down the road – where you did precisely nothing. It's because worms are infectious and children play in close proximity – so deworming children in one school reduces the chance of them infecting children in other schools as they play together, so the other schools' attendance improves too. The figure of $1,000 for adding a year of education through conditional cash transfers, and $100 through school uniforms comes from More Than Good Intentions, p. 208. This gives the cost of adding a year of education through deworming as below $4. Another report suggests that deworming in India is 25 times cheaper than conditional cash transfers. (See Bossuroy, T., Delavallade, C., 2008, 'Deworming improves school attendance, says report' OneWorld South Asia, http://bit.ly/mZDEYa, accessed 28 October 2011.) GiveWell, the independent charity analyst, has raised concerns about one set of published figures for costs of deworming, concluding that they could be $30-80 per school year added. (Berger, A., 2011, 'Errors in DCP2 cost-effectiveness estimate for deworming', GiveWell http://bit.ly/qFBRXD, accessed 28 October 2011.) Based on GiveWell's range and the 25 multiple cited, I am using $40, though the actual cost may be as little as a tenth of that.

p5 'When we think we are doing good': Goldacre, Bad Science, p. 108.

p6 'Jews and Christians are asked': Singer. P., 2009, The Life You Can Save, London: Picador, p. 21.

p6 'Toby Ord, an academic': Geoghegan, T., 2010, 'Toby Ord: Why I'm giving £1m to charity?', BBC News Magazine www.bbc.co.uk/news/magazine-11950843, accessed 2 September 2011.

p12 'Don't say philanthropy is giving it away': Bishop M., Green M., 2008, Philanthrocapitalism, London: A&C Black, p. 97.

p15 'Start with your heart': Alderton, D., 2011, 'Sweet Charity – it's the way that you give that gets results', London Evening Standard www.thisislondon.co.uk/lifestyle/article-23964545-sweet-charity---its-the-way-that-you-give-that-gets-results.do ,accessed 28 October 2011.

p16 'Areas in which charities operate': UK Legislation, Charities Act 2006, The National Archives www.legislation.gov.uk/ukpga/2006/50/introduction.

p18 '90% of global health research spending': Goldacre, Bad Science, p. 187.

p18 'Gallup measures people's well-being': Ray, J., 2011, 'High Wellbeing Eludes the Masses in Most Countries Worldwide', Gallup, www.gallup.com/poll/147167/high-wellbeing-eludes-masses-countries-worldwide.aspx, accessed 28 October 2011.

p19 'the annual spend by UK charities for various types of 'beneficiary'': The figure here for donkeys includes only the Donkey Sanctuary, and includes only the figures it gives for the costs of its 'donkey care' work and its estimate of the number of donkeys it looks after in the UK. The Donkey Sanctuary also does public outreach work – as do many mental health and cancer charities, which will reach and benefit people who don't have mental health problems or cancer. The mental health figure here excludes spending by government which is a major player in mental health: however, if that is included, the total is only £1,477 per person. The calculation is given at www.giving-evidence.com

p19 'Even the Bill and Melinda Gates Foundation with its $56 billion': This includes the $26 billion donated by Bill and Melinda Gates, plus the Berkshire Hathaway shares pledged by Warren Buffett in 2006, valued at the time at $30 billion. www.gatesfoundation.org.

p19 'Even adjusting for inflation': Maidment, P., 2008, 'Giving It Away', Forbes www.forbes.com/2008/03/05/philanthrophy-gates-buffett-pf-philanthrophy-billionaires08-cx_pm_0304givingitaway.html.

p20 'Many donors report feeling pressure': I'm indebted to Mark Kramer of FSG Social Impact Advisors for this observation.

p23 'Professor Dean Karlan of Yale University did the maths': Karlan, D., 2011, 'Why Ranking Charities by Administrative Expenses is a Bad Idea', Freakonomics www.freakonomics.com/2011/06/09/why-ranking-charities-by-administrative-expenses-is-a-bad-idea/ accessed 20 June 2011.

p23 'Chance UK': Brookes, M., 2009, 'Measuring impact, why it matters and why so many organisations need to sharpen up their performance', Speech at CharityComms seminar 'Measuring Impact, Communicating Results' www.philanthropycapital.org/downloads/pdf/CharityComms_why_measuring_impact_matters_FINAL.pdf accessed 2 April 2011.

p23 'Overhead costs can be classified as illustrated': Fiennes, C., Langerman C., Vlahovic, J., 2004, Full Cost Recovery, a guide and toolkit on cost allocation, London: ACEVO and New Philanthropy Capital.

p24 Google's offices: Google, undated, 'The Google Culture' www.google.com/about/corporate/company/culture.html, accessed 28 October 2011.

p25 'The worst way to pick a charity': Holden, 2009, 'The Worst Way to Pick a Charity', GiveWell http://blog.givewell.org/2009/12/01/the-worst-way-to-pick-a-charity/, accessed 2 December 2010.

p25 'Susan Hitch': private correspondence, used with permission.

p27 'the Disability Law Service': Copps, J., Vernon, B., 2010, The Little Blue Book: NPC's guide to analysing charities, for charities and funders, London: New Philanthropy Capital.

p29 'raising money is much cheaper for companies': Bishop and Green, Philanthrocapitalism.

p30 'Philanthropy is commendable': National Committee on Responsive Philanthropy, Criteria for Philanthropy at Its Best, p. 4.

p30 'placing charitable activity on a triangle': Langerman C., Worrall E., 2005, Ordinary Lives: Disabled children and their families, New Philanthropy Capital, p.5.

p33 'a quarter of the destruction of rainforest': The Food Programme, 30 October 2011, BBC, www.bbc.co.uk/programmes/b016kgv1, accessed 28 November 2011.

p34 'around half of all trial results are unpublished': Correspondence with Ben Goldacre, used with permission. Dr Goldacre discusses this 'publication bias' in his TED talk: www.ted.com/talks/ben_goldacre_battling_bad_science.html.

p34 'published studies funded by pharmaceutical companies': Goldacre, Bad Science, p.194.

p34 'a tiny, tiny little organization': Bishop and Green, Philanthrocapitalism, p. 51. Microsoft and Apple market cap from Yahoo, 2011, 'Yahoo Finance', http://finance.yahoo.com.

p35 'in a poll': undated, 'Loud and Clear', Charity Times, www.charitytimes.com/pages/ct_features/august06/text_features/ct_august06_feature3_loud_and_clear.htm, accessed 28 October 2011.

p35 'Instead of giving alms': Fleishman, J., 2007, The Foundation: A Great American Secret, New York: PublicAffairs, pp. 101 & 105-106.

p36 Charitable donors' greatest achievements: Breeze, B., 2006, UK Philanthropy's Greatest Achievements, London: Institute for Philanthropy.

p37 'Activity associated with human genome sequencing projects': Battelle, 2011, '$3.8 billion investment in human genome project drove $796 billion in economic impact creating 310,000 jobs and launching the genomic revolution' www.battelle.org/spotlight/5-11-11_genome.aspx, accessed 28 October 2011.

p38 'Lack of clarity is a sin': Popper, K. R., 1972, Objective Knowledge: an Evolutionary Approach, Oxford: Oxford University Press, p. 44.

p43 'lentils are a good tool for immunisation': The Global Poverty Project, 2010, 'Esther Duflo's 2010 TED talk', www.globalpovertyproject.com/blog/view/126, accessed 28 October 2011.

p43 'The Lucy Faithfull Foundation quotes 'Steve'': see video on www.lucyfaithfull.org

p45 'an essay in photojournalism': Riis J., 1890, How the Other Half Lives: Studies Among the Tenements of New York: New York: Charles Scribner's Sons.

p45 'the research and development arm of society': Grossman, A., Letts, C., Ryan, W., 1997, 'Virtuous Capital: What Foundations Can Learn from Venture Capitalists', Harvard Business Review http://hbr.org/1997/03/virtuous-capital-what-foundations-can-learn-from-venture-capitalists/ar/1.

p50 'The problems philanthropy seeks to address': Buchanan, P., 2010, 'Here's some philanthropy advice for Mark Zuckerberg', The Center for Effective Philanthropy. www.effectivephilanthropy.org/blog/author/philb/page/4/ accessed 28 October 2011.

p52 'The private sector spends more than a billion dollars': Ross, J. A., Parker, S., 2010, Lessons from the Field: from understanding to impact, The Center for Effective Philanthropy.

p53 'the problems of philanthropy are not experienced as problems by philanthropists': from an unpublished but rather brilliant paper by Katherine Fulton, president of the Monitor Institute, used with permission.

p53 'From 1987 to 1999, Paul Brest was the dean of Stanford Law School': Brest, P. and Harvey. H., 2008, Money Well Spent, New York: Bloomberg, p. 83.

p54 'do not think of charities as just another sector': The ideas about feedback loops in charities and the public sector is from Owen Barder, and is discussed in Harford T., (2011) Adapt: Why Success Always Starts With Failure, London: Little, Brown.

p56 'Over half of UK personal giving is by people giving less than £100 a month': 'UK Giving 2010 Trends and Characteristics', slide 14, www.slideshare.net/NCVO/101202-uk-charitable-giving-2010-final, accessed 21 October 2011.

p57 'impact = idea x implementation': Adapted from: Karlan, D., 2011, 'Why Ranking Charities by Administrative Expenses is a Bad Idea', Freakonomics www.freakonomics.com/2011/06/09/why-ranking-charities-by-administrative-expenses-is-a-bad-idea/, accessed 21 October 2011.

p58 'Six questions which any good charity can answer': Based on a set produced by New Philanthropy Capital (private conversation with Head of Strategy Tris Lumley), and a set collectively produced by Independent Sector, BBB Wise Giving Alliance, and GuideStar USA: Gose, B., 2010, 'A Move to Encourage Charities to Focus on Results', The Chronicle of Philanthropy, http://philanthropy.com/blogs/conference/a-move-to-encourage-charities-to-focus-on-results/27602, accessed 28 November 2011.

p58 'it actually reduces self-esteem': DuBois, D.L., Keller, T.E. & Wheeler, M.E., 2010, 'Review of Three Recent Randomized Trials of School-Based Mentoring', Sharing Child and Youth Development Knowledge 24 (3).

p59 'Some programmes don't make any difference at all': GiveWell, undated, 'Social Programs that Just Don't Work', www.givewell.org/giving101/Social-Programs-That-Just-Dont-Work, accessed 21 October 2011.

p59 The Bangladesh Integrated Nutrition Project: Preston, C., 2011, 'Why It Matters That Donors Evaluate Their Work', The Chronicle of Philanthropy, http://philanthropy.com/blogs/conference/why-it-matters-that-donors-evaluate-their-work/27941, accessed 21 October 2011.

p59 'Educational Software Products': Anderson, D. , 2008, 'Proven Programs are the Exception, not the Rule', The GiveWell Blog, http://blog.givewell.org/2008/12/18/guest-post-proven-programs-are-the-exception-not-the-rule/, accessed 21 October 2011.

p59 'diarrhoea is a major killer of children': Abdul Latif Jameel Poverty Action Lab, undated, 'Child Diarrhea', www.povertyactionlab.org/policy-lessons/health/child-diarrhea, accessed 21 October 2011.

p62 'Giving money is one of the few things people do alone': The Beacon Fellowship, 2005, 'Dr Frederick Mulder Wins Judges' Special Beacon Prize', The Beacon Fellowship, www.beaconfellowship.org.uk/press_releases.asp?rel=1054, accessed 21 October 2011.

p64 Comic Relief: 'A Just World Free from Poverty: UK Grants Strategy 2009-2012', www.comicrelief.com/sites/all/assets/documents/resources/UK-full-Grants-Strategy.pdf, accessed 21 October 2011, and 'A Just World Free from Poverty: International Grants Strategy 2009-2012', www.comicrelief.com/sites/all/assets/documents/resources/International-Grants-Strategy.pdf, accessed 21 October 2011. Comic Relief's Achievement Report: 'The Difference We've Made', www.comicrelief.com/how-we-help/the-difference-we-have-made, accessed 21 October 2011.

p66 'BBC Radio 4 Charity Appeal': 'BBC Charity Appeals Advisory Committee', BBC, www.bbc.co.uk/charityappeals/about/aac.shtml, accessed 21 October 2011.

p66 'funding from eBay co-founder': 'The eBay Way', 2004, Bloomberg Business Week www.businessweek.com/magazine/content/04_48/b3910407.htm, accessed 26 September 2011.

p68 Charity Navigator: www.charitynavigator.org

p69 'based on a process designed by New Philanthropy Capital': Joy, I., 2010, 'How I'd Analyse a Charity in Two Hours', New Philanthropy Capital's Blog, http://newphilanthropycapital.wordpress.com/2010/03/23/how-id-analyse-a-charity-in-two-hours/, accessed 21 June 2011, and The Charity Commission, 2008, 'The Hallmarks of an Effective Charity', www.charitycommission.gov.uk/Publications/cc10.aspx, accessed 10 April 2011.

p73 'The team with the best players wins': Welch, J., Welch S., Winning, 2005, slide 73 www.slideshare. net/Batjaa_sh/jack-welch-winning, accessed 21 October 2011.

p76 'the Disasters Emergency Committee (DEC)': Raising funds for six months and spending the funds over two years: www.dec.org.uk/item/492; criteria for member organisations: www.dec.org.uk/cgi-bin/ item.cgi?ap=1&id=256; requirement for independent evaluations from those who receive funds www.dec. org.uk/item/356, all accessed 10 June 2011.

p77 'The Little Blue Book': Copps and Vernon, The Little Blue Book.

p78 'several British Army chaps': The Scott-Amundsen Centenary Race, http://scottamundsenrace.org, accessed 6 December 2011.

p78 'six soldiers who served in Iraq': Row2Recovery, www.row2recovery.com, accessed 6 December 2011.

p79 'to demonstrate defensible 'public benefit'': Bates Wells and Braithwaite, 2011, 'Outcome of Public Benefit Tribunal case – BWB analysis confirmed', www.bwbllp.com/Updates/Outcome-of-Public-Benefit-Tribunal-case-BWB-analysis-affirmed.html, accessed 19 October 2011.

p79 'Admissions Policy': 'Durham University's Admissions Policy' www.dur.ac.uk/news/newsitem/?itemno=8077, accessed 10 June 2011.

p80 'further questions available from GiveWell': www.givewell.org/DIY/united-states, accessed 21 October 2011.

p80 'More than a third of us leave money to charity in our Will': Charity Choice, 2011, 'Leave Money to a Charity in Your Will', www.charitychoice.co.uk/willbequest.htm, accessed 21 October 2011.

p82 'National Trust': 'How to Leave a Gift in your Will', www.nationaltrust.org.uk/main/w-trust/w-support/w-giftinwill/w_giftinwill_how_to.htm, accessed 21 October 2011.

p83 'University of Wisconsin': Foleya, R.J., 2010, 'Judge: UW-Madison's donors can stay anonymous', The Chippewa Herald, http://chippewa.com/news/article_370c9c8f-bd14-5b2c-a5ee-d3b04b4c5c1a.html, accessed 21 October 2011.

p83 'Bill Gates on this matter': a private email to Steve Kirsch, http://skirsch.com/charity/philanthropy/ anonymous_giving.htm, accessed 4 April 2011.

p84 'Pride and vanity have built more hospitals': Bishop and Green, Philanthrocapitalism, p. 39.

p84 'For £11 Oxfam can deliver a bednet in Kenya': Oxfam Unwrapped, undated, www.oxfamunwrapped. com.au/gift-171-mossie-net, accessed 21 October 2011

p85 'charities normally can't recover their VAT': Charity Tax Group, 2005-2011, 'Representing Charities on Tax - Welcome', www.ctrg.org.uk/home, accessed 5 May 2011.

p85 'you don't pay VAT if you get a boob job': 'Facelift and breast enlargement bills to rise under new VAT guidelines', www.guardian.co.uk/uk/2011/oct/16/vat-rules-raise-cosmetic-surgery-cost, accessed 17 October 2011.

p86 'there are pockets of surprising deprivation': a great story of such is told in Dickson M., 2010, Please Take One, London: The Generous Press.

p86 'I was not lucky': Bishop and Green, Philanthrocapitalism, p. 47.

p88 'The book Nudge': Thaler. R. and Sunstein, C., 2008, Nudge, London: Penguin p. 189. See also for comparison of organ donor systems and aversion to loss.

p90 'the way to manage risk': Dawkins, R., 2006, The Selfish Gene, Oxford: Oxford University Press.

p90 'Put all your eggs in one basket': Carnegie, A., 2001 [1902], Empire of Business, Books for Business, p. 17.

p90 "unrestricted' donations are worth just over half as much again': Garvey, B., Sutherland, L., 2006, 'Restricted and project funding survey, nfpSynergy', p. 7, www.nfpsynergy.net/includes/documents/ cm_docs/2008/m/may06_resticted_income_survey.pdf, accessed 21 October 2011.

p91 'No-strings money': Coady, T., 2008, 'University of Manchester Scientists win Nobel Prize for Physics', 18th Century Diary, http://18thcenturydiary.org.uk/university-of-manchester-scientists-win-nobel-prize-for-physics/, accessed 5 May 2011.

p91 'unrestricted money from the Global Fund for Women': Kanyoro, M., 'A Nobel Victory for No-Strings-Attached Grants', Chronicle of Philanthropy, December 6, 2011.

p92 'restricted giving unintentionally becomes a vote of no-confidence': Panahpur, 2011, The End of Charity: ...and the Renewal of Welfare http://panahpur.files.wordpress.com/2011/04/the-end-of-charity. pdf, accessed 2 March 2011.

p92 'continual vote of no confidence': Pallotta, D., 2008, Uncharitable: How Restraints on Nonprofits Undermine Their Potential, Tufts University.

p92 'Jim Collins rigorously analyzed thousands of corporations': Tierney, T. J., 2007, 'Higher-Impact Philanthropy', The Bridgespan Group www.bridgespan.org/LearningCenter/ResourceDetail.aspx?id=320, accessed 6 May 2011.

p93 'Restricted giving misses a fundamental point': Collins, J., 2005, Good to Great and the Social Sectors: A Monograph to Accompany Good to Great, London: HarperCollins.

p93 'we pretend to believe them': Comment by Fiona Ellis at 2008 event at the Association of Charitable Foundations, used with permission.

p94 'veteran venture capitalist Sir Ronald Cohen': 'Interview: Sir Ronald Cohen', Alliance, 1 January 2011, www.alliancemagazine.org/node/3596, accessed 28 November 2011.

p95 'in a dispute with his neighbours': The Beacon Fellowship Charitable Trust, 2008, 'Biography: Dr Frederick Mulder', www.beaconfellowship.org.uk/biography2004_fmulder.asp, accessed 2 June 2011.

p96 'A customer comes into the shop': J.P. Morgan Private Bank, 2011, Philanthropic Lives: the unique experiences of eight UK philanthropists.

p96 'Collect only pennies': Pennies for Peace, 2009, 'For Kids', www.penniesforpeace.org/for-kids/, accessed 21 October 2011.

p96 'You give but little': Gibran. K., 1923, 'On Giving'. In A. A. Knopf (ed.) The Prophet.

p98 'The curious incident of the goat in the catalogue': 'How we Spend Your Money', www.oxfam.org.uk/ shop/content/unwrapped/how_we_spend_your_money.html and Good Gifts Catalogue www.goodgifts. org, both accessed 2 August 2011.

p100 'The author JM Barrie': Great Ormond Street Hospital Charity, 'Peter Pan and the hospital', www. gosh.org/gen/peterpan/history/peter-pan-and-the-hospital/, accessed 21 October 2011.

p100 'everyone can give something': Clinton, B., 2008, Giving: how each of us can change the world, London: Arrow Books.

p102 'Stuff We Don't Want': The Best In #SWEDOW 2010, Tales from the Hood, http:// talesfromthehood.com/2011/01/19/announcing-the-winners/, accessed 28 October 2011.

p104 'How the Honours System Works': Private Eye, 2011, No. 1279, p. 7.

p105 'The Methodist Church has long screened out': 'Ethical Investments', www.ethicalinvestment.co.uk/ Socially_Responsible_Investment.htm, accessed 21 October 2011.

p105 'churches divested stock in Caterpillar': 'Church of England pulls out of Caterpillar', www.waronwant. org/campaigns/fighting-occupation/palestine/inform/16455-divestment-campaign-builds-as-companies-profiteering-from-the-occupation-come-under-pressure, accessed 21 October 2011.

p105 'Bill Gates thinks this is nonsense' : Bishop and Green, Philanthrocapitalism, p. 163. On the Gates Foundation and Nigerian oil: Dixon, R., Piller, C., Sanders, E., 2007, 'Dark cloud over good works of Gates Foundation', Los Angeles Times, www.latimes.com/news/la-na-gatesx07jan07,0,2533850.story, accessed 3 September 2011.

p106 'pension trustees will have to consider ethics': Green Consumer Guide, 2011, 'Pension Funds', www. greenconsumerguide.com/domesticll.php?CLASSIFICATION=88&PARENT=85, accessed 21 October 2011.

p106 Spectrum of investments diagram closely based on one in Panahpur, The End of Charity.

p108 Triodos Bank: www.triodos.co.uk/en/personal/investments/, accessed 4 April 2011.

p108 'A meta-study': United Nations Environment Programme Finance Initiative and Mercer, 2007, Demystifying Responsible Investment Performance: A review of key academic and broker research on ESG factors www.unepfi.org/fileadmin/documents/Demystifying_Responsible_Investment_Performance_01. pdf, accessed 5 February 2011.

p114 'his heart should be in the work': Fleishman, The Foundation, p. 116.

p114 'process with the stages shown below': slightly adapted from De Las Casas, L., Fiennes, C., 2007, Going Global: An review of international development funding by UK trusts and foundations, London: New Philanthropy Capital.

p115 'deeply ingrained best practices': Criteria for Philanthropy at its best, p. 44.

p117 'NatWest has a giving programme which will reject 14 of every 15 applicants': discussed in more detail on my blog post 'NatWest's Community Force programme is crushingly awful', http:// carolinefiennes.com/2011/10/18/natwest-community-force/, accessed 21 October 2011.

p117 'Net grants': Criteria for Philanthropy at Its Best.

p117 'An experimental physicist at Columbia University': 'Dr. No Money: The Broken Science Funding System', Scientific American, April 25, 2011.

p118 'First of the British Army's Principles of War': Ministry of Defence (2008), British Defence Doctrine.

p119 'How to manage $1 billion': Ditkoff, S. W., Tierney, T. J., 2010, 'Donating $600 Billion is Just Step One', The Bridgespan Group, www.bridgespan.org/donating-600-billion-just-step-one.aspx, accessed 21 October 2011.

p119 'MELMAC … funds statewide educational initiatives in Maine': MELMAC Education Foundation, 2003, 'Education Needs Assessment and Strategy', MELMAC Foundation with Foundation Strategy Group, www.melmacfoundation.org/publications/Needs_Assessment.pdf, accessed 21 October 2011.

p120 'Voluntary organisations themselves have selected': Diana, the Princess of Wales Memorial Fund, 2005, A Consultation Document.

p120 'there is an unlimited amount of injustice and suffering': Buchanan, P., 2011, 'Here's some philanthropy advice for Mark Zuckerberg'.

p120 'My favourite book is Disease Control Priorities in Developing Countries': Bishop and Green, Philanthrocapitalism, p. 68.

p121 'Last night a banker saved my life': the IFFIm bond: www.iff-immunisation.org/index.html, www.iff-immunisation.org/donors.html, www.iffim.org/about/origins-of-iffim/; that Goldman Sachs worked pro bono: www.gavialliance.org/resources/Financing_Country_Demand_March_2010.pdf, p. 21, footnote 3; quote from Michael Sherwood www.gavialliance.org/vision/in_financing/iffim/iffi_capital_markets_view. php, all accessed 11 August 2011.

p121 'The bond itself is credited with saving at least 3m lives': Gavi Alliance, 2011, 'Innovative Finance', www.gavialliance.org/funding/how-gavi-is-funded/innovative-finance/, accessed 28 November 2011.

p123 'We came up with the name Sentebale': 'Prince Harry's Story', www.sentebale.org/home/ PrinceHarry.html, accessed 5 May 2011.

p123 'It's possible that whatever I do': Kirsch, S., 2007, 'Waldenstrom's Macroglobulinemia: My story', http://skirsch.com/wm/wm.htm, accessed 2 April 2011.

p125 'a huge study': Ruvinsky, J., 'Global Diseases, Local Needs', Stanford Social Innovation Review, Winter 2012.

p126 Wikimedia Foundation strategy development: Wikimedia Foundation, 2011, Wikimedia Strategic Plan: a collaborative vision for the movement through 2015, http://upload.wikimedia.org/wikipedia/ foundation/c/c0/WMF_StrategicPlan2011_spreads.pdf, accessed 21 October 2011.

p126 'you might use a process of elimination': process roughly based on that in Martin, R., 1997, 'Strategic Choice Structuring', www.rogerlmartin.com/library/articles/strategic-choice-structuring#on

p128 'We didn't want to be limited to one tool': Bishop and Green, Philanthrocapitalism, p. 116.

p128 'You really need to play all the keys on the keyboard': National Public Radio, 2009, 'Will $100 Million Solve World's Problems?', www.npr.org/templates/story/story.php?storyId=103842147, accessed 11 June 2011.

p130 'as pro-poor enterprises become financially viable': Shell Foundation, 2005, Enterprise Solutions to Poverty: opportunities and challenges for the international development community and the big business, www.shellfoundation.org/download/pdfs/Shell_Foundation_Enterprise_Solutions_to_Poverty.pdf

p130 GlaxoSmithKline and the Gates Foundation: GlaxoSmithKline, 2009, 'World's largest malaria vaccine trial now underway in seven African countries', www.gsk.com/media/pressreleases/2009/2009_pressrelease_10124.htm, accessed 21 October 2011, and The Economist, 22 Oct 2011, 'Not swatted yet, A new vaccine is one step towards a distant goal'

p130 'Meth is a consumer product': Montana Meth Project, 2005-2011, 'Results', www.montanameth.org/ About_Us/results.php, accessed 2 May 2011.

p131 Royal Society Wolfson Research Merit Awards: University of Warwick , 2011, 'University of Warwick chemist honoured with prestigious award by the Royal Society', http://bit.ly/vLgEjX, accessed 28 November 2011, and The Royal Society, 2011, 'Royal Society Announces Prestigious 2011 Wolfson Research Merit Awards', http://bit.ly/lucLW7, accessed 28 November 2011.

p131 Paul Hamlyn Foundation's partners: 'Musical Bridges: Transforming Transition', www.phf.org.uk/page. asp?id=770, accessed 15 August 2011; and PHF programme around supplementary education, tackling school exclusion and truancy: Children and Young People's Partnership in Somerset (CHYPPS), 2010, 'Paul Hamlyn Foundation Funding to Tackle School Exclusion and Truancy', www.chypps.org.uk/funding-now/paul-hamlyn-foundation-funding-to-tackle-school-exclusion-and-truancy.html, accessed 21 October 2011.

p131 'The Alfred P. Sloan Foundation': Fleishman, The Foundation, p. 147.

p132 'Panahpur also invests across the spectrum': 'Our portfolio', http://panahpur.org/portfolio/, accessed 28 November 2011.

p133 'Napoleon offered a prize': Harford, T., 2008, 'Cash for Answers', http://timharford.com/2008/01/cash-for-answers/, accessed 2 August 2011, and Civitello, L., 2003, Cuisine and Culture: A History of Food and People, Wiley.

p133 'The founder of the modern-day X Prize': Bishop and Green, Philanthrocapitalism, p. 110.

p134 'Nobel Prizes bring the gift of life itself': Dubner, S., Levitt, S., 2009, Superfreakonomics, London: Penguin, p. 82.

p135 'Warren Buffett on the logic of giving his $31 billion through the Gates Foundation': see www.gatesfoundation.org/leadership/Pages/warren-buffett.aspx, accessed 21 October 2011; 'I sat down and thought about who could do a better job of dispersing wealth than myself': Bishop and Green, Philanthrocapitalism, p. 77; and 'What can be more logical': Fleishman, The Foundation, p. 46.

p136 'At Eurostar': Correspondence with Eurostar, used with permission.

p136 'Robbie Williams' charity Give It Sum': see www.robbiewilliams.com/news-blogs/robbies-give-it-sum-fund-celebrates-10-years, accessed 28 November 2011.

p136 'Pew's respected machine': see www.pewtrusts.org/giving.aspx, accessed 21 October 2011.

p137 'EJAF itself outsources part of its work': De Las Casas and Fiennes, Going Global. See also for details of The Baring Foundation and John Ellerman Foundation working together.

p137 'Edna McConnell Clark Foundation initiated a fund with $39m': Brest and Harvey, Money Well Spent, p. 199.

p140 Shell Foundation: Enterprise Solutions to Poverty.

p143 PVF and the 'fax grant program': Kramer, M. E., Porter, M. R., 1999, 'Philanthropy's New Agenda: Creating Value', Harvard Business Review 77 (6).

p146 'Nissan thinks it takes £1,200': www.carmagazine.co.uk/News/Search-Results/Industry-News/News-watch-Feb-2011-todays-auto-industry-news/ (Dollar value converted to sterling at exchange rate given by oanda.com on 27 July 2011).

p146 'There are just over 50m adults in the UK': Beaumont, J., 2011, 'Population', Social Trends 41, Office for National Statistics.

p147 'Coca-Cola's value has grown by a fizzy 14%': Data on for total nominal value of KO (normal stock) from 'Yahoo Finance' http://uk.finance.yahoo.com Calculation of CAGR and inflation adjustment at www.giving-evidence.com.

p147 'The best indicator of future behaviour is past behaviour': Jackson, S. E., Schuler, R., Werner, S., 2008, Managing Human Resources, Cengage Learning.

p149 The City Bridge Trust public decision-making: City Bridge Trust, 2009, The Knowledge, Learning from London www.citybridgetrust.org.uk/CBT/Publications/TheKnowledge.htm, accessed 21 October 2011.

p149 'Money alone is seldom the answer': Philanthropy UK, 2005, A Guide to Giving, 2nd ed., Philanthropy UK, p. 125.

p150 'US research shows small grants are much more expensive than larger ones': The Center for Effective Philanthropy, 2004, Listening to Grantees: What Nonprofits Value in Their Foundation Funders.

p150 'The median grant made by America's larger foundations ': Tierney, 'Higher-Impact Philanthropy'.

p151 'John D. Rockefeller receiving a request': Fleishman, The Foundation, p. 247.

p151 'a survey of nearly 2,000 non-profit executives in the US': Criteria for Philanthropy at its best, p.34.

p151 'a decent and widely-endorsed toolkit': Fiennes, C., Langerman C., Vlahovic, J., Full Cost Recovery.

p152 'Why conduct rigorous evaluation?': Ogden T., 'Thoughts from day one of Global Philanthropy Forum', Alliance, www.alliancemagazine.org/node/3692, accessed 25 April 2011. (Note that Howard White is mis-named in this article as Edward White.)

p152 'Learning with a purpose': Kramer, M., Fisk, L., Graves, R., Hirschhorn, J., 2007, From Insight to Action: New Directions in Foundation Evaluation, FSG Social Impact Advisors, p. 39.

p152 'monitoring looks at implementation whereas evaluation looks at the idea': This concept comes from discussion with Dean Karlan.

p152 'A staff member at one leading evaluation firm': Forti, M., 2011, 'Best of Both Worlds: Bridging the Gap Between Monitoring and Evaluation', The Bridgespan Group www.bridgespan.org/bridging-the-monitoring-and-evaluation-gap.aspx?resource=Conversation%20Starters, accessed 21 October 2011.

p153 'A randomised control trial of primary health care provision in Uganda': Bjorkman, M., Svennson, J., 'Power to the People, evidence from a randomized field experiment on community-based monitoring in Uganda', Quarterly Journal of Economics, http://people.su.se/~jsven/PtP_QJE.pdf, accessed 21 October 2011.

p153 'Vanessa Kirsch laments that': private correspondence, used with permission.

p154 'Futurebuilders published research into its own performance': Futurebuilders England, 2005, Investment with a Difference: a first learning report http://bit.ly/dSshup, accessed 21 October 2011, and Futurebuilders England, 2007, Second Learning Report http://bit.ly/hLTEU0, accessed 21 October 2011.

p154 Measles out-break in Indonesia: Barder, O., 2011, 'What Would Google Do?', Owen Abroad, www.owen.org/blog/4999, accessed 28 November 2011; International Aid Transparency Initiative, 2011, www.aidtransparency.net, accessed 28 November 2011.

p155 Letter attributed to the Duke of Wellington: International Military Forums, 2000-2011, 'About Lord Wellington's Letter to British Foreign Officer- 1812', www.military-quotes.com/forum/lord-wellingtons-letter-british-foriegn-t1566.html, accessed 2 March 2011.

p157 'The following feedback is not atypical': quotes from: The Center for Effective Philanthropy, Listening to Grantees.

p158 'It is amazing what you can accomplish': De Jager, P., 2005, 'Credit Legerdemain for Managers', www.technobility.com/docs/article087.htm, accessed 27 October 2011.

p158 'You and your grantee will seldom': Brest and Harvey Money Well Spent, p. 112.

p161 'the inability of organisations to discuss risky and threatening issues': Argyris, C., 'Making the Undiscussable and its Undiscussability Discussable', Public Administration Review 40 (3).

p161 'The Hewlett Foundation has an annual prize for the worst grant': Fleishman, The Foundation.

p161 'Many of the small schools that we invested in': First Annual Letter, 2009, 'Bill Gates Annual Letter, pp. 11-12, www.scribd.com/doc/11425495/2009-Bill-Gates-Annual-Letter, accessed 21 October 2011.

p162 Frequency and helpfulness of management assistance activities diagram: The Center for Effective Philanthropy, 2005, 'S. H. Cowell Foundation Grantee Perception Report', www.shcowell.org/docs/

Granteeperceptionstudy.pdf, accessed 21 October 2011.

p163 Example feedback in Grantee Perception Reports:
'I'm not aware of any impact': Paul Hamlyn Foundation, 2010, 'Grantee Perception Report', (www.phf.org.
uk/page.asp?id=1031, accessed 21 October 2011).
'They have been approachable, practical and direct in their suggestions': ibid.
'They are one of very few funders that understands': The Center for Effective Philanthropy, 2009, 'Grantee
Perception Report, for the William and Flora Hewlett Foundation', (www.hewlett.org/uploads/files/
Hewlett_2009_Grantee_Perception_Report_PUBLIC.pdf, accessed 21 October 2011).
'The Foundation provides opportunities for us': The Center for Effective Philanthropy, 2009, 'Grantee
Perception Report, for the Cleveland Foundation', (www.clevelandfoundation.org/uploadedFiles/
GrantMaking/2009%20Grantee%20Perception%20Report_Public%20Version.pdf, accessed 21 October
2011).

p164 'Stewart Hudson': Kramer, Fisk and Graves, From Insight to Action: New Directions in Foundation
Evaluation, p. 18.

p164 'In a survey at the beginning of 2011': Buteau E., 2011, 'Data Point: Learning from failure', The Center
for Effective Philanthropy, www.effectivephilanthropy.org/blog/2011/10/data-point-learning-from-
failure/, accessed 25 October 2011.

p164 'Drilling for data': Shell Foundation, Enterprise Solutions to Poverty.

p165 'Few phrases are as overused and poorly defined as 'strategic philanthropy'': Kramer, M. R., Porter, M.
E., 2002, 'The Competitive Advantage of Corporate Philanthropy', Harvard Business Review.

p166 This chapter draws on: Kramer, M. R., Porter, M. E, 2006, 'Strategy and Society: The Link Between
Competitive Advantage and Corporate Social Responsibility', Harvard Business Review; and Kania, J.,
Kramer, M. R., 2006, 'Changing the Game', Stanford Social Innovation Review.

p167 'When a well-run business applies its vast resources': Porter, M., 2002, 'The Importance of Being
Strategic', Harvard Business Review.

p167 'Coca-Cola in Africa': 'Leveraging Core Competencies to Combat HIV/AIDS in Africa', Case Western
Reserve University, worldinquiry.case.edu/bankGetFile.cfm?idFile=328, accessed 21 October 2011.

p167 'The acid test of good corporate philanthropy': Kramer and Porter, 'Strategy and Society: The Link
Between Competitive Advantage and Corporate Social Responsibility'.

p168 Sony's Open Planet Ideas competition: www.openplanetideas.com, accessed 2 August 2011.

p168 'Iodine Deficiency Disorder is the world's most prevalent cause of brain damage': Foster, W., Kundu,
S. and Singh, A., 2005, 'Corporate Social Responsibility: Through the Supply Chain: MNCs to SMEs', School
of International and Public Affairs, New York: Columbia University.

p169 On James Timpson and offenders, see J.P.Morgan, Philanthropic Lives; for the 'unusually high
autonomy' given to Timpson staff see Harford, Adapt, p.227.

p171 Apple's philanthropy: Carry, J. and Martin, C. E., 2011, 'Apple's philanthropy needs a reboot', CNN
Opinion, http://bit.ly/tHZqiN, accessed 5 October 2011.

p174 'as simple as possible': 'On the Method of Theoretical Physics', the Herbert Spencer Lecture, Oxford,
June 10, 1933. Oxford University.

p174 'Not everything that counts': Cameron W.B., 1963, Informal Sociology: A Casual Introduction to
Sociological Thinking, Random House.

p179 'Apparently '70% of [its] graduates': Goldman Sachs advert in Stanford Social Innovation Review,
Summer 2011, back inside cover.

p180 'Randomised control trials currently creating interest in the UK': Allen, G., Smith, I.D., 2008, 'Good Parents, Great Kids, Better Citizens', Centre for Social Justice, www.centreforsocialjustice.org.uk/client/downloads/EarlyInterventionpaperFINAL.pdf, accessed 29 October 2011.

p181 Methods of randomisation: Goldacre, Bad Science, pp. 49-50.

p183 'Michele Bachmann seemed to think so': Whitwell L., 30 Aug 2011, "Hurricane was message from God to Washington politicians': Michele Bachmann says He is angry with government policies', Daily Mail.

p183 Correlation and causation cartoon: from www.xkcd.com.

p184 'Global Cool Foundation... an innovative campaign': , 'Global Cool Campaigning Impact January 2009 – June 2010', p.10, http://globalcoolfoundation.org/wp-content/uploads/2010/11/Global-Cool-Impact-Assessment-September-2010.pdf, accessed 28 November 2011.

p184 'Age Concern Swansea helps older people claim welfare benefits': Charlton, H., 2007, 'Getting more from your giving', Rathbones Review, Rathbones Investment Management, p. 4, (http://production.investis.com/rat/publications/review/autumn07/autumn07_n.pdf, accessed 29 October 2011).

p185 'the building trades are overwhelmingly male': Construction Skills, 2011, 'Diversity Expo for Construction Industry', www.cskills.org/aboutus/newsandevents/news/diversityexpo.aspx, www.cskills.org/aboutus/newsandevents/news/diversityexpo.aspxaccessed 29 October 2011.

p188 'a third-party tool': CORE-OM (Clinical Outcomes in Routine Evaluation Outcome Measure), a 34-item questionnaire recommended by the National Family Parenting Institute. It covers well-being, symptoms, functioning and risk, and is not associated with a particular school of therapy.

p189 Quality-Adjusted Life Years: NHS Institute for Health and Clinical Excellence, 2008, 'Guide to the methods of technology appraisal', London, www.nice.org.uk/media/B52/A7/TAMethodsGuideUpdatedJune2008.pdf, accessed 10 March 2010.

p190 'the human brain computes it very strangely': Thaler and Sunstein, Nudge.

p195 'This phenomenon is well-documented': It is discussed in Goldacre, Bad Science.

p195 'What we observe is not nature itself': Heisenberg , W., 1952, Physics and Philosophy, London: Penguin.

p195 'A study reported recently in Nature': Kahan, D. M., 2010, Fixing the Communications Failure, Nature, 463, pp. 296-297.

p197 'Tom Ross': Kramer, Fisk and Graves, From Insight to Action: New Directions in Foundation Evaluation, p. 31.

p198 'John Conant': Motoko, R., 2010, Fairies, Witches and Supply and Demand, The New York Times . www.nytimes.com/2011/08/21/opinion/fairies-witches-and-supply-and-demand.html.

p198 'we are missing a lot of what goes on': Chabris, C., Simons, D., 2010, 'The Invisible Gorilla', www.theinvisiblegorilla.com, accessed 29 October 2011.

p200 Distribution of charities in England and Wales by size: NCVO, 2010, The UK Civil Society Almanac, Question 14.

p200 Marks & Spencer annual revenue: Marks and Spencer, 2011, 'Investors: financial highlights', M&S, http://corporate.marksandspencer.com/investors/fin_highlights, accessed 29 October 2011.

p200 BP annual income: BP, 2011, 'Financial and Operating Information 2006-2010', BP, www.bp.com/liveassets/bp_internet/globalbp/STAGING/global_assets/downloads/F/FOI_2006_2010_full_book.pdf, accessed 2 November 2011.

p201 Market shares:
Food retailers: Holz-Clause M., Geisler M., 2011, Grocery Retailing Profile, Agricultural Marketing Resource Center.
Soft drinks: UK Soft Drinks, 2009, Zenith International.
UK audit market: Oxera 2011, Competition and choice in the UK audit market.

p202 'The UK has about 190,000 registered charities': Charity Commission, 2011'Facts and Figures', www.charitycommission.gov.uk/About_us/About_charities/factfigures.aspx, accessed 2 November 2011; Northern Ireland data for 2007/08.
(162,415 in England & Wales at the end of 2010; and Scotland had 23,286. Most recent data on Northern Ireland was for 2007/8, of 4000 from The UK Civil Society Almanac, Question 1.)

p202 Number of UK companies in comparison to charities: Office for National Statistics www.statistics.gov.uk/cci/nugget.asp?id=1238, accessed 5 May 2011.

p202 Charity mergers: Article by The Bridgespan Group cited in Fleishman, The Foundation: p. 29.

p202 Imperial Cancer Research Fund joining with the Cancer Research Campaign 2002: BBC News, 2011, 'Cancer Charity Mega-Merger', BBC, http://news.bbc.co.uk/1/hi/health/1703612.stm, accessed 2 November 2011.

p203 'Mergers have failure rates of more than 50 percent': Wharton University of Pennsylvania, 2011, 'Mergers and Acquisitions', http://executiveeducation.wharton.upenn.edu/open-enrollment/finance-programs/mergers-acquisitions-program.cfm, accessed 2 November 2011.

p203 '35%-50% of all cancers are rarer forms': Rarer Cancers Foundation, 2011, 'Rarer Cancers', www.rarercancers.org/index.php?option=com_content&view=article&id=1&Itemid=2, accessed 2 November 2011.

p206 'Charity spend as percentage of government spend': Various sources. BBC (on gov't spend), CAF Charity Trends (on charity sector spend), NPC on both government and charity sector spend on child abuse. Details at www.giving-evidence.com

p207 'Private charitable foundations can try out things, take risks': 'Interview – Lord David Sainsbury: confessions of a 'hands-on' donor', Alliance www.alliancemagazine.org/node/3413, accessed 2 November 2011.

p207 ZeShan and Hepatitis B in China:
Discrimination in China: China Daily, 2011, 'Hepatitis B Discrimination', www.chinadaily.com.cn/opinion/2011-02/18/content_12036220.htm, accessed 15 August 2011.
ZeShan Foundation website : ZeShan Foundation, 2008, 'Health', www.zeshanfoundation.org/family/programsdetails.asp@programid=25.htm, accessed 15 August 2011.
Government vaccinating all children: CRIEnglish, 2009, 'Free Hepatitis B Vaccination to Cover all Children', Jiang Aitao ed., http://english.cri.cn/6909/2009/06/18/189s494485.htm, accessed 15 August 2011.
Number of children under 15 in China: total population = 1345.8m, of which population under 15 is 19.9%: The Economist, 2012, 'Pocket World In Figures', London: The Economist.

p208 Correspondence with IncomeMax, used with permission.

p208 Correspondence with IPSEA, used with permission.

p209 Save the Children and school meals: seewww.savethechildren.org.uk/en/102.htm, accessed 3 November 2011.

p209 'Charity Commission ordered the closure of Atlantic Bridge': Neate, R., 5 Oct 2011, 'Charity created by Liam Fox axed after watchdog issues criticism', The Guardian.

p209 'Nearly three-quarters of the money which charities receive': Wilding, K., 2011, 'The Seven deadly charity myths', NVCO, www.ncvo-vol.org.uk/networking-discussions/blogs/209/11/08/08/seven-deadly-charity-myths, accessed 3 November 2011.

p210 'The costs in the criminal justice system': New Philanthropy Capital, 2007, 'Circle charity recommendation', www.philanthropycapital.org/download/default.aspx?id=337, accessed 28 November 2011.

p211 Social Impact Bonds: this passage draws on www.socialfinance.org.uk, Social Investment Task Force, 2010, 'Social Investment Ten Years On: Final Report of the Social Investment Task Force', www.socialinvestmenttaskforce.org/downloads/SITF_10_year_review.pdf, accessed 28 November 2011, and correspondence with Social Finance, used with permission.

p215 Fundraising tennis match for Haiti raised £114,000: 'Roger Federer & stars play tennis match in aid of Haiti', BBC,http://news.bbc.co.uk/sport1/hi/tennis/8462953.stm, accessed 3 November 2011.

p216 'they can be vastly misleading': the statistics of incidences in samples of varying sizes is discussed in: Goldacre B., 28 Oct 2011, 'DIY statistical analysis: experience the thrill of touching real data', The Guardian, www.guardian.co.uk/commentisfree/2011/oct/28/bad-science-diy-data-analysis, accessed 28 November 2011.

p220 'Four Acre Trust': Institute for Philanthropy, 2010, 'The Power of Now: spend out trusts and foundations in the UK', www.instituteforphilanthropy.org/cms/pages/documents/The_Power_of%20Now_Spend%20Out_Trusts_in_the_UK.pdf, accessed 3 November 2011.

p221 'I think over time it would cease': Alliance, 'Interview – Lord David Sainsbury: confessions of a 'hands-on' donor'.

p223 Charity Commission and regulators: Charity Commission for England & Wales www.charity-commission.gov.uk; Office of the Scottish Charity Regulator www.oscr.org.uk; The Charity Commission for Northern Ireland www.charitycommissionni.org.uk/; IRS, 2011, Charities and Non-Profits www.irs.gov/charities/article/0,,id=96136,00.html or www.irs.gov/app/pub-78/

p224 Charities and VAT: Charity Tax Group, 2005-2011 www.ctrg.org.uk/home, accessed 3 November 2011.

p225 'people who work for charities are not paid an appropriate salary': Panahpur, The End of Charity. p.19.

p225 'The RSPB spends over £½m managing its volunteers': Lake, H., 2004, 'Two charities invest over £1m in volunteering', UK Fundraising, www.fundraising.co.uk/node/158462, accessed 28 November 2011.

p226 'It doesn't much matter what people call things': Alliance, 2011, 'Interview – Sir Ronald Cohen'.

p227 'Your local Age UK': www.ageuk.org.uk/about-us/local-partners/, accessed 28 November 2011.

p229 'I am not just being philanthropic in the sense of giving money away': Alliance, 'Interview – Sir Ronald Cohen'.

p229 'Many voluntary organisations are unincorporated': National Council for Voluntary Organisations, 2010, 'UK Civil Society Almanac 2010', Table 1.1.

p230 The Fundraising Promise: Drawn up by the Fundraising Standards Board, see www.frsb.org.uk/english/give-with-confidence/how-we-can-help/fundraising-promise/, accessed 3 November 2011.

p231 The 10 largest voluntary organisations in the UK by total expenditure, 2007/08: 'UK Civil Society Almanac 2010', Question 14.

p231 Membership within various organisations: UK Civil Society Almanac 2010, Section 1, Membership of National Trust for Scotland: National Trust for Scotland, 2010, 'Fit for Purpose: Report of the Strategic Review of the National Trust for Scotland', Edinburgh: National Trust for Scotland, www.nts.org.uk/Downloads/trustees/fit_for_purpose.pdf, accessed 28 November 2011.

Index